Fields of the First

A history of aircraft landing grounds in Essex used
during the First World War

Paul A. Doyle

Forward Airfield Research Publishing ≫

First published in 1997 by
Forward Airfield Research Publishing
2 Carmelo Court, Beamish Close
North Weald Bassett, Essex CM16 6UA
England

ISBN 0 9525624 1 3

Typesetting by
West 4 Printers Ltd.
8 Essex Place, London W4 5UT

Printed and bound in England by
Woolnough Bookbinding Ltd.
Express Works, Church Street
Irthlingborough, Northants NN9 5SE

By the same author/publisher
Where the Lysanders were . . . (the story of Sawbridgeworth's airfields)

Front cover photograph:

Of all the landing grounds to have been laid down in the County during the First World War, Stow Maries remains the most complete. This 1997 aerial view of the technical and regimental sites shows the 24 buildings still existing at this former Flight Station. The light-coloured square with the track leading from the buildings is the flying ground for the Anglia Model Flying Club, the 'current' flying unit. In the left background is Flambirds Farm.

Contents

Acknowledgements

Principal thanks are due to:

John Barfoot (Cross & Cockade), Mr & Mrs Bovill (The Grange, Woodham Mortimer), Chelmsford Borough Council, Essex County Council Planning Department (for supporting this work financially), the Essex County Record Office, Ian Oliver & Les Smith, the Public Record Office (Kew), Strutt & Parker (Chelmsford) who manage many of the (now) farm sites, my children Christopher and Kirsten, and finally Dr Ron Blake who, as a fellow member of the Airfield Research Group and senior lecturer in Town and Country Planning at Trent Polytechnic, Nottingham, made sure I had the right location in each case.

Also to the many people who helped with each site, including:

Beaumont – Roger Freeman (Colchester), Ann Gorman and Patience Sullivan (Walton on the Naze library), Laura 'Pearl' Lonsdale (Thorpe-le-Soken history recorder)

Blackheath Common – Jon & Trevor Hodder, Colchester Military Headquarters

Bournes Green – Ken Crowe (Southend Museums Department), Michael Hills (British Gas Museum, Bromley-by-Bow), Rob Lindel, The Museum of Army Flying (Middle Wallop), Gwen Rawlinson (Great Wakering)

Braintree – John and Mrs Hawkes (Stebbing), Tom Scott (Stanford Farm)

Broomfield Court – Richard Hudson, Gary Kite, Ken Searles, Michael & Mrs Stacey

Burnham-on-Crouch – June & John Jolly (Mangapps Farm), Henry Potten, Douglas & Mrs Smith (Burnham Wick Farm)

Chingford – Chingford Library, Leonard Davies (Historical Society), Brian Mardall (Vestry House Museum, LB Waltham Forest)

Clacton – *Clacton Graphic* newspapers, the Fleet Air Arm Museum (RNAS Yeovilton), H.M. Coastguard & Rescue (Frinton-on-Sea), Norman Jacobs (Local Historian), Judith Robson (Central library), Ray C. Sturtivant (RNAS/FAA historian)

East Hanningfield – Bill Benson, Mrs W. Fish (Galleywood), Trevor Laurence (Hill Farm)

Easthorpe – Jack Bishop, Ian Melrose (Scotties Farm)

Fairlop – Ian Dowling (Ilford Central Library), The London Playing Fields Society, Chris Wright (Redbridge Council)

Fyfield – Joyce McArthy, the Revd Morgan, Julian Read, Brenda Walker (Bundish Hall)

Goldhanger – Ivor Dallinger and Stephen Nunn (Maldon), *Southend Standard* newspapers

Hainault Farm – John Barfoot (Cross & Cockade), Bert Harman, Silver Lady Vehicles staff

Horndon-on-the-Hill – Brentwood Borough Council Information Centre, David Campbell, Jackie Firman & John Wordley (Orsett), Alan McCheyne (Shenfield), Alan Webb (RAF retd, Gidea Park)

Little Clacton – Stuart McKay (DH Moth Club, Berkhamsted), Brian Naylor, Barry Sayer

Mountnessing – John Cross, Frank Mason, the Rt Hon Lord Petre, Harold Smith

North Benfleet – John & Mrs Wordley (Orsett)

North Ockendon – Geoff Jones, Roger Mee (Bulphan), Joy and Daniel Scott (Upminster)

North Weald Bassett – Paul Francis (ARG, Ware, Herts), North Weald Airfield Museum

Orsett – Robert Fearby (Bulphan), John & Mrs Wordley

Rochford – Stephen Nunn, Carole Ryan (English Heritage), *Southend Standard* newspapers

Runwell – Carina Bristow, Joanne Cullen (Wickford library), James Gould (Manor Park), Peter Hall (Wickford), Jean Willis (Leigh on Sea)

Shenfield – Alf Dobson, Gerald, Janet & Alan McCheyne (Palmers Farm)

Sible Hedingham – Terry Gladwell (Halstead), John and Mrs Lewis (Pevors Farm)

Stow Maries – Ivor Dallinger, Michael Marsh, *Southend Standard* newspapers

Thaxted – Margaret Caton, Wilfred Challis, John and Mrs Heywood, Messrs J F Knights

Widford/Writtle – George Bewers, Miss Ethel Chinnery, Bob & Doris Collison, Wendy Hibbert (Historical Society), Tessa Lambert & Paul McBride (Chelmsford Borough Council Environmental & Planning Services), Ray Rodwell (Great Baddow), John Sapsford (Sawbridgeworth, Herts), Tim Wander (Earls Colne), staff at Writtle College and Garden Centre

Wormingford – Roger Freeman (Colchester), Richard Lindsey, John V Nicholls.

Plus – the many other residents local to the sites who offered directions or assistance.

Introduction

The idea for this book came about following research into the First World War aspect of an airfield site just over the border in Hertfordshire. Many people are not aware that such places exist in their locality, due to even less visible remains than from similar locations in the Second World War, and if such sites are not recorded and made known to the general public they will be lost for ever.

Most readers are familiar with the heroic deeds carried out from the well-chronicled First World War aerodromes in Essex such as Hainault Farm, North Weald Bassett, Rochford and Suttons Farm, and to a lesser degree those at Chingford, Goldhanger and Stow Maries, but do not realise that these sites were less than a quarter of thirty-one landing grounds available for the Army, Royal Flying Corps (later the Royal Air Force) and Royal Naval Air Service across the county during that conflict.

Whilst the aerodromes given above had buildings of a more permanent nature others raised as an emergency measure were little more than farm fields clear enough to give a suitable landing area for the fragile machines of the period, but however the landing ground was classified traces of most have been swept away or changed dramatically over the years. Exceptions are Hainault Farm, as well as Stow Maries (with most of its original buildings still intact), North Weald Bassett and Rochford, the latter three remaining as active flying sites. It is noted with some satisfaction that certain lessons learnt from the aerial strategies of the First World War were borne in mind by planners at the Air Ministry when it can be seen that, of all these sites, the most suitable were utilised in part or total subsequent to that conflict.

Those with an architectural as well as a historical mind can derive further satisfaction by visiting these locations and, in dreams, picture what they were like in their heyday some 80 years ago when the air above them echoed to the crackling sound of under-powered aircraft engines, or the view 'over the fence' was that of fabric-covered machines parked in front of canvas or timber aeroplane sheds, or merely standing next to a solitary tent in the corner of a farm field. Whatever the dream, these sites remain in essence what they were, places where history was fought and made.

Paul A Doyle
North Weald Bassett 1997

To my children
For once again putting up with my ramblings,
over now-empty fields and overgrown hedgerows
generally in the most inclement weather conditions.

Although at first sight this 1997 aerial view of the former Flight Station at Hainault Farm appears to show lots of period buildings, only a few are in fact survivors from the First World War; these being marked with white discs. Hainault Farm is on the left whilst just visible in the right background is one of the lakes formed for leisure activities on the site of the Second World War airfield at Fairlop. New buildings are on the Officers' Mess site, whilst to this side of Hainault Road the two-chimneyed houses are private dwellings not absorbed into the flight station site.

Air Defence of Great Britain in the First World War

Late in 1911 the Imperial Defence Committee, under the chairmanship of Lord Haldane, proposed the formation of a 'British Aeronautical Service' to provide support by aerial means for the already existing land and naval forces. In March 1912 Royal approval was given and, on 13 April 1912, this flying corps was properly constituted by Royal Warrant under the name 'Royal Flying Corps'.

The initial role for the newly-formed Corps was aerial reconnaissance without any thought being given to using the aircraft in an attacking mode, indeed early sorties only carried the lightest of hand weapons for self defence. Two years later the First World War started, in the first months of which there were barely enough aircraft of a suitable standard to equip the four Expeditionary Force squadrons in France, let alone maintain a force for aerial defence of the UK mainland. On 3 September 1914 the Admiralty took on the responsibility for air defence with the priority for the Royal Naval Air Service, the branch appointed to the task as having somewhat longer experience in the operation of aircraft, being the protection of the Capital. It must be realised that the civilian manufacturing sites at Barking Creek and Fambridge, and the experimental flying ground at Dagenham, had all closed by 1914 and at this time there were no permanent aerodromes in the county, therefore aircraft had to be despatched from the major training stations west of London to temporary locations in East Anglia as required.

By early 1916 aircraft production had increased sufficiently to meet demands and, although the majority of aircraft available to the Royal Flying Corps were of the B.E.2c type, in February that service took over the role for defence of the homeland from the RNAS with the flying units given the classification of Home Defence squadrons. Aircraft types such as the F.E.2b and Sopwith 1½-Strutter subsequently came into service and proved themselves more suitable for the task to hand.

By September 1916 two Home Defence (HD) squadrons were based in Essex as part of 6th Brigade, South East Area, these being Nos. 37 & 39 with separate Squadron Headquarters at Woodham Mortimer and Woodford respectively. Each squadron comprised three flights which for purely operational, not space, reasons were detached to six aerodromes known as Flight Stations; No 37 having its 'A' Flight at Rochford, 'B' at Stow Maries and 'C' at Goldhanger, whilst No 39 had 'A' Flight at North Weald Bassett, 'B' at Suttons Farm and 'C' at Hainault Farm.

From these bases aircraft flew daily against expected incursions by German airships and bombers but whilst in the Second World War defensive operations were aided by that all-seeing eye RDF, Radio Direction Finding and Ranging or 'radar', to direct fighters to any incoming hostile aircraft the situation for Home Defence squadrons in the First World War was quite different. Without any form of advance warning as to the location of airships or Gotha 'giants', or the route they were taking, the defending fighters were tasked to fly on set patrol lines which they were forbidden to leave unless actually attacking the enemy or if a heavy concentration of AA guns, or searchlights at night, led the pilot to the indicated location of the enemy.

In accordance with Home Defence Order No. 1, on receipt of the order 'Aeroplane Attack Patrol' aircraft on readiness would take off and climb to operational height over their own flight station before proceeding to the the patrol line, the locations of which are given in Appendix 1. If an airship raid occurred at the same time as an aeroplane raid the GOC 6th Brigade would, in accordance with Home Defence Order No. 3, telephone certain aerodromes or landing grounds to have them fire red rockets. The locations were those nearest to the last known position of patrolling fighters, the highest of which on seeing the signal would climb as high as possible and attempt to find the airship. Having aircraft in the right area to make contact with the enemy was extremely difficult, especially when it was realised that it required 12 aircraft per day to have one in the air at any one time, but as more squadrons were formed or returned from the Western Front the greater numbers of available aircraft eased the situation.

By August 1917 the active day defences, AA guns and fighters, against both airships and aeroplanes had proved themselves but the matter of countering night raids was still not perfected. The Gotha G5 bomber came into use for formation day bombing in June 1917 and was quickly countered by two

S.E.5-equipped fighter squadrons withdrawn from the Western Front, therefore tactics changed and it was employed as a 'lone wolf' night raider. With this aircraft being as fast, if not faster, than current British night fighters the defenders now had to seek out raiders flying at speeds much greater than the airships had the previous year.

During daylight hours navigation was a simple matter but by night it was quite different and, until 1917 when the early wireless telephony sets were tested and 1918 before they started to be used with any degree of success, an extremely difficult task for the pilots who carried no form of homing apparatus to find their home station. In the event of any night-flying pilot on this early form of 'cab rank' patrol becoming disorientated due to bad weather or loss of bearings, suffering engine failure or becoming low on fuel and not being able to find their own, or any, flight station due to not seeing its 'aeroplane lights' (see 'Aids to operations'), provision was made for them to use any of the prepared emergency night landing grounds close to their patrol line. Once one was found the pilot was then able to make as safe a landing as possible, this being the reason why all the smaller sites in this book came into existence.

At the end of August 1917 the nine Home Defence squadrons in the London Air Defence Area, which also had control of the anti-aircraft guns and searchlights, were raised to Brigade level with three Wings (Southern, Eastern and Northern) and the number of squadrons increased to a total of seventeen by November 1918.

These defensive measures remained basically unchanged, except for fine improvements, until the Armistice in 1918 but other changes were taking place inside the very organisation of the RFC itself. On 24 August 1917 the War Cabinet met and accepted, in principle, the recommendation that a separate service for the air be formed, and accordingly Lt General Smuts headed a panel known as the Air Organisation Committee to investigate details of its formation and prepare the draft legislation prior to a Bill being submitted to Parliament.

The War Cabinet approved the Bill on 6 November 1917 and decided that it should be laid before Parliament, it received Royal assent on 29 November and Orders in Council of 2 January 1918 stated that the Air Council would come into being the next day. They in turn decreed that the Royal Air Force would come into being on 1 April 1918 (in itself a rather inappropriate date) although the lighter-than-air service would not be taken over from the Admiralty until October 1919. Thus by June 1918 the RAF had control of 1,736 machines of all types on the Western Front and 336 for HD duties, 144 of the latter being single-seat fighters and another 144 night flying machines, but not including training aircraft.

In addition to active fighter defence further measures were instigated to protect primarily London, as well as other areas, against air attacks. In the belief that aircraft flying at a great height could be seen more clearly by the defending guns a ring of barrage balloon aprons were placed on a line running – Winchmore Hill railway station - Mossford Green church - Vallence House (near Becontree Heath) - due south to the Greenwich-to-Dartford main road - Eltham Palace.

Balloons were flown with cables up to 9,000 feet, which forced intruders to fly above this height, and Home Defence aeroplanes were instructed not to cross this line at an altitude less than 11,000 feet (for obvious reasons). Thus the guns and defending fighters knew the minimum height at which to expect raiders to be at and could react accordingly. Additionally, single balloons were moored in St James's Park and Kensington Gardens for 'special' observation work, but these also provided reassurance for Londoners.

Control for all balloon operations was exercised by No. 7 Balloon Wing, South East Area, No. 1 Training Group, with its wing headquarters at the Royal Forest Hotel, Chingford (NGR TQ 396948), next to the historic Queen Elizabeth's hunting lodge.

The wing composed three squadrons, No. 1 being based at Longbridge Road, Barking (NGR TQ 452852) and controlling balloon aprons 1-4 plus two detachments, whilst No. 2 was at 'Banavie', Woodford Green (NGR TQ 412915) and controlled aprons 5-8. No. 3 Sqn was based at Shooters Hill, SE15 and operated in Kent, controlling two aprons.

Each apron had its three balloons flying 500 yards apart with their suspension cables linked to form the basis of a curtain of vertical cables 25 yards apart. A further depot for experimental work and training in the use of kite balloons for apron defence of London was set up in 1917 at Loughton (NGR TQ 424970) but this closed in the summer of 1918.

Outside the balloon barrage lay two bands of anti-aircraft guns with the inner limit of fire or 'Green Line' of the Outer London Barrage running from Shenfield railway station - High Ongar church - Ware - St Albans - Kings Langley - Uxbridge - Weybridge - Effingham - north west corner of Chevening Park - Hartley - Orsett - Shenfield railway station. The outer limit comprised gun stations between Coalhouse to Hadham (under control of AADC, Chelmsford), Batsham to Chalfont St Peter (under St Albans), Gerrards Cross to Wotton, excluding Farnborough, Newhaven and Portslade (under Staines), Westcott to Southwood (under Redhill) and those as far east as Allhallows (under Thames and Medway).

The Air Defence of Great Britain system ceased to exist in July 1936 when four completely new commands – Bomber, Fighter (including Army Co-operation and the Observer Corps), Coastal and Training – were formed. The Admiralty had by then resorted to matters of a purely naval nature, and instigated the use of a carrier-borne strike and reconnaissance force continuing as the Royal Naval Air Service but later renamed the Fleet Air Arm.

Aids to operations

Aeroplane Lights

By the end of 1916 searchlights were installed near, or on, the Flight Stations in order to help pilots on night patrol find the aerodrome. Six were allocated to each Home Defence squadron and operated by them completely separately from those used with the anti-aircraft batteries. When lit they were directed vertically upwards and proved so successful as to form the basis of the Sandra System used in the Second World War.

To assist the separate flights of 37 (HD) Sqn in locating their flight stations, lights were placed at Poplar Grove Farm ($2\frac{1}{8}$ miles WNW of Goldhanger), Woodham Mortimer Lodge (3 miles N of Stow Maries) and Plumberow Mount (3 miles NW of Rochford), as well as one each on the stations themselves. Whilst the 39 (HD) Sqn squadron station at North Weald Bassett had one searchlight and another at Stapleford Tawney (3 miles SE) the other two squadron stations had none on site, searchlights for Hainault Farm being at Stapleford Abbotts and Noak Hill (4 miles NE & ENE respectively), with Suttons Farm using Harold Wood and Great Warley Hall (4 miles NNE & NE).

Ground Arrows

During daylight operations in 1918 nineteen of the Essex sites displayed a ground signal in the form of a large white arrow 200 yds long x 50 yds wide. This was orientated to indicate the current direction of any hostile aircraft that would be visible to aircraft on patrol lines. (See Appendix 4)

Ground Signals

Early in 1915 1st Lt H. Ingram from RNAS Westgate devised a ground-to-air signalling system which was initially shunned but eventually adopted by the RNAS. This was based on a central letter 'T' to which up to three discs could be added in varying positions to pass a specific message to patrolling fighters. As the 'T' was 20'0" wide with a tail 40'0" long and 4'0" broad, and the discs 8'0" in diameter, messages were intended to be seen in daylight at altitudes up to 14,000 ft although under exceptional conditions they could be read from over 17,000 ft. (See Appendix 4)

Money Flare

This comprised a steel cage enclosing an asbestos wick soaked in paraffin, which burnt at the rate of 1¼ gallons per hour and was effective in showing through mist or low cloud as well as being widely used during night operations. Three were laid out on the upwind boundary of an emergency landing ground in an 'L'-shaped pattern with the vertical leg pointing downwind, the landing direction being up the vertical leg of the 'L'.

At first lighting on the landing grounds was laid out and maintained by civilian volunteers but this arrangement proved to be unsuitable for various reasons, therefore at the end of 1916 this duty was taken over by detachments from the Royal Defence Corps allocated to the site. Both Flight and Squadron Stations also used the flares to delineate flarepaths but no standard spacing was specified (See Appendix 4).

Wireless Telegraphy

Known for ever afterwards in its shortened form as 'W/T' this was the method first tried at Biggin Hill in 1915 as a means of communicating with aircraft aloft and vice versa. Standard radio valve equipment was used and the first airborne sets were bulky and heavy, as a result aircraft performance suffered and only a small number in a Flight on operations at any time were thus equipped. No 37 (HD) Sqn first made use of the new equipment on 12 August 1917 when one of their stable B.E.12 aircraft, known as a wireless tracker, relayed information during defensive patrols over the Thames Estuary against eleven Gothas raiding Chatham. By 1918 technology had improved such that airborne sets were lighter and more compact, thus the aircraft's performance was not affected.

Status of landing grounds by operational limitations

By definition – A 1st Class site had no restrictions to landings in any direction, whilst a 2nd Class site had buildings and/or trees which were hazardous to landings in any one direction (note – all Flight Stations had to satisfy requirements for 1st Class status).

3rd Class sites had such landing difficulties in more than one direction, and when in operation at night a flare path comprised of Money Flares was used to show both wind direction and the safest approach onto the usable portion of the field.

Ah, the things you can still find on First World War landing grounds! (Fibreglass replica Spitfire wing on 1830 (Tendring Hundred) Sqn ATC land at Little Clacton.)

The Landing Grounds

Note

1. Apart from Clacton advanced seaplane base, of the land sites active in the county over various periods during the First World War only 20 were still so at the time of the Armistice on 11 November 1918.

2. The site maps show field boundaries as depicted on the 1843-1849 tithe awards held at the County Record Office, Chelmsford. This was the most detailed survey available prior to the First World War but as a result of local surveys carried out just prior to each flight station, and most of the landing grounds, being set up changes in the boundary situation were recorded and where relevant these have been incorporated on the maps.

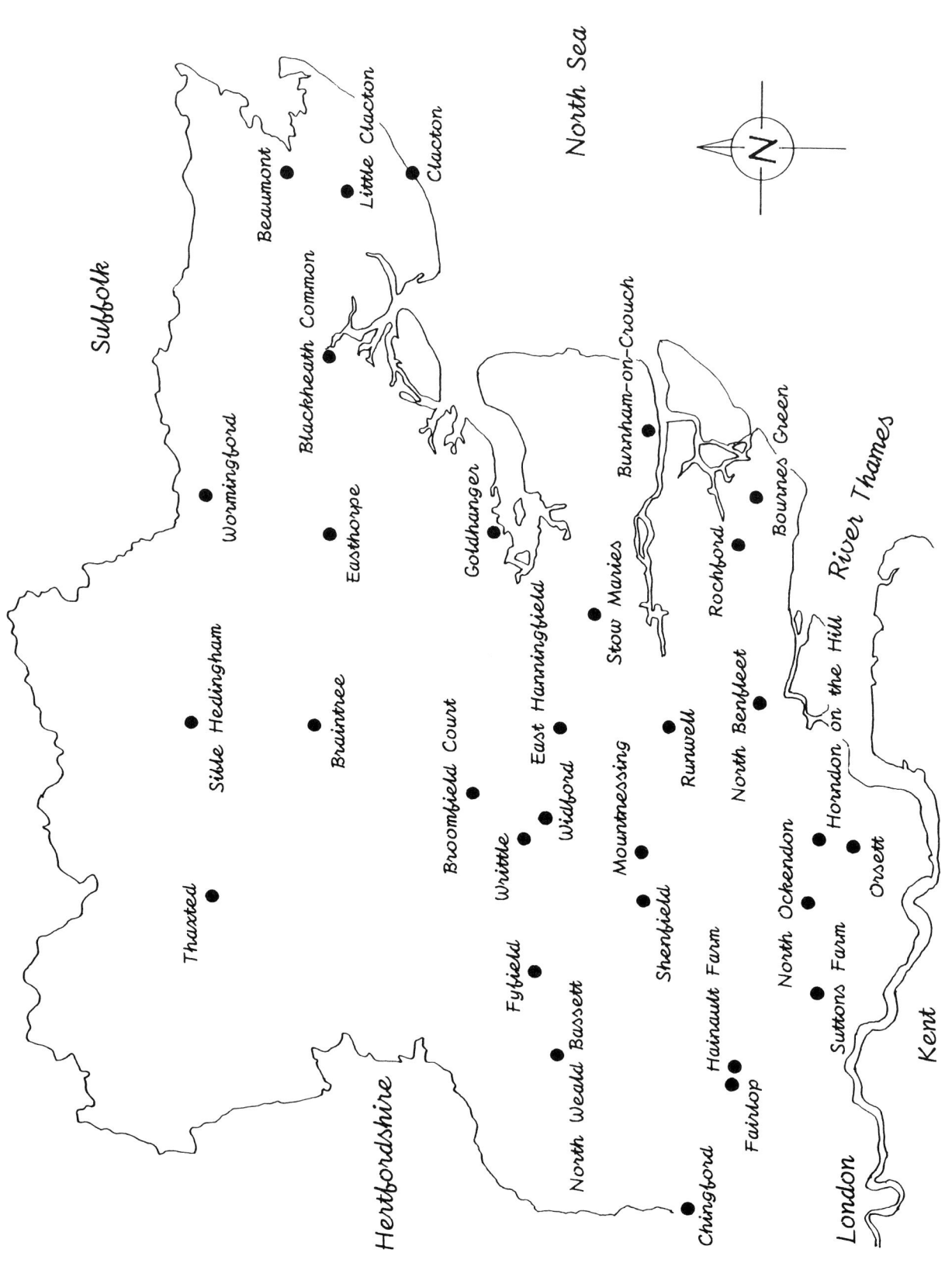

Map of Landing Grounds

One of the least-known sites in the county, this location was selected early in 1916 as a very advanced night landing ground to serve detached flights or pairs of aircraft operating anti-Zeppelin patrols. The need for the site, as with others selected for the same purpose, arose after the defending fighters based at stations nearer to London had failed to intercept numerous intrusions by airships and 'lone wolf' raiders before they reached their targets, therefore it was necessary to operate fighters on patrol lines nearer to the coast in order for them to be more successful.

The fields south of the village, between the parish church of St Leonard and St Mary in the grounds of Beaumont Hall and Golden Lane to the south, had been tithe land owned by Guy's Hospital in 1850 but were being farmed by the Salmon family when the Royal Flying Corps requisitioned them. Located just south of the church at 50' above sea level the site had a clear view of Hamford Water which ran in from the North Sea north of The Naze up to the wharf on the east side of the Harwich Road at Beaumont Quay, this being routinely patrolled against sea-borne entry by enemy forces. The quayside here is quite historic, being built of stones recovered from the original London Bridge, whilst the author Arnold Bennett once lived at Beaumont Hall.

The two fields making up the 43-acre landing ground, Wood Field and Lower Wood Field, had a clay sub-stratum and gave useful landing dimensions of 450 x 350 yards but whilst tents for bad weather shelter, plus pyrotechnics and a windsock, were provided no ground arrows or signals were placed on the site to warn patrolling pilots of hostile aircraft approaching. No classification of status for the landing ground is recorded, this being possibly due to its rather rapid establishment and short usage period, although the altitude and relatively open surroundings adjacent to the site should have placed it in at least a 2nd Class category even though a slope to the south existed.

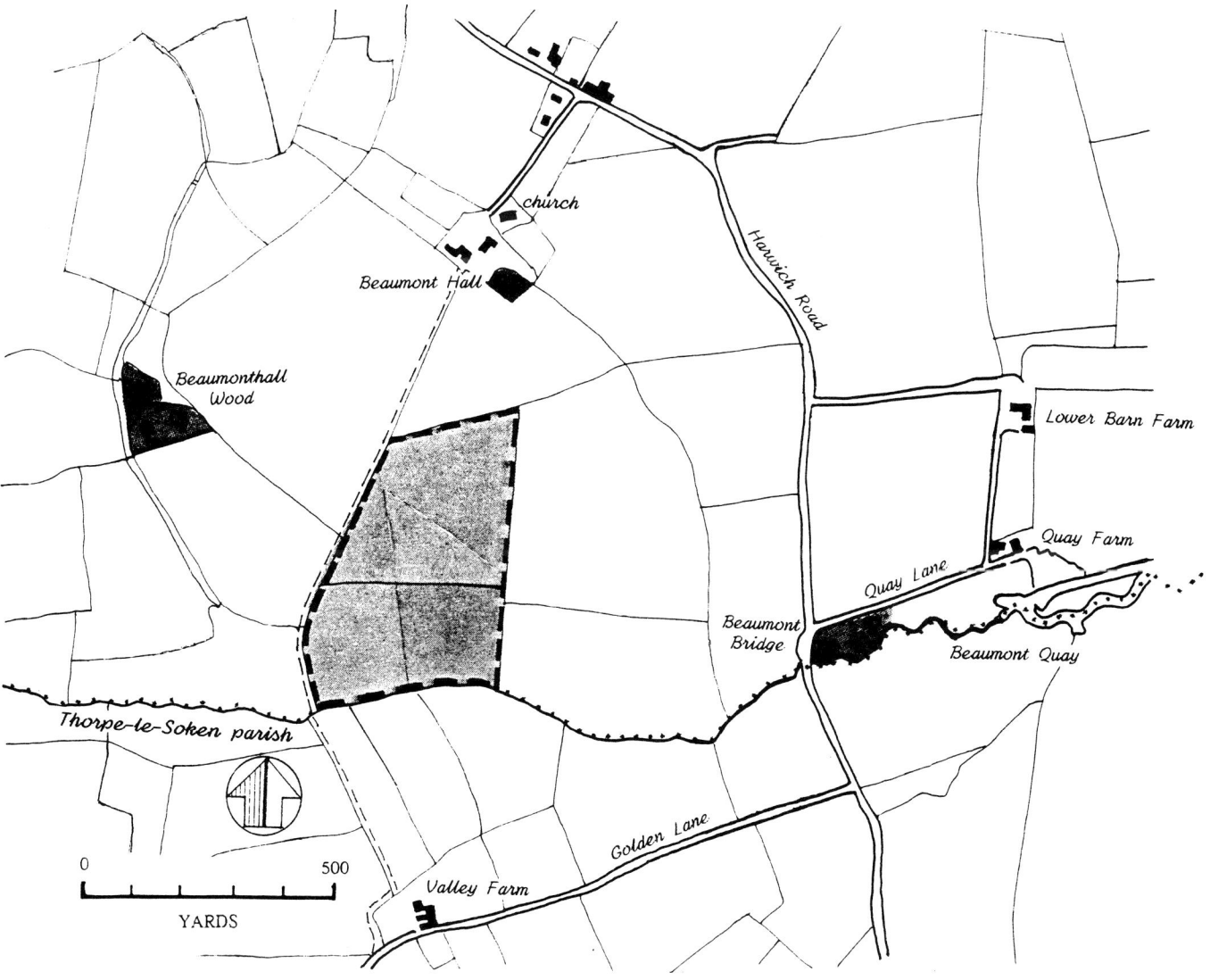

The landing ground opened in April 1916 and was allocated to No. 39 (HD) Sqn, in 49th Wing, South East Area. Based at Hainault Farm and Suttons Farm in the south-western part of the county the squadron had been formed on 15 April by the amalgamation of HD detachments sent there from No. 19 Reserve Aeroplane Squadron at Hounslow.

Little use was made of the landing ground, due mainly to the reduction in enemy airship activity brought about by the shorter nights following its setting-up, and when occupation of the site ceased in August 1916 it returned to agriculture. Although a forced-landing was recorded the following month the need for such a facility was transferred to a new landing ground which opened that October at Plough Corner, Little Clacton to serve 'C' Flight of 37 (HD) Sqn, a unit recently established at Goldhanger as part of 50th Wing.

Apart from occasional forced landings, such as the RAF biplane bomber which arrived one Friday in 1928 and left the next day after being refuelled, no notable mid-war flying took place on the site, the nearest aeronautical event being the 'Astra' show of Alan Cobham's National Aviation Day Display which visited Walton-on-the-Naze on 9 July 1935.

The next notable occasion for Beaumont-cum-Moze (the proper name, which came about when the parishes of Moze and Beaumont were united by Act of Parliament in 1678) was on 12 June 1938 when Her Royal Highness Queen Mary came to the parish church for the Sunday morning service. Plaques inside the church record her visit that day (as well as the fact that Viscount Byng of Vimy, leader of the Canadian forces in World War One, and his wife are buried in the churchyard) but no such memorial in any form exists to the brief but longer use by the RFC of the farm fields near the church.

The landing ground, like other fields here, slopes down to the stream running to the north of Valley Farm. Stable Yard Field, the slightly darker one to the north of the LG, is completely level and took the 1928 forced-landing. The lane running east of the Harwich Road leads to Beaumont Quay.

In the Second World War flying did not return to the area, but it did gain the doubtful distinction of being bombed by the Italian Air Force. Between mid-October and the end of December 1940 a detachment from the *Regia Aeronautica* based in Belgium made over 200 bomber and fighter sorties against the East Coast ports of Great Yarmouth, Lowestoft and Harwich. After a raid on the latter target during the evening of 24 October four bombs were jettisoned just west of the church, no casualties resulted but damage was caused to a house and overhead wires. The following month pairs of bombs were dropped on Golden Lane and just outside the area of the WW1 landing ground at Pond Farm to the west.

Fields immediately to the north of Oldhouse Farm in Beaumont village were next earmarked as the possible location of a bomber airfield for the United States 8th Air Force based in East Anglia. The bomber airfield construction programme for the USAAF proposed 11 in Essex which would have taken in all, or part, of the First World War sites at Beaumont, Burnham on Crouch, Little Clacton, Stow Maries and Wormingford (as well as locations at Bulphan, High Roding, Ingatestone, Maldon, Southminster and Weeley, but only the High Roding site drawing has come into the author's possession so far).

Given the USAAF Station number 148, Beaumont was allocated to the 8th Air Force on 10 August 1942 and confirmed the next month but, after initial survey work had been carried out, construction was postponed indefinitely early in December and never came to fruition as the need arose to complete other airfields in the county which had fallen behind schedule due to a season of bad weather conditions. Had work gone ahead three concrete runways and the associated buildings on many dispersed sites required for a Class 'A' airfield would have been laid down there, quite a contrast to the lack of facilities provided in 1916 at the RFC site one mile to the south.

Land on both the First and proposed Second World War sites has remained agricultural ever since, farms in the area being managed by Strutt and Parker, the fields to the south of Beaumont church being as they were prior to 1916.

Blackheath Common   TM 006213

As one of only two night emergency landing grounds in Essex chosen directly by the War Office for the RFC, the other being at the southern end of the county at Horndon-on-the-Hill, it was located two miles south of Colchester railway station on part of a military exercise area lying opposite Roman Hill Farm on the road to Mersea Island. The positions of most of the night landing grounds were generally given from railway stations or large towns, the reason being that at night or in bad weather pilots would be more likely to spot these and thus plot the distance and direction to the lighted LG.

Originally set up in March 1915 to support Home Defence squadrons who were patrolling in an attempt to counter incoming raiders it was promptly given the telephone number of Colchester 307, although it was located in the very northern part of the parish of East Donyland. With an area of some 55 acres of grass on a loamy soil at 105' amsl, and good approaches from all directions onto a landing area of 500 x 700 yards, the surroundings were somewhat wooded but nevertheless it was designated a 1st Class site.

After being set up nothing is recorded of any aerial activities at Blackheath Common until February 1917, when No. 37 (HD) Sqdn based at Goldhanger as part of 50th Wing, South East Area, was noted as the prime user, the most northerly extent of their Northern patrol line being the LG at Easthorpe. By the end of May it had been added to the list of landing grounds available but its only recorded use was on the night of 19/20 October 1917 when a B.E.2e of No. 37 (HD) Sqn, flown by 2nd Lt Armstrong on an occasion when 78 sorties were launched against Zeppelins attacking Northern England, force-landed here with engine failure. Armstrong survived this incident but lost his life exactly four months later when his aircraft crashed and burnt near Goldhanger whilst on a similar duty.

Postwar the site was retained for RAF use until July 1919 when it returned to the Army and flying left the area until Alan Cobham's National Aviation Day display visited the field. This happened on three occasions, the first tour coming on 19 May 1932, the No. 1 Tour of 1933 on 4 May (when two simultaneous tours were operated around the country that year) and the last on 26 June 1934.

Between 1936-39 the field at Fridaywood Farm, one mile due west, was used by No. 2 (AC) Squadron for its summer camps with Hawker Hector and Westland Lysander aircraft, and in May 1943 Abberton reservoir one mile to the south-west was one of the waterways used by the Lancasters of No. 617 Squadron whilst training for the Ruhr dams raid. Blackheath Common itself saw no more flying activity, with Cherry Tree Army Camp being established on the northern part of the landing ground.

Following military land disposals after 1956 Cherry Tree Camp was demolished and Cherry Tree Infants school built there in the 1960s, with private housing of the Monkwick Estate between it and the B1025. The rest of the landing ground is now a mixture of pasture or woodland managed by the Ministry of Defence.

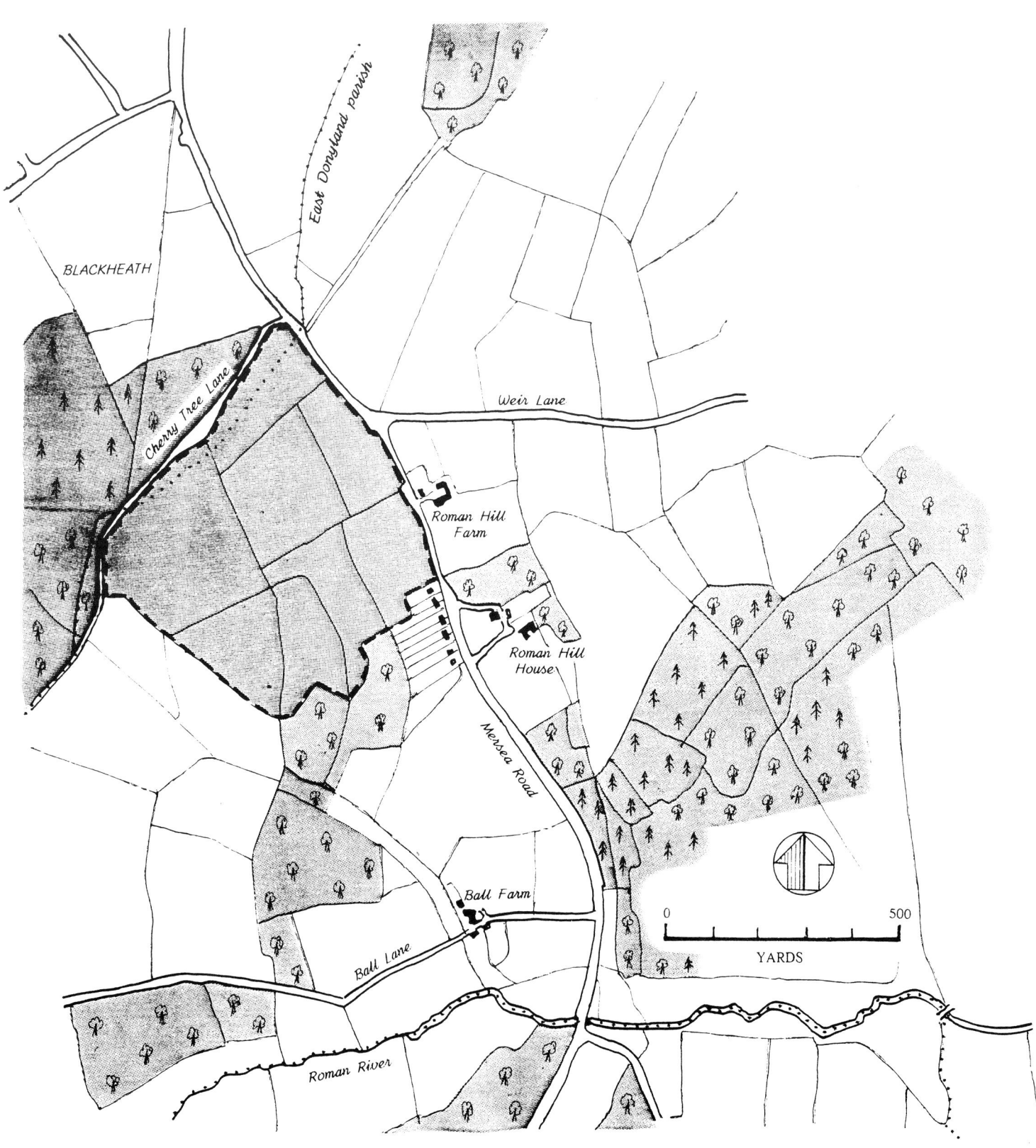

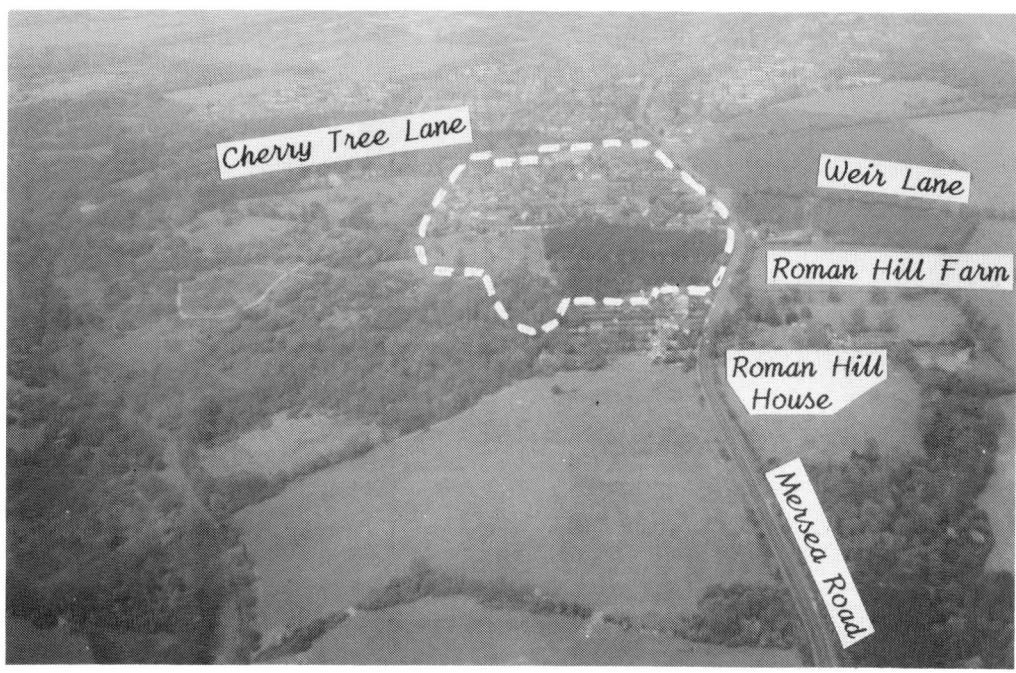

The Mersea Road runs up the picture, past Roman Hill Farm and into Colchester. Part of the former LG is either farmed or woodland whilst the rest is covered with housing.

Bournes Green   TQ 917873

With the dubious honour of having been the most short-lived of all the landing grounds it still looks much as it was 80 years ago, except for the nearby roads and farms which have been modernised.

The site was brought into use in May 1917 for aircraft using the artillery ranges at nearby Shoeburyness ('Gunners Town') when it was thought beneficial to have a landing ground close by. Ground-to-air firing over the offshore mud flats had previously been achieved by firing at kites flown from moving locomotives or small balloons towed by aircraft, but in the latter case the aircraft were operating from further afield with only a short period of time actually available for useful range work.

Set up ¼ mile to the east of Silchester Corner and one mile north of Thorpe Bay railway station the site encompassed an area of some 32 acres on the John Burgess Jnr estate. At 40' amsl the landing area was level arable land on a clay loam stratum but only had usable landing dimensions of 425 x 325 yards. Although generally the surroundings were open with reasonable-sized fields the restricted landing directions led to it being placed in the category of a 2nd Class landing ground for day use only.

It was just another part of a steady expansion of accommodation and training facilities in the Shoeburyness area by the War Office who, amongst other things, had been the original producers there of coal gas for domestic use. To store the produced gas a gasholder was built in the late-1860s at North Shoebury one mile south-east of the landing ground and, as well as the chimneys of Sutton brickworks to the east, proved an ideal inland landmark for locating it in bad weather.

Another well-known local landmark in 1917 was the Rose Inn on the other side of the road running past the landing ground, this had been there since around 1799 with the licence first issued to a Thomas Salt and well known by personnel manning the site. The 'ground sorties' to this objective however were curtailed somewhat by the introduction of licencing laws brought in during the First World War, mainly to stop workers at munitions factories from getting too drunk to produce explosive shells properly.

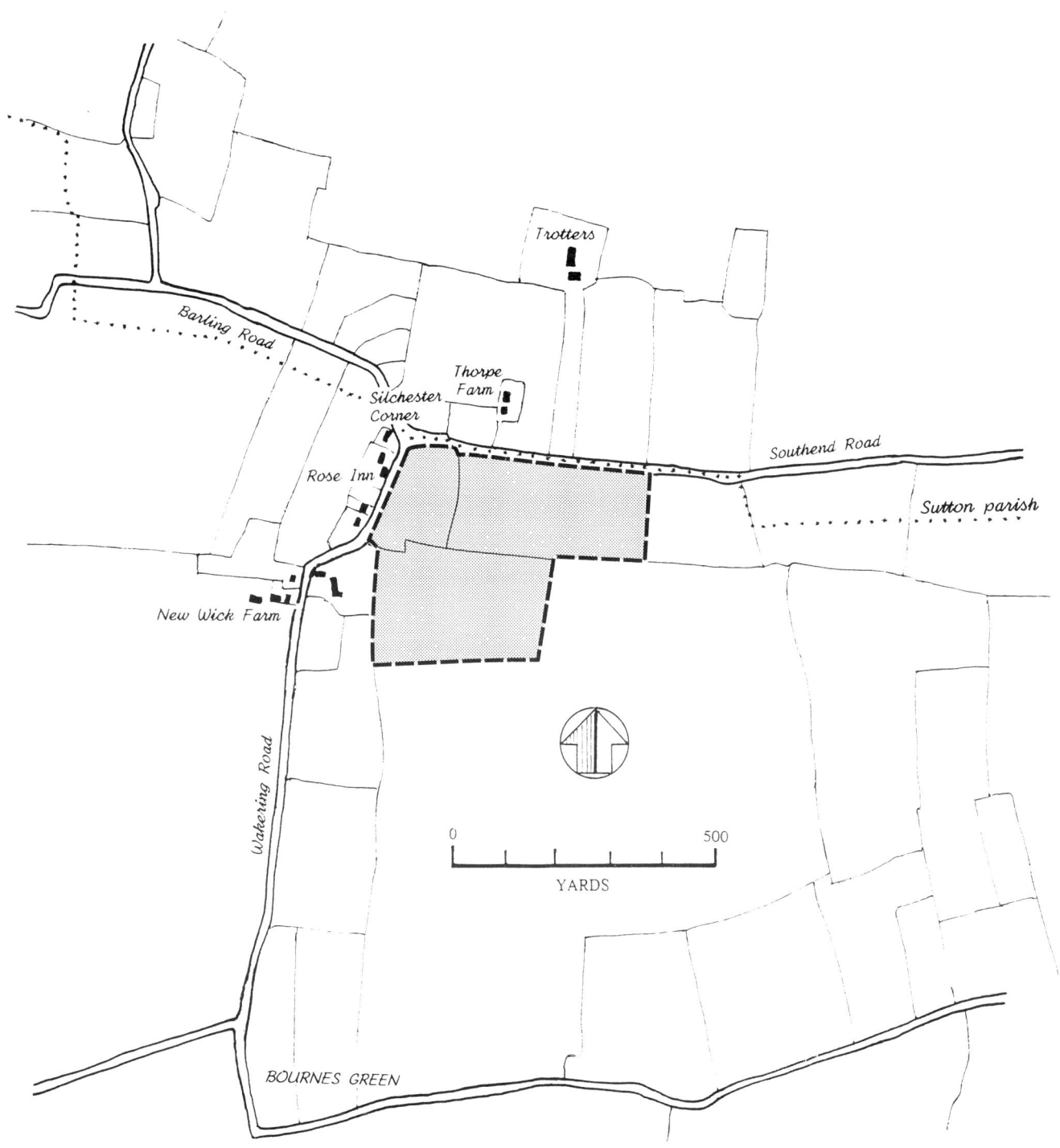

No facilities except a windsock and tents for accommodation were provided and the landing ground functioned perfectly satisfactorily, but operations were brought to a halt when it was realised that the activities resulting from regular air gunnery flights over the area were not entirely conducive with the close proximity of Thorpe Bay and Shoeburyness town. Operational only for 3½ weeks, occupation of the site ceased in June 1917 when the need for such a facility was transferred to the landing ground at Marine Town, to the east of Sheerness on the other side of the River Thames in Kent, and the site returned to farming.

No further aviation activities took place in the area, the closest 'arrival' during the Second World War being Messerschmitt BF110c 3U+KR of 7/ZG26 which force-landed at North Shoebury House after being shot down during an escort sortie on 3 September 1940. The only other remaining sign of any military presence in the area of the landing ground is the Second World War Type FW3/24 pill-box sited on the northern boundary to protect the Silchester Corner road junction.

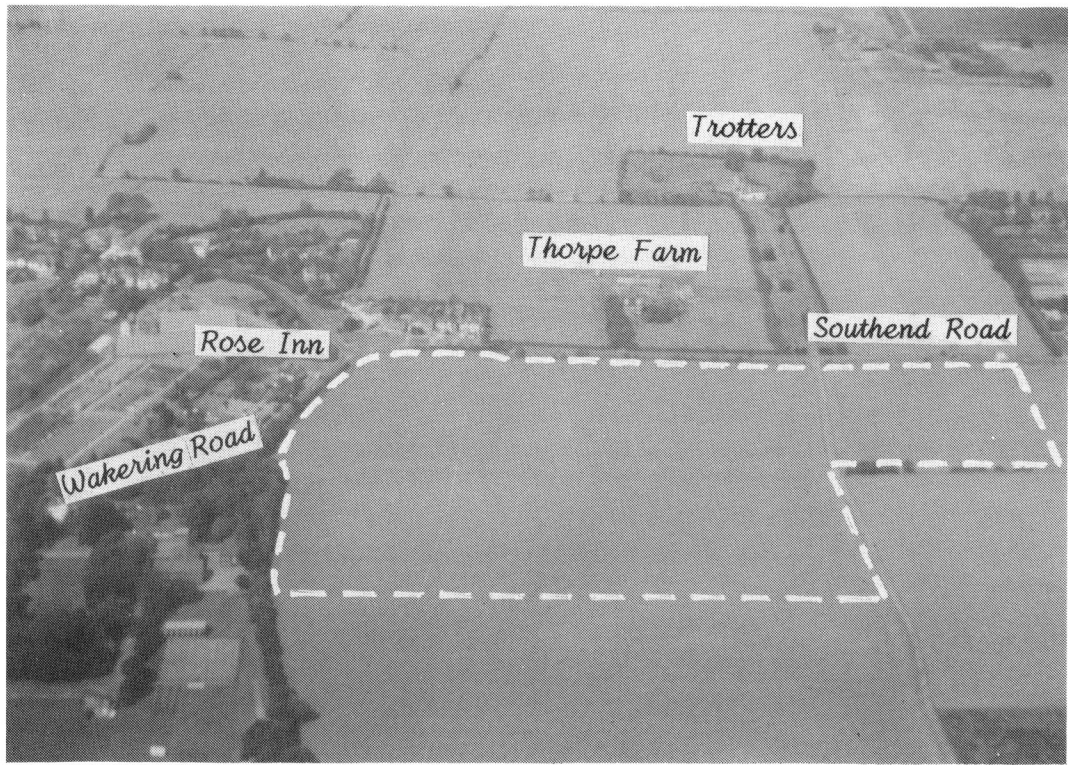

The fields next to Silchester Corner once used as an Army Co-operation day landing ground are still open.

Braintree   TL 738218

This site on the south side of Queenborough Lane 1½ miles south-west of the town centre was located next to a small hamlet known locally as Braintree Green, itself half a mile south of the comparatively larger village of Rayne on the Bishops Stortford road. Six fields in pasture belonging to Stamfords Farm and two to Slamsey Farm had the dividing hedges taken out to form a flying field of 60 acres with useful landing dimensions of 700 x 400 yards. At 230' amsl on a boulder clay sub-soil the site was fairly level, but the dwellings and heavily wooded surroundings in the northern quadrant put it in the category of a 3rd Class night landing ground when it was added to the list of sites available at the end of January 1917.

Allocated to No. 39 (HD) Sqn, in 49th Wing, South East Area it was intended to serve the northernmost patrol lines flown initially by 'A' Flight based at North Weald Bassett, but little has been recorded of its use by the squadron. It continued to be manned during the change from Royal Flying Corps to Royal Air Force in April 1918 until October of that year when, having been kept open for use by other units, it was deemed to be not worthy of retention and shortly afterwards the whole site was returned to its owners for farming to resume.

Fifteen years later the sight and sound of a dozen aeroplane engines was experienced at the field on the same day when the flying circus of Alan Cobham's National Aviation Day 1933 tour came to town. Two separate tours of the United Kingdom were operated by Cobham for the whole of that year only, with the town of Braintree scheduled for the 29 May stop by the No. 1 tour. Apart from newly-opened civil aerodromes in or close to town centres many locations used by air circuses had been landing grounds in the First World War and Braintree was no exception, but by 1933 the dividing hedges had grown back such that the air circus fleet were only able to use an area of 22 acres made up by four fields on what had been the eastern corner of the RFC night landing ground.

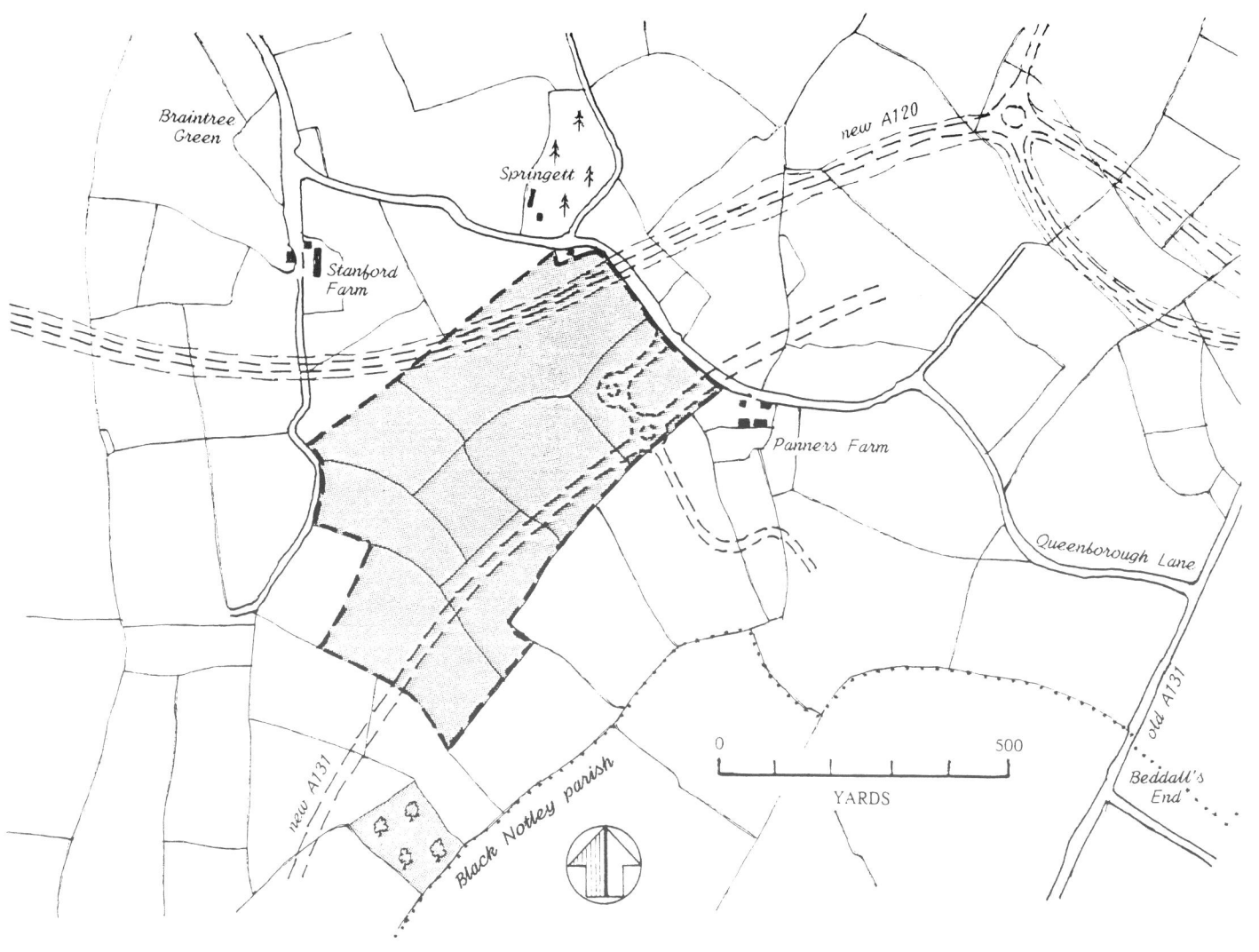

The format used successfully by Cobham was to start each display with the whole fleet arriving in formation, in this case from the previous day's display at Earls Hall, Clacton, the fleet would then stream for fly-pasts before coming in to land on the prepared site for the opening ceremony. The public paid to get into the screened-off flying ground and the day's programme remained basically the same at all locations, with precise aerobatics and formation work, then crazy flying and daring low-level feats such as handkerchief pick-ups being demonstrated. Cobham was a showman and always kept his audience enthralled then, for those members of the public that could afford it, flights over the area could be had for 5/- (25p) in one of the machines that had previously been seen cavorting in the sky above them. When the display finally came to an end the public left and the pilots helped clear up before picketting the aircraft and sleeping under them or in caravans inside the field. The ground crew meanwhile started work on dismantling the fences and public address facilities, this work continuing into the night before the vehicles were loaded up to go to the site of the following day's venue (Huntingdon) where the next display was to be given. Prior to flying off the aircraft would be checked, fuelled up and readied for the next venue where they would arrive on time, in formation, and the show would start all over again.

After this visit by the National Aviation Day display no further flying took place on the site, the agricultural use continuing in the ownership of the Hawkes family. In 1995 a new dual carriageway to replace the original A120 road and bypass Rayne was taken across the north-western corner, whilst the new A131 and junctions serving the housing areas built to the south of Braintree bound the site on the east side.

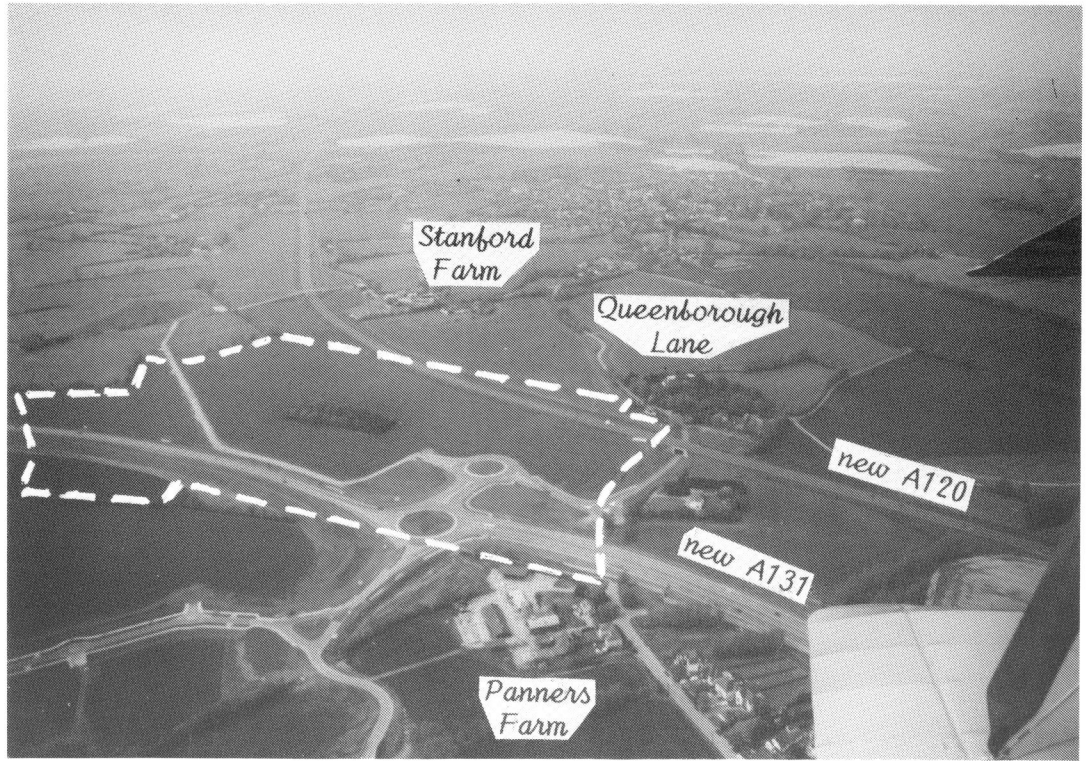

This shot was taken from the east to show both the landing ground and new roads built over the area in recent years. Queenborough Lane runs from behind the lower wing up the centre of the picture to the right of Panners Farm, past the wooded area at Springett and into Rayne village. Between Panners Farm and the remains of the tree belt on the site (the missing portions being due to new saplings planted in the 1950s having been stolen by gypsies) are the roundabouts built on the new A131.

Below the top wingtip is the disused railway line running into Rayne with the new A120 Rayne by-pass running rearwards from the wing strut.

Typical line-up at a daily air display, this being the British Hospitals Air Pageant, with DG60X Moth G–EBZL in front of a Phillips and Powis (Woodley) Spartan two-seater, another Moth and Desoutter Mk 1 G–AAVO. The Desoutter was taken out of service in December 1936 whilst G–EBZL served with the RAF when impressed as AW159 in June 1940. The lady is Pauline Gower, who flew with the BHAP and was appointed a Commandant in the Air Transport Auxiliary, the civilian-staffed aircraft ferry organisation of the Second World War. (Paul Fahie photo)

Broomfield Court

Situated 3½ miles north of Chelmsford railway station and on the Broomfield Court estate, the site was established in August 1916 on some 36 acres of farmland 'borrowed' for the duration of hostilities. Although at 200' amsl, due to its location being just west of the Court itself and with rather heavily wooded surroundings to the north-west, it fell into the category of a 2nd Class night landing ground when allocated to the RFC.

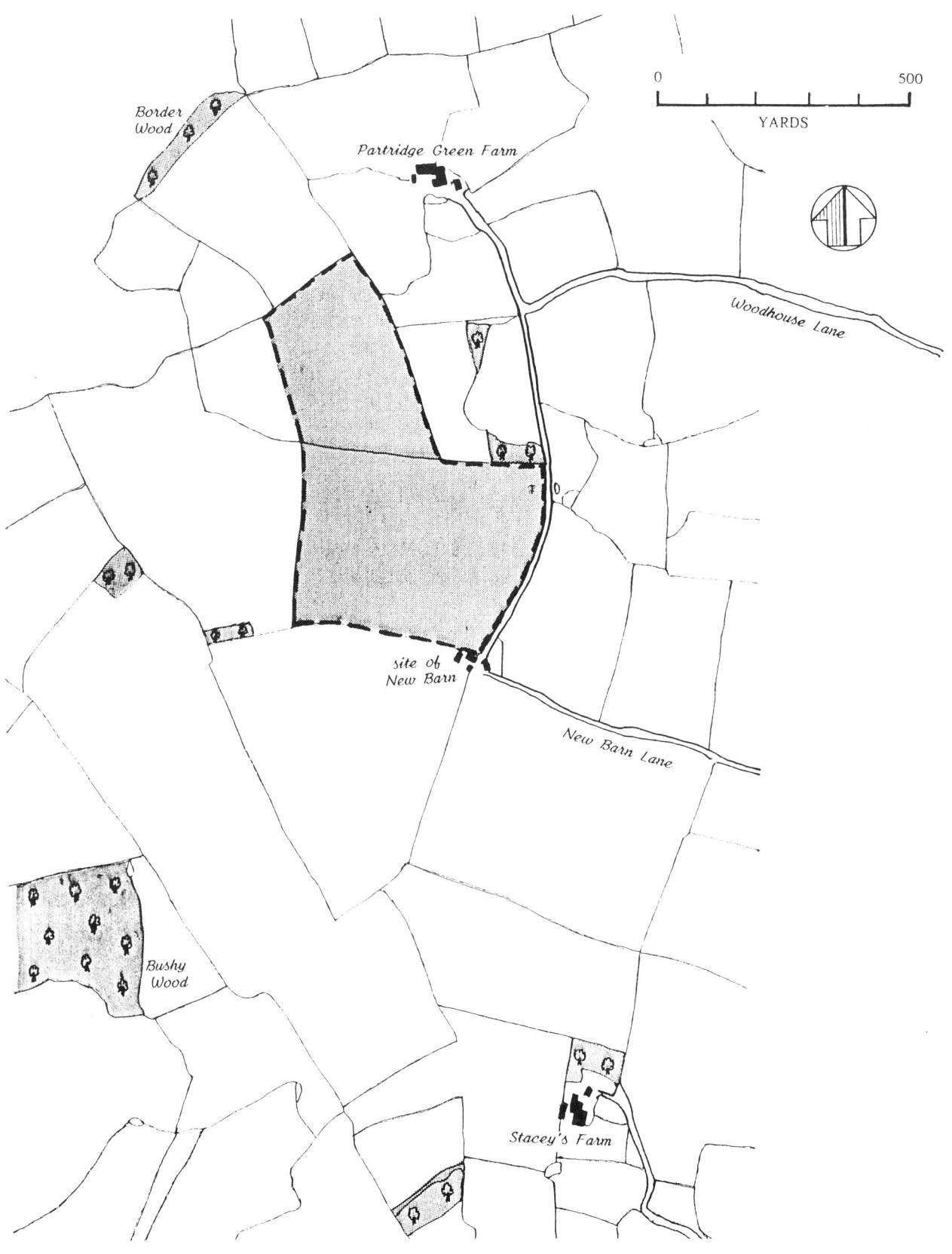

Whilst it was intended to be allocated to No. 37 (HD) Sqn in 50th Wing, South East Area, the use of such night landing grounds was not solely limited to aircraft from the units designated to them. After an abortive pursuit of Zeppelin LZ98 on the night of 2/3 September 1916 Flt Cdr A.R. Arnold, flying a Farman F.56 from RNAS Grain in Kent, saw the wooden-hulled SL11 held in searchlights to the north-west and headed towards them. As he arrived Leefe Robinson from No 39 (HD) Sqn at Suttons Farm was in the process of shooting it down at Cuffley so, having lost his bearings, Arnold promptly made for the NLG flares lit at Broomfield but lost them due to bad visibility whilst on his final approach and crashed into a nearby field.

In January 1917 the status of the landing ground was reduced to 3rd Class but, with the acquisition of further pasture on the estate near to the farm cottages at Partridge Green, the area of the landing ground was increased to 45 acres and at the end of March it was once more reclassified as a 2nd Class site. Noted as having a usable landing area of 700 x 500 yards on clay soil and now fairly open surroundings to the larger landing field it was duly given the unusual telephone number of Little Waltham 2a. Still primarily for use by No. 37 (HD) Sqn it was used occasionally, the site being retained by the Royal Air Force up to the time of the Armistice but finally closed in August 1919 and the land returned to pasture.

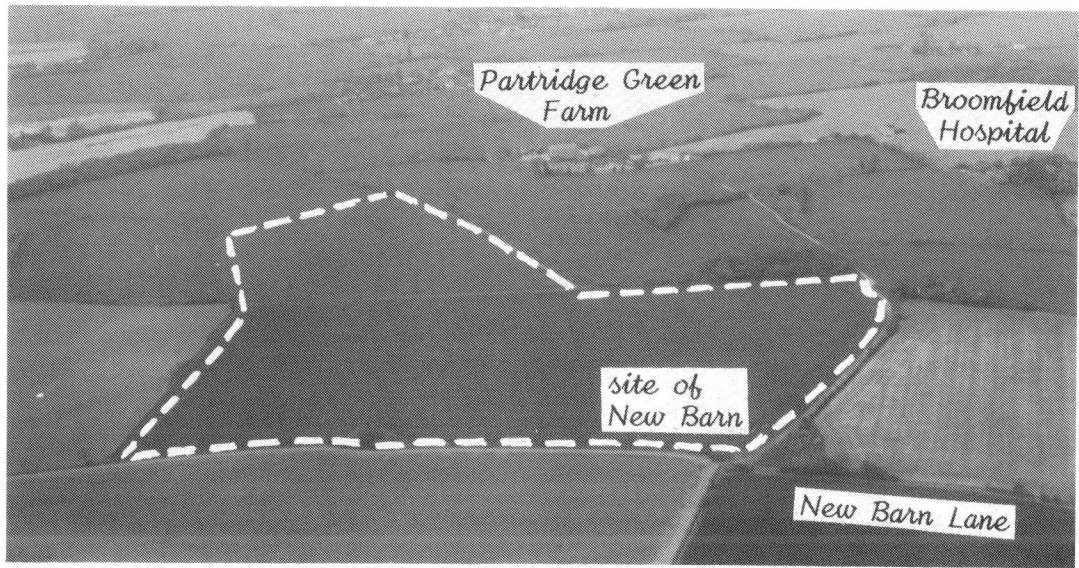

Broomfield Court today, with no trace of any aerodrome buildings. The site of New Barn is marked only by a crossroad on New Barn Lane whilst to the north Partridge Green Farm is still prominent. Staff quarters to the enlarged Broomfield hospital can just be seen at centre right.

With the upsurge of public interest in aviation in the 1930s the aerodrome was opened up on 26 November 1931 for passenger flying by Aviation Transport Sales and Services Ltd, whose 'fleet' comprised two Avro 504K aircraft originally erected in an Orsett garage, but the venture was not successful and operations ceased after a short while.

On 18 May 1932 the aerodrome then became active once more as Broomfield/Chelmsford aerodrome, when it was officially opened by Brigadier-General R.B. Colvin, the then Lord Lieutenant of Essex. The occasion was marked by a visit from Alan Cobham's National Aviation Day display, in its first year of operation, and included various DH Gipsy Moths as well as other larger passenger-carrying types and the small Comper Swift G-ABPY. One week later, on 25 May, the new aerodrome hosted a royal visit when HRH the Duke of York arrived in the 3-engined Airspeed Ferry G-ABSI, 'Youth of Britain II', to open the Widford-Springfield section of the Chelmsford bypass. The Duke was driven by car to the town and later returned to take his leave by air.

In June 1932 the main clubhouse was replaced by another wooden structure, this coming from Brooklands in Surrey. On 18 September a hangar fire brought operations to a stop and although the aerodrome lease was taken up by a German, Franz Lehman, in 1933 it lasted for less than two years and lapsed in October 1934. The Broomfield Flying Club was then formed and club flying went on until the club itself ceased to exist at the start of the Second World War when the aerodrome, in common with most civil sites, was closed on 3 September 1939.

After the war the aerodrome never re-opened, all traces of the previous operations have disappeared including the fuel tanks and their concrete base, and the barn at the end of New Barn Lane where aircraft engines were once serviced and stored. With later changes in land ownership the house at Broomfield Court itself and the area around it then became an annexe to the Broomfield Hospital which exists today in a much enlarged form, whilst the aerodrome site is back to agriculture.

Burnham-on-Crouch   TQ 962961

The need, so their Lordships at the Admiralty thought, to have a Flight Station on the most likely route that raiders would take in approaching London from the East Coast led to the site at Burnham-on-Crouch being established as a Branch Station of the RNAS. This came about following a change in strategy on 27 December 1914 when, for the defence of London, it was anticipated that a screen of aircraft from bases sited between Lincolnshire and London itself would be able to intercept airships from Northern Germany or aircraft from locations in Belgium, and accordingly new Branch Stations were placed at Burnham-on-Crouch, Chelmsford, Chingford, Maidstone and Ramsgate.

Situated one mile east of the town railway station, and three-quarters of a mile north of the River Crouch, the landing ground lay directly between Burnham and Dammer Wick farms at 12' amsl with the surroundings low-lying and marshy. Operations began with two Bristol T.B.8 aircraft from Eastchurch being positioned here but whilst no successes were recorded, nor indeed any contacts made by the patrolling aircraft, Burnham served the RNAS as a Flight Station (night) for over a year until transferred over to the RFC when that service took over the responsibility for aerial defence of mainland Britain in 1916. Although it had previously been categorised as a Flight Station by the RNAS this was a completely different method of classification to that used by the RFC in determining the status of a site.

When the RFC took over the tenancy in April 1916 the clay soil fields were opened up by hedge removal to increase the landing ground to 102 acres and give useful landing runs of 750 x 600 yards. A line of elm trees was taken out along the eastern boundary and, with the open surroundings making forced landings simple, the site achieved the status of a 1st Class Home Defence night landing ground when it was designated for use primarily by No. 37 (HD) Sqn in 50th Wing, South East Area with the telephone number of Burnham-on-Crouch 15. No permanent facilities of any kind were erected, personnel being provided with tents placed on the northern edge of the site near to Dammer Wick Farm.

One of the occasions on which the site was used in the emergency role occurred on the night of 24–25 August 1916 when the Navy Zeppelin L31, commanded by the experienced Kptlt Mathy, had been chased by 2nd Lt J.I. Mackay of No. 39 (HD) Sqn in a B.E.2c from North Weald Bassett. Mackay lost the Zeppelin after a few miles, then after becoming lost himself landed at Burnham at 0300 but in doing so damaged his undercarriage.

The landing ground also catered for aviators caught out much further away from their own station and in need of its facilities. On the morning of 24 May 1917 2nd Lt J.G. Goodyear of 'A' Flight, No. 50 (HD) Sqn, flying a B.E.2e from Bekesbourne in Kent against the L42, was blown well off course by strong winds whilst patrolling between Dover-Margate and force-landed at 0425 hrs. As part of a total of 76 Home Defence sorties flown against an armada of six airships which started incursions the previous night this was his second sortie, he having taken off earlier but been forced to return to Bekesbourne due to rain then went off again later only to arrive at Burnham. The following day Flt Lt H.C. Lemon, flying Sopwith Baby N1025 from RNAS Westgate, had taken off after 23 Gothas attacking Folkestone in daylight but force-landed on the sea with engine trouble and had to be towed into the harbour at Burnham-on-Crouch.

The RFC/RAF retained use of the site ostensibly with the allocation still to No. 37 Sqn until July 1919 when it was given up and returned to the Croxon family, from whom it had been originally requisitioned, and arable farming resumed on the land.

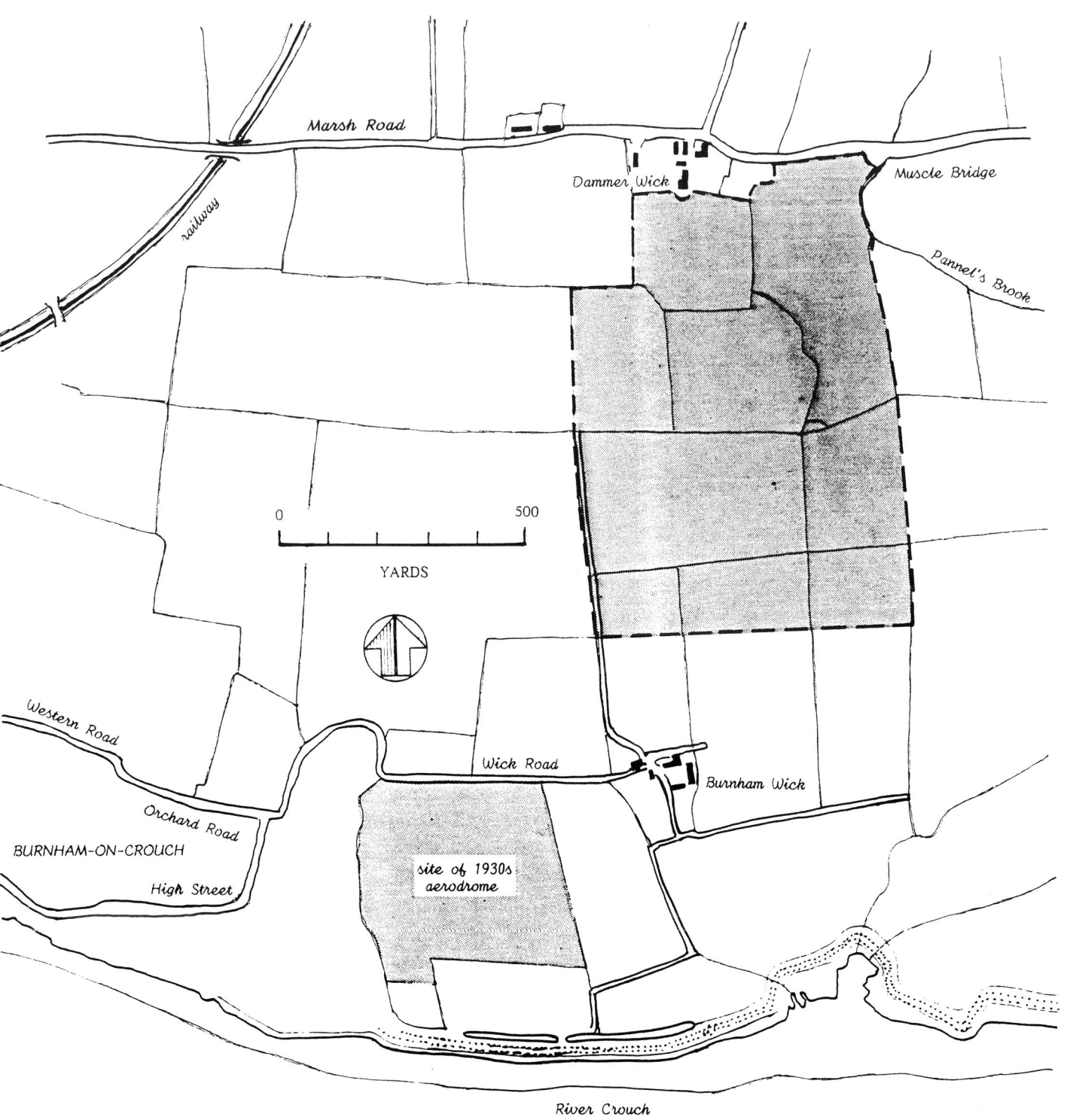

This was not the end of aviation in the area, for less than half a mile mile to the south-west a civil aerodrome was opened in 1932. Registered for operations in the name of Douglas B. Smith, JP, esq, living at Wickham Hall, Witham and referenced 'DB' by the inspecting Automobile Association the square field was located between Burnham Wick farm and the sewage works on the riverside to the south next to the Royal Corinthian Yacht Club House. Although of only 29 acres in size by comparison with the First World War landing ground this new site provided a maximum landing run of 370 yards. In use only up to the beginning of the Second World War it was, like most British civil aerodromes, closed on 3 September 1939 and indeed orders from the Air Ministry of 26 May 1940 decreed that it be obstructed to prevent landings by airborne enemy forces. The much larger area of the First World War landing ground however escaped the need for such precautions.

Despite other developments nearby both flying sites have reverted to farming.

No airfield was established at Burnham during the Second World War but the conflict saw much air activity around the area, articles dropped in the vicinity of the WW1 aerodrome including some 150 incendiary bombs at Burnham Wick on 27 December 1940, 72 onto Dammer Wick farm on 19 March 1941, and RAF Sgts Coker, Grubb and Perrin of 51 Sqn who landed safely by parachute near the town after baling out of their Whitley bomber T4224 (NH-B) which had force-landed on the south side of the river at Paglesham Rectory on 4 May 1941. Further aviation interest came about in August 1942 when Burnham was surveyed as a possible location for a bomber base to serve the United States 8th Air Force, but this did not happen after only preliminary survey work had been carried out.

No traces of aerial activities remain at either site except for the windsock from the civil aerodrome which has ended up in the barn at Burnham Wick farm, this holding now being worked by Douglas Smith, grandson to D.B. Smith of Wickham Hall. The WW1 site remains farmland whilst the southern part of the 1930s civil aerodrome now plays host to a holiday caravan park.

The one Essex landing ground which changed so dramatically after the First World War opened at the western county boundary on 27 December 1914 when it was designated as a Branch Station of the RNAS. Here, in the low-lying area between Chingford and Ponders End, four Bristol T.B.8 aircraft were placed on readiness against Zeppelin raiders, as were the RNAS stations at Burnham on Crouch and Widford which each had two machines despatched there for the same purpose.

On 15 April 1915 the site was then one of two in the county selected by the Admiralty for pilot training, the other being Widford, but was re-categorised a 2nd Class landing ground by virtue of the enclosed surroundings which made approaches bad from most directions except over Flanders Weir to the south. Along the north side ran the high embankment of the King George's reservoir (opened in 1913), whilst housing and higher ground existed to the east, and across the middle of the site ran the Old River Lea with a 200' wide bridge near the north boundary. A further branch of the Lea from just north of Flanders Weir followed the western site boundary up to the Pike and Anchor public house south of Ponders End lock on the River Lea Navigation. Forced landings due to engine failure after takeoff were therefore only recommended to the south and south-west, indeed to cater for such eventualities to the north a power boat was permanently moored in the reservoir.

The site area was 150 acres but all the topographical restrictions resulted in a triangular landing area with usable dimensions of only 1500 x 400 yards. At 45' amsl the northern half of the site was on Chingford Marsh, with another part on reclaimed ground, and while the clay soil surface was generally good it was noted as becoming soft in wet weather.

With the telephone number of Chingford 131 for the station all the buildings were sited around the northern boundaries, off site were the Photographic Section at White Hall, near Whitehall Road, and the Station Sick Quarters at Sewardstone Lodge, near Daws Hill on the Sewardstone Road.

Pilots under training first completed a disciplinary course at the Crystal Palace, they then were posted for preliminary flying training to either Chingford, Eastbourne, Eastchurch or Redcar. After 20-24 hours solo they then went to Cranwell for advanced training in a full syllabus comprising cross-country flying, engines, navigation, aerial gunnery, bombing, photography and wireless-telegraphy. (Seaplane pilots went from Crystal Palace to Calshot, Felixstowe or Killingholme, thence to Cranwell where they graduated in all subjects except flying.) Amongst the instructors from 1915 onwards were Flight Lieutenants Hubert Broad (later chief test pilot for the de Havilland Aircraft Co), F. Warren Merriam (later author) and Ben Travers (later playwright).

Chingford was, by standards at the time, a permanent station and this was reflected in the social and sporting activities carried out there. Regular plays and concerts were held in the YMCA hut and the annual sports day, with the novel 100 yard race by the station band a great favourite, was enjoyed by all and reported in the station journal both in words and pictures (courtesy of the Photographic Section). With the title of 'Chingflier' the journal was started in 1916 by three Naval Air Service ratings and at 3d (1p) per issue was very popular not only with those at Chingford but also other RNAS stations who did not have one. 'Chingflier' was also the name given to pilots under training whilst recruits were known as 'Chingboys', but names for the ladies of the RNAS have not been recorded.

Many later well-known personalties were stationed at Chingford, amongst them Flight Sub Lieutenants Norman Blackburn (of the aircraft company), Egbert Cadbury (of the chocolate family), Sidney Cotton (inventor of the Sidcot flying suit) and David Ivor Davies, the last being popular at the piano during the nightly sessions at the 'King's Head' in the town and subsequently as a composer under the name Ivor Novello. These nightly antics enhanced the nickname given to the RNAS of 'Rather Naughty After Sunset'.

Additionally, Roy Brown, the Canadian pilot who reputedly shot down Richthofen and rose to the rank of Flight Commander, trained at Chingford.

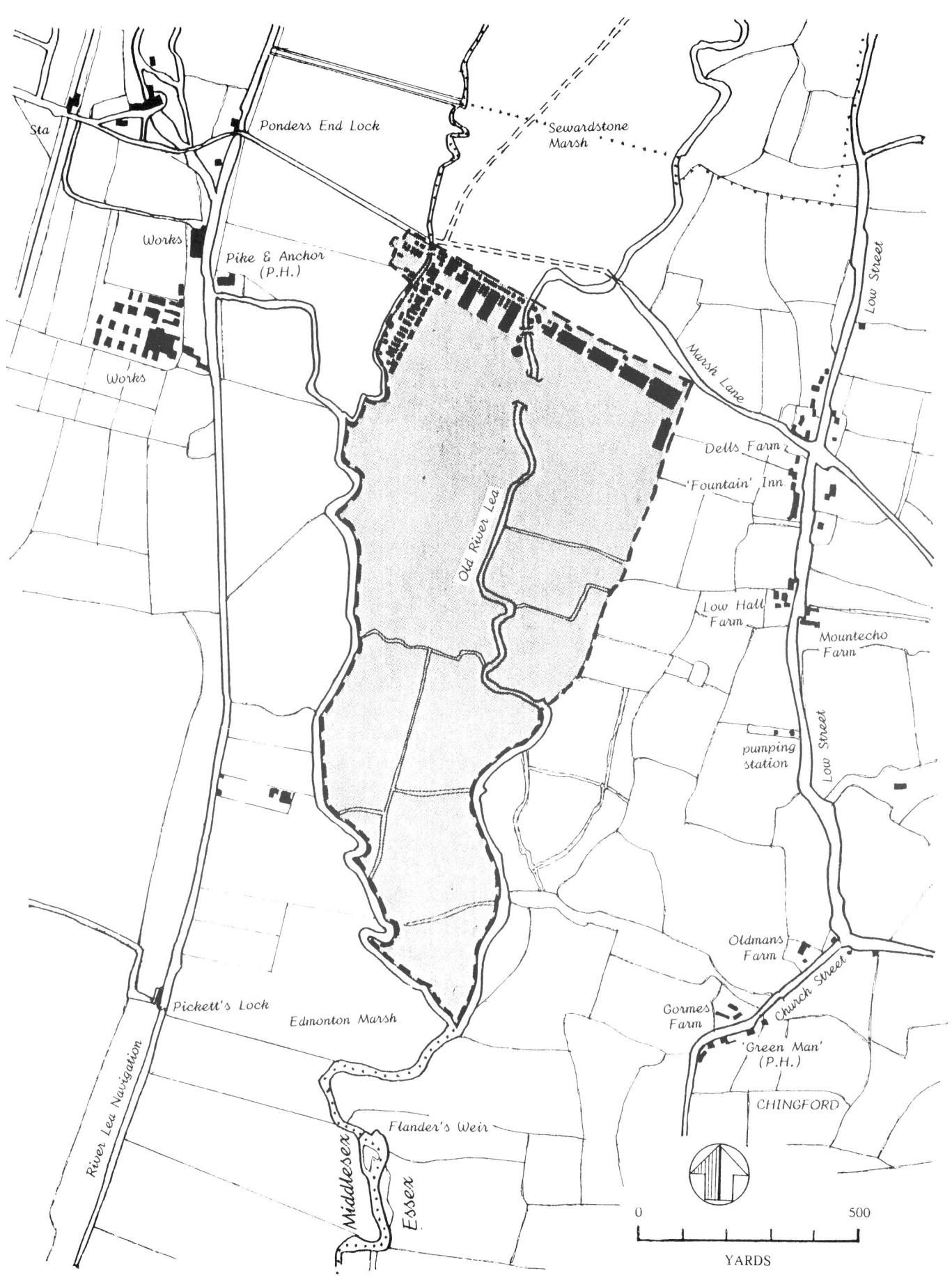

Sta

Ponders End Lock

Sewardstone
Marsh

Works

Pike & Anchor
(P.H.)

Marsh Lane

Low Street

Works

Dells Farm

'Fountain' Inn

Old River Lea

Low Hall
Farm

Mountecho
Farm

Low Street

pumping
station

Oldmans
Farm

Pickett's Lock

Edmonton Marsh

Gormes
Farm

Church Street

'Green Man'
(P.H.)

River Lea Navigation

CHINGFORD

Flander's Weir

Middlesex

Essex

0   500

YARDS

22

The RNAS training role continued until March 1918 when the RAF took over Chingford, in August of 1918 building works were finally complete and it was redesignated a Mobilisation Station for three squadrons. Due to America now also having been drawn into the world-wide conflict, and with units in need of combat training prior to being transferred to action on the Western Front, by the end of the year a detachment from the United States Army Air Corps was based there with billets at the Jubilee Retreat in Bury Road.

On 1 February 1919 the station ceased to be a military base and closed the next month. It reverted to dairy farming and remained as such until 1923 when the easternmost 36 acres then reopened as a civil aerodrome with the name of Hall Lane (after the farm on nearby Low Street, now the north end of Mansfield Hill, to the east). The aerodrome operated quietly until 1932 when the major event was a visit from Alan Cobham's National Aviation Day display, which in the first year of operation held its last display of the year there on 16 October. Just six months later a similar flying organisation, the British Hospitals Air Pageant, displayed on 23 April 1933 but after this Hall Lane slowly ran down and closed in the autumn of 1934.

The vast expanse of the William Girling reservoir separated from the King George V to the north by Lea Valley Road. The county boundary with Essex and Middlesex runs along the west side of the old landing ground. At centre left is Picketts Lock (the sports centre being south of the circular lake) and Flanders Weir is at the confluence of the two canals on the east side.

The First World War aerodrome started its disappearing act in 1935 when, with the River Lea being so low after a very dry summer in 1933 as to cause a drought, the Metropolitan Water Board decided to build a second great Chingford reservoir. The old East London Company had planned this long before when the King George's reservoir was opened and although contracts were placed in 1935 work was slow due to flooding and two slips of the embankment. Damage sustained during the Second World War, particularly three V2 long-range rocket impacts within the construction area, delayed matters further with the result that the reservoir was not brought into use until September 1951. Named after the then Chairman of the Board the William Girling covers an area of 334 acres with a capacity of 3500 million gallons, with the depth at 43 feet having a surface level 30 feet higher than that of the old landing area.

Clacton TM 175143

In July and August of 1912 Claude Grahame-White embarked on an aerial tour of England, which he hoped would stir the British nation into becoming aware of the importance of the (then new) aeroplane. After obtaining the backing of Lord Northcliffe and the *Daily Mail* the tour, labelled the 'Wake up, England!' campaign, started at Manchester then went on a circuit of coastal towns commencing with the South coast before going into East Anglia. For the coastal tours special emphasis was given to the use of 'waterplanes', as they were then called, and Clacton was the venue on 28 August when Grahame-White and his wife flew up from Southend in a Henry Farman biplane fitted with floats.

On arrival the Farman, painted sky blue with struts lined in gold and the legend 'Wake up, England!' emblazoned on it, landed on the sea and taxied onto West Beach just below the Grand Hotel. The Grahame-Whites first took lunch with Lady Gooch and others at the 'Grand' (two months earlier Lady Gooch had hosted Grahame-White's wedding reception at her country home of Hylands, near Chelmsford) before a flying demonstration was given along the shoreline, one of many displays staged during the tour which visited a total of 121 towns. A further tour was made in 1913 but the initial impact had already been made.

The following year saw a very important personage visit, again by air, when Winston S. Churchill arrived on 25 April 1914 as a result of an emergency. Due to a combination of bad weather and engine problems the Short Admiralty Type 74 Seaplane (No. 79) he was travelling in had to make a forced landing at West Beach. At this time two piers existed, one at each end of West Beach, the main one and another built originally for off-loading barges and known as the Jetty. Churchill waited on this one for another aircraft to arrive and took the opportunity to enjoy one of the cigars he was later to become so famous for, the jetty attendant then assisted him to dress for the return flight, made in Short Biplane S.38 (No. 19) which was despatched from RNAS Grain to collect him.

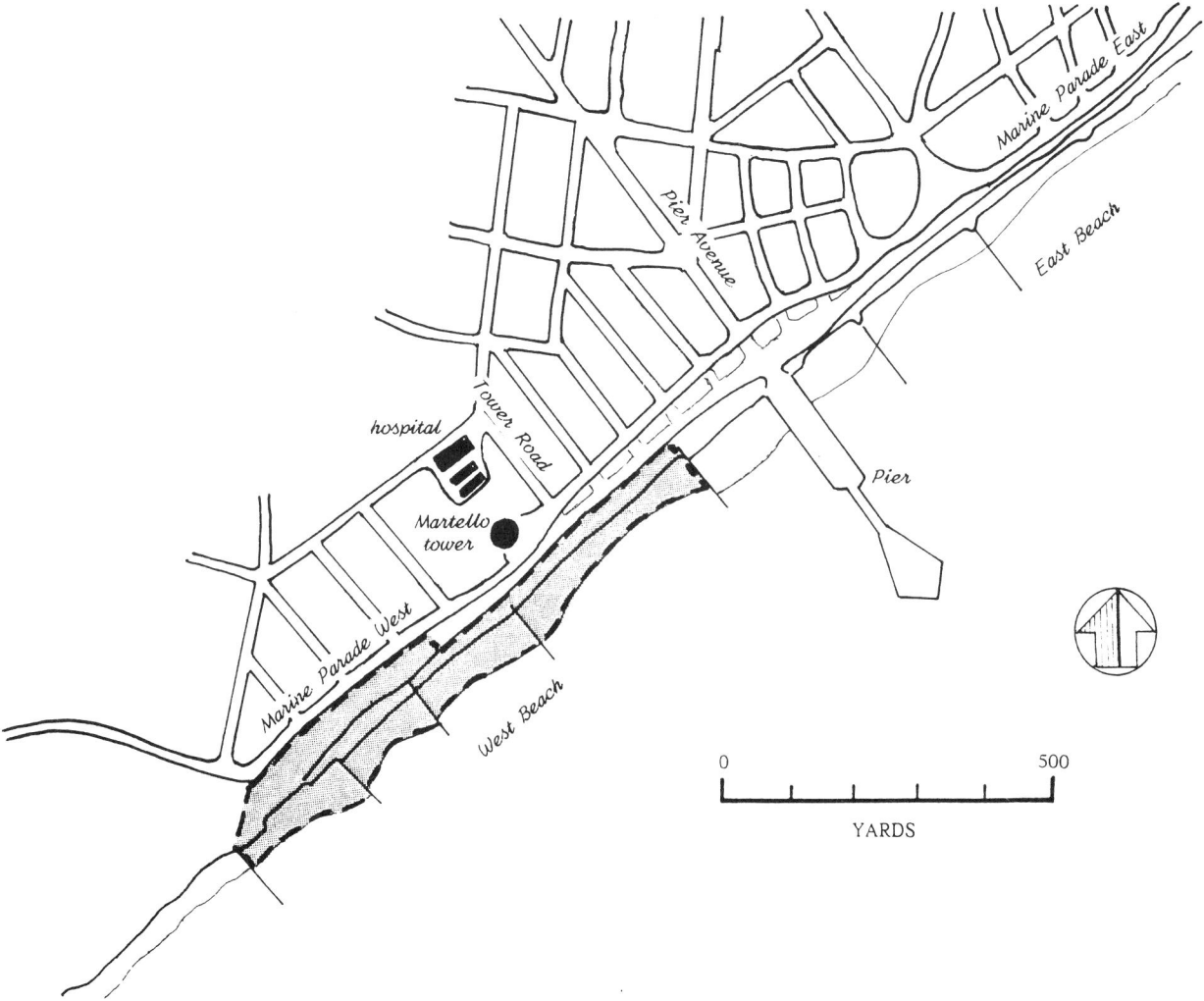

24

In August 1914 Clacton, like so many other coastal towns, prepared itself for war with the Army establishing coastal defences and the 'Naval Flying Corps' settling in on West Beach below Marine Parade West. The coastguard station at the Martello tower in Tower Road was taken over as the Station HQ whilst the seaplane landing area itself was located on the foreshore at the end of the sea wall to the west of the town pier. The guard was provided initially by the Essex Territorials who patrolled the landward limits of the station and were issued with loaded rifles, fixed bayonets and the order that, after one challenge only, they were to open fire on intruders (a bit on the over-zealous side for 1914!). Later guarding of the seaplane station was taken over by a detachment from the 5th Essex Battalion.

Opened on 2 August as one of two sub-stations to RNAS Grain, Kent (the other being at Westgate near Margate) its role was to be that of an advanced operating base where, in addition to carrying out normal patrols over the Thames Estuary, its seaplanes could also be used to provide air defence for the naval bases at Sheerness and Chatham. Three Short Admiralty Type 74 seaplanes arrived next morning as the first detachment and with only five pilots on strength routine patrols began. One aircraft was lost on patrol that first day in a crash at Buxey Sands, off the coast to the south between the rivers Blackwater and Crouch, to be replaced by another held in reserve at Grain.

After a number of uneventful patrols the seaplanes were withdrawn to Grain but, following a German raid on 24 December when a single bomb was dropped on Dover, a further two aircraft were sent to Clacton on 27 December with orders to be on permanent readiness over the holiday period in order to counter any intrusions by the Germans who might assume defences would be relaxed during the festive season. It may seem that an endless supply of floatplanes was available for the station until it is realised that no offensive weapons at all were carried by any of the aircraft. Had any intruders been detected a radio message would be sent via the very basic form of w/t carried to RNAS Eastchurch, from which station land-based aircraft would deal with the situation.

West Beach, which offered ideal beaching facilities for seaplanes from 1912 onwards. On the esplanade, in front of the hospital behind the central breakwater, is the Martello tower used as Station HQ. The white field at the top left is the site of the 1930s Earls Hall airstrip, whilst between it and the seafront is the current Clacton airstrip. Only one boat in sight, but you can almost smell the sea air!

Many uneventful coastal patrols were flown by the RNAS from the seaplane station which was operated only by a beach officer and an Intelligence Officer. It was still on the list of seaplane stations in April 1916 and retained as a sub-station to RNAS Grain until closing that autumn, all aircraft and personnel being transferred back to Grain, and whilst the naval establishment vacated the foreshore it still retained its anti-invasion beach defences. The two piers lasted until the Second World War when the main pier was cut in two and the Jetty demolished as anti-invasion defences.

Apart from military incidents the sea front seems to have had a fatal attraction for aviators over the years. In April 1949 an Olympia glider G-ALLD, BGA No. 530, came down just off the beach, whilst in the most recent incident on 20 August 1996 Tiger Moth G-ANPK crashed on the esplanade after engine failure on take-off from Clacton airstrip just inland.

East Hanningfield   TL 763007

As part of the facilities required by the RFC, who were now tasked with mainland defence of Great Britain, a Home Defence night landing ground was hurriedly set up here in April 1916. For fighters flying defensive patrols of long duration so that positive interception of intruding airships and aircraft could be made the need for such fields in an emergency was twofold, first to enable pilots to land safely and secondly to ensure that the machine could be recovered without much damage. The pilot was irreplacable, and at 1916 prices the cost of even an ungainly aircraft such as the B.E.2c costing £1,072.10.0 with its 150 hp Hispano Suiza engine at £1,004 was a lot of money to waste.

Situated three miles south of Danbury, the highest point in the county, and half a mile mile west of the village the landing ground of just under 67 acres occupied ten fields belonging to various landowners and had usable landing dimensions of 450 x 650 yards. On a clay strata at 190' amsl the site was generally level but sloped down noticeably to the south, where access was gained from Pan Lane which ran past the southern edge.

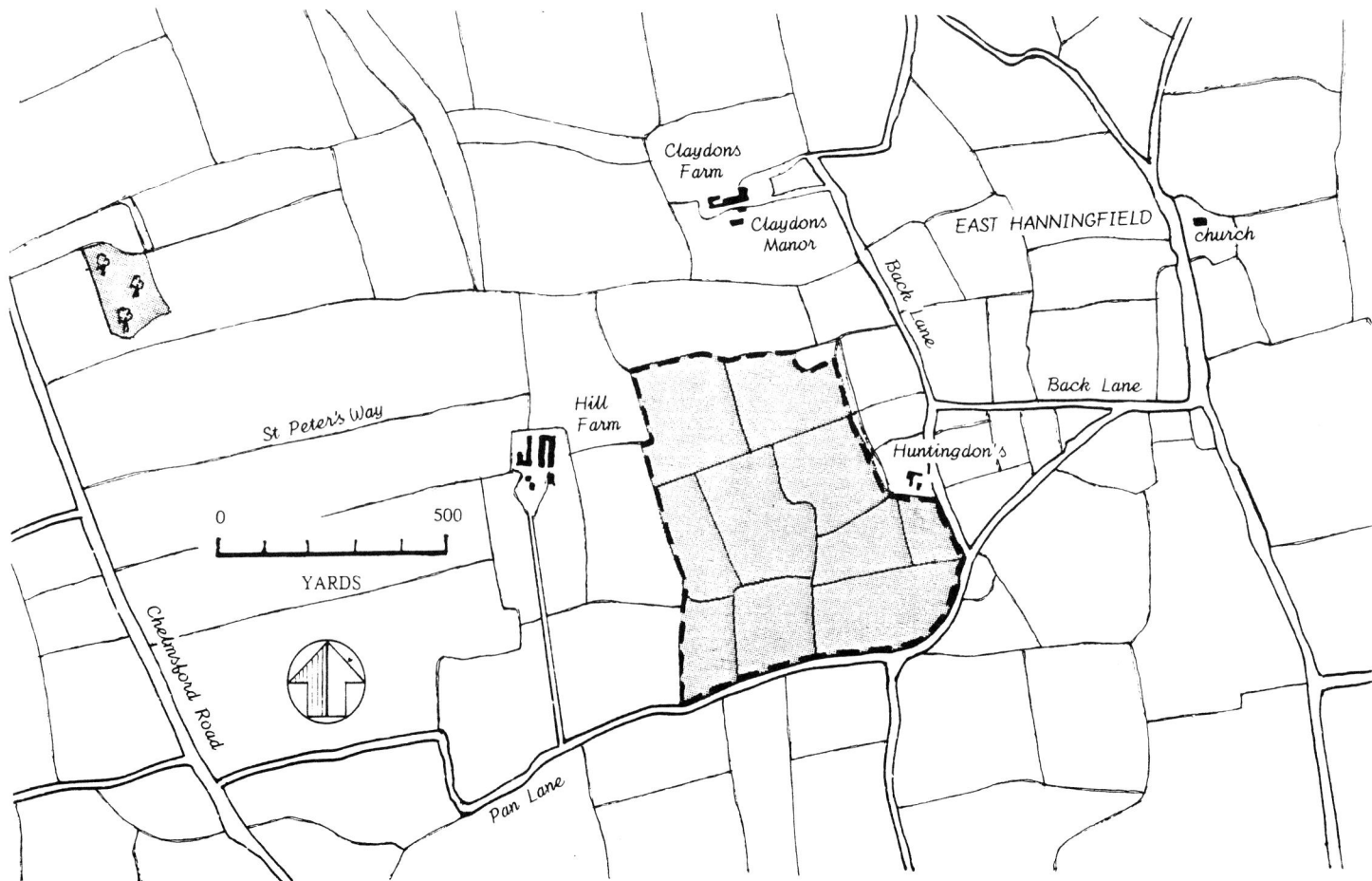

Due mainly to a combination of adjacent woodland and undulating fields which sloped down appreciably on all sides and would have made forced landings dangerous the landing ground was categorised as a 3rd Class site. No facilities were provided, apart from the tents used as bad weather shelter for those setting the landing flares, nor were any ground signals displayed on the site.

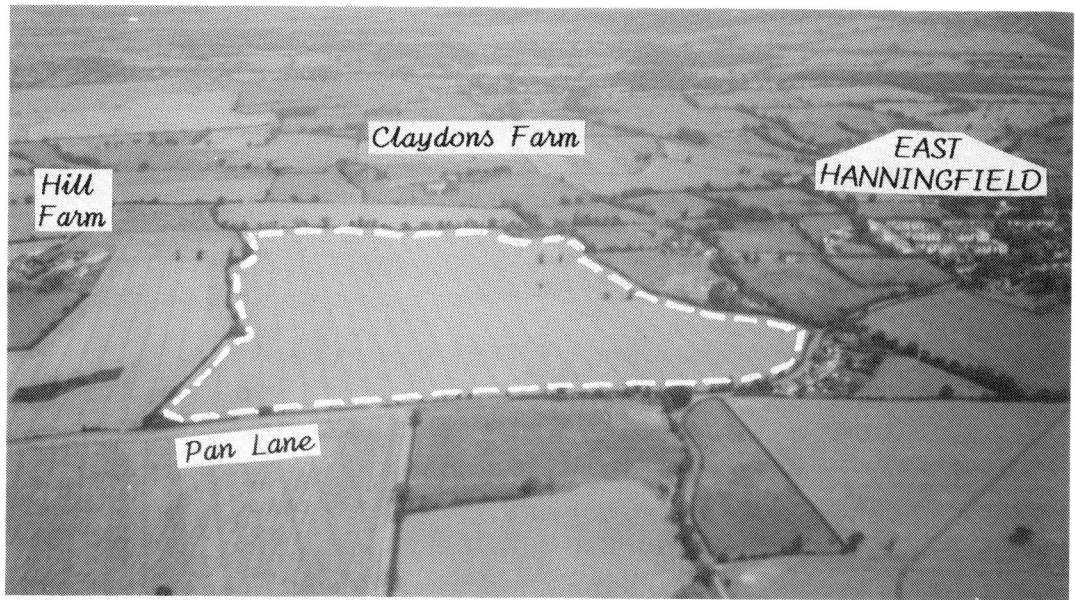

Prior to being used as a night landing ground the site was ten fields but is now just one, due to the larger-field farming system in use.

Intended primarily for use by all three flights of No. 39 (HD) Sqn in 50th Wing, South East Area, based in the south-western part of the county, as an alternative location to the site at Mountnessing it is also recorded as having been allocated to No. 37 (HD) Sqn, based in the south-eastern part of the county, but no instances of emergency landings from either, or any, unit have been discovered.

The value of the landing ground for night operations can be gauged by the fact that it was not lighted after the middle of October 1916, and by the end of December the site party had been posted away. The tenancy was given up by 5 January 1917 after Stow Maries was established just three miles away and 'B' Flight of No. 37 (HD) Sqn then used newer night landing grounds located closer to the East coast. The land returned to agriculture and has remained such ever since, no further aviation use having been made of it.

Easthorpe   TL 895214

Another of the landing grounds opened during the 'panic' period early in 1916, when the need arose for Home Defence fighters to be able to patrol nearer to the coast for longer periods of time in order to ensure earlier interceptions of incoming raids, Easthorpe was located two miles south-west of Marks Tey railway station on part of what was then called Scott Lives Farm immediately north of the Roman Road which led to the village from the main A12.

Four fields were combined by the employment of Canadian lumberjacks to fell trees on field boundaries and fill in ditches, the resulting landing ground being an irregular-shaped area of just 29 acres on a clay soil overlying gravels. A large field, First Rowley at 15½ acres, was amalgamated with the adjacent 2 Acres, 4 Acres and Little Elbuds to make a site with usable dimensions of only 400 x 380 yards. At 120' amsl the immediate surroundings were fairly open and unrestricted with Little Domsey farmhouse to the west and Domsey Brook running past the north-eastern corner of the slightly-sloping site.

As at East Hanningfield, opened at the same time, Easthorpe had no structures of any kind apart from tents and a windsock but it did have the capability to display ground signals for the benefit of patrolling aircraft. On becoming operational in April 1916 it was classified a 2nd Class night landing ground with an initial allocation to No. 39 (HD) Sqn in 50th Wing, South East Area and the telephone number of Marks Tey 9.

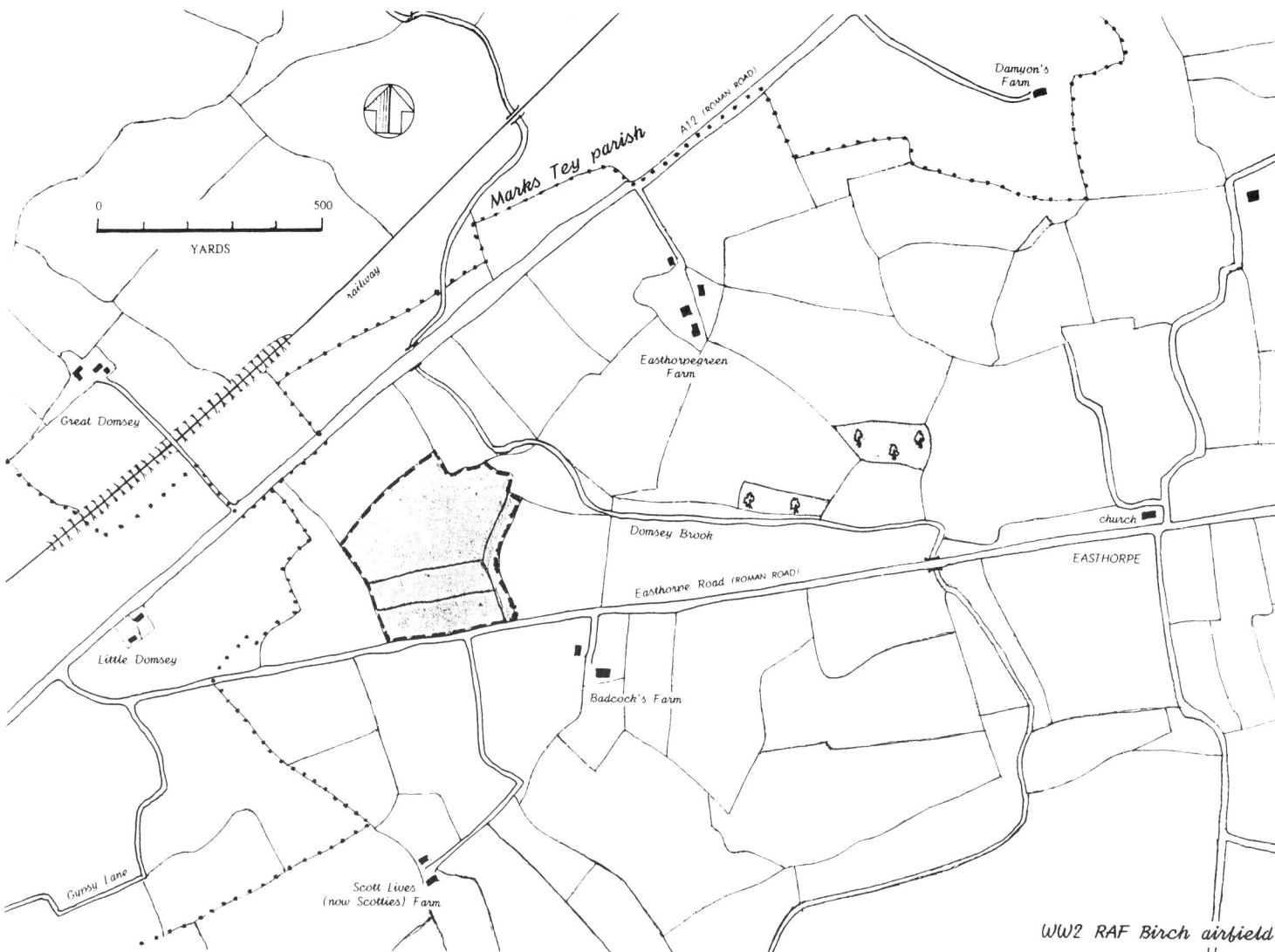

WW2 RAF Birch airfield
II

No. 39 (HD) Sqn gave up their use of the site in September 1916 when it was re-allocated instead to No. 37 (HD) Sqn to serve the most northerly limit of their northern patrol line, although by the middle of October no flares for night landings were in operation and the site function reverted primarily to that of a day landing ground.

On the morning of 23–24 May 1917 it received apparently its only recorded emergency landing when Captain W. Sowrey from 'C' Flight at Goldhanger safely landed a B.E.12a after the engine started to misfire due to sooted-up plugs whilst on patrol. This was the second unsuccessful sortie William Sowrey had been on that night as one of seven aircraft ordered up against an armada of six airships, his earlier flight in another B.E.12a having resulted in him breaking both the propellor and lower port wing on landing in bad visibility back at Goldhanger.

The landing ground remained for use primarily for No. 37 Sqn until December 1919 when it was handed back to farming and apart from it being occasionally used by the field sports fraternity aviation left the area.

The need for further airfields in Essex during the Second World War led to a bomber base being constructed at Birch, some two miles to the south-east, in October 1943. Although built to Class 'A' standards for the U.S. 9th Air Force it was sadly under-used and duly handed over to the 8th Air Force. It then passed to the RAF who used it on only one day in March 1945 for launching towed Horsa gliders for the Rhine crossing then, after short periods of use by ground organisations, it lay idle until it closed later that year.

The two fields on the southern portion of the landing ground, Little Elbuds and Four Acres, are now one, whilst part of First Rowley is linked to Further Rowley (seen here covered by horse trails) and extends up to the A12 road. Badcocks Farm is to the far right.

It has been reported by an elderly Easthorpe farm worker that a chalk shape, possibly the remnants of a ground signal pad, was present on the WW1 landing ground, as fragments had been brought to the surface by ploughing. The practice of ploughing the field stopped in the mid-1960s when hunting returned to the area in the form of the Hunnable (now the East Essex) Hunt who used the old landing ground, sightings of the shape therefore ceased and although the field is now worked again no recent reports have been received.

The last known aviation activity to occur on the site happened on 3 April 1972 when the author, by chance, landed an Olympia 2 glider after a one hour 25 minutes cross-country flight from the Essex Gliding Club base at North Weald airfield.

Whilst Little Domsey farmhouse is now gone the filled-in ditches remain to leave the field in its enlarged state, worked as part of (now) Scotties Farm by the Melrose family.

Fairlop   TQ 458913

In 1911 Handley Page Ltd, the aeronautical engineers, used the 30-acre Fairlop Oak Playing Field here as a flight test ground but gave it up in the summer of 1912. 1916 then saw an RNAS Training Depot Station open up, as a sub-site to Chingford, on the north-west part of what was the large estate of Hainault Forest. With the railway station at Fairlop on the Great Eastern network one mile to the west, and a siding coming to within 300 yards of the aerodrome, it was half a mile due west of the RFC Home Defence squadron station already existing at Hainault Farm.

The rectangular landing ground of 110 acres occupied what had been five playing fields and gave useful landing runs of 900 and 600 yards, whilst at 100' amsl the surface was level with a loamy soil overlaying gravels thus adequate drainage was assured. The surroundings were fairly open and undulating, with nearby fields noted as being small but considered more than suitable for forced landings.

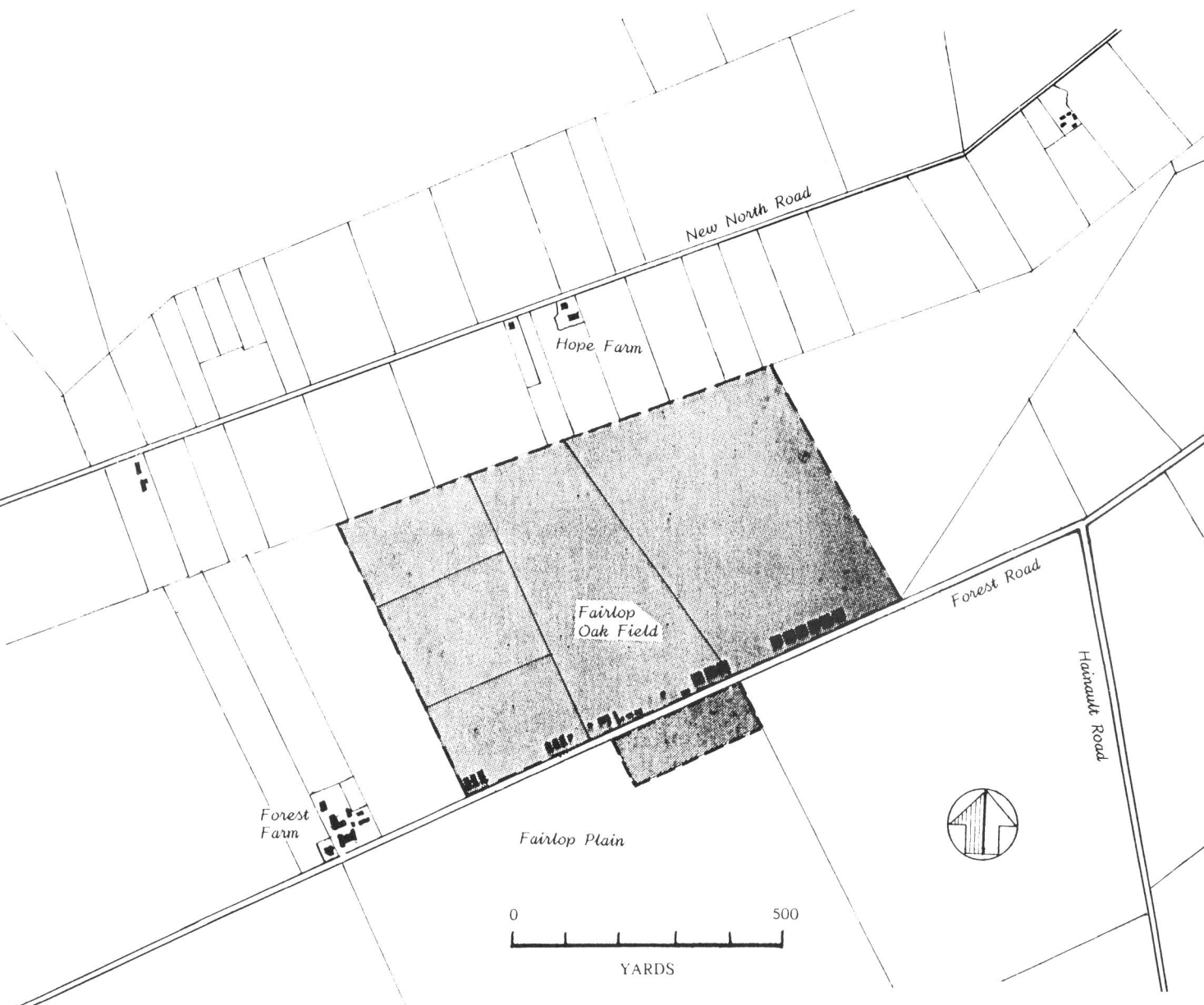

A total of 26 aerodrome buildings, including some already existing on a two-acre plot, were located along the full length of the southern boundary immediately next to Forest Road and eventually comprised:—

Technical	Regimental
9 canvas hangars (Bessonneau)	3 officers' quarters
workshop	dining room
technical store	Regimental store
oil store	3 men's huts
petrol store	3 men's baths
office and latrines	3 men's latrines and ablutions

Fairlop was operated by the RNAS until the end of March 1918, then the Royal Air Force came into being on 1 April 1918 and immediately took it over as a training base with an establishment at 24 each of Avro trainers and Sopwith Camels, although until the end of May it was still known as No. 207 Training Depot Station of the RNAS. Of all the stations in the county Fairlop was the only pure RAF training establishment, and whilst it had but limited accommodation there were as many personnel attached to it as the Training Station at Rochford with its two full squadrons based there. Further billets in the form of single-storey bungalows were then built on the western boundary for officer instructors.

The station continued in the training role until February 1919 when the site was vacated by the RAF. By that summer it had finally returned to its previous use as playing fields, after a lengthy period whilst the hangars and other buildings were removed and the surface made good. The central field, Fairlop Oak, then became known as the London Playing Field and industry established itself along Forest Road between it and the officers' bungalows.

Now mostly covered with sports fields the former TDS has changed little, by comparison with the total destruction on the other side of Forest Road of the Second World War site of RAF Fairlop.

Another aviation-associated site nearby was the Kelvin Hughes factory, Husun Works, that opened in 1916 on New North Road a quarter of a mile to the north-west. Arthur Joseph Hughes had formed the company to produce compasses and navigational aids for the RFC, and for his work in inventing the aperiodic compass was later awarded the OBE.

Between 1920-23 an area of 25 acres off the western end of the landing ground became a civil aerodrome known as Forest Farm after the farm outside the south-west corner. At this period in time civil aerodromes were checked and certified for operation by the police and Forest Farm came under the jurisdiction of Barkingside Metropolitan Police station. When the aerodrome licence was not renewed that area returned to farming.

Whilst Alan Cobham brought his National Aviation Day Displays to the Ilford area on three occasions he only visited visited the aerodrome once, other previous tours having used the nearby Goodmayes Park in April and May of 1932. When the tour split into two for the latter part of 1935 the 'Astra' Show came on Thursday, 26 September, using as the display site the easternmost 46 acres of the WW1 TDS which by now was known as the Hainault Recreation Ground. Apart from the usual free flight competition other events included a parachute drop by Miss Naomi Heron-Maxwell, the only female exponent of the art at that time in Britain, aerobatics by Fl Lt Geoffrey Tyson and a demonstration by Mr T. Bullmore of a new type of aeroplane, the Cierva C24 autogiro. A Mignet Flying Flea was also flown painted with the legend 'Ilford Recorder', after its sponsors.

The area to the south side of Forest Road known as Fairlop Plain was purchased in the late-1930s for the City of London airport and as late as November 1939 was shown on planning maps as such, but in September 1940 the Air Ministry took it over and it became RAF Fairlop. It was host to Hurricane, Spitfire and Typhoon squadrons before becoming a balloon barrage site in 1944. It then closed in August 1946 and, although zoned as open space in 1950, negotiations began once again to build a civil airport in its place. These disputes ended in 1953, when the application was rejected on the grounds that industrial and domestic haze would create hazards to operations, and the airfield site was bought two years later by Ilford Council for gravels extraction.

The TDS, Forest Farm and WW2 Fairlop sites are now recreational centres and very little remains from their previous lives, except at the TDS where the bungalows on the western boundary that served as RAF officer accommodation are now private residences. The sports pavilion on Fairlop Oak field which served as the officer's dining room still remains.

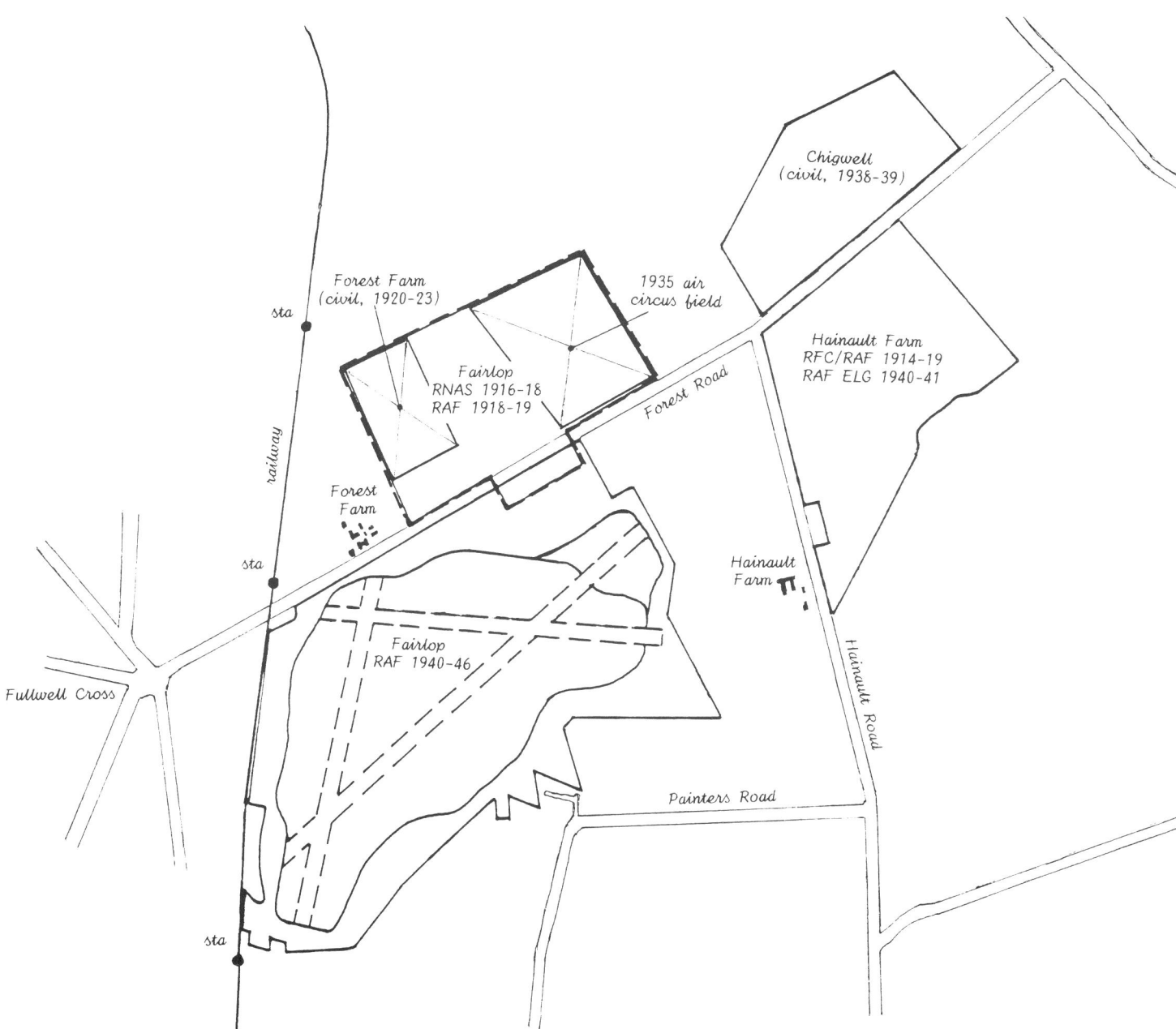

To clear up any confusion which has existed over the years as to which were Fairlop and Hainault Farm aerodromes this map shows the locations and usage periods for all flying sites in the area, coincidentally all along Forest Road.

Fyfield

At 25 acres this was one of the smaller sites in the county and, according to the gazeteer of landing grounds, located 1½ miles due north of Chipping Ongar railway station. Sited as it was though between Bundish Hall and the church at Shelley it was actually in the parish of Moreton some 1½ miles from Fyfield village, from which it was separated by the small hamlet of Clatterford End.

The single field which made up the landing ground had been part of the Thomas Chaplin estate in 1840 and was being arable farmed when 'borrowed' for the duration of hostilities by the RFC from the Eve family at Bundish Hall in October 1916. Its use was to be as a further night landing ground for No. 39 (HD) Sqn in 49th Wing, South East Area who, stationed at North Weald Bassett five miles to the west, already had by then two 1st, two 2nd and six 3rd Class sites allocated to it.

At 220' amsl the landing area had usable dimensions of 370 x 350 yards on a clay soil sub-stratum and had comparatively open surroundings, but suffered from an appreciable slope down to the south towards the church at Shelley. This, along with the wooded areas close to the eastern boundary and the proximity of farm buildings at Bundish Hall itself, led to it being categorised as a 3rd Class site with the telephone number of Ongar 12.

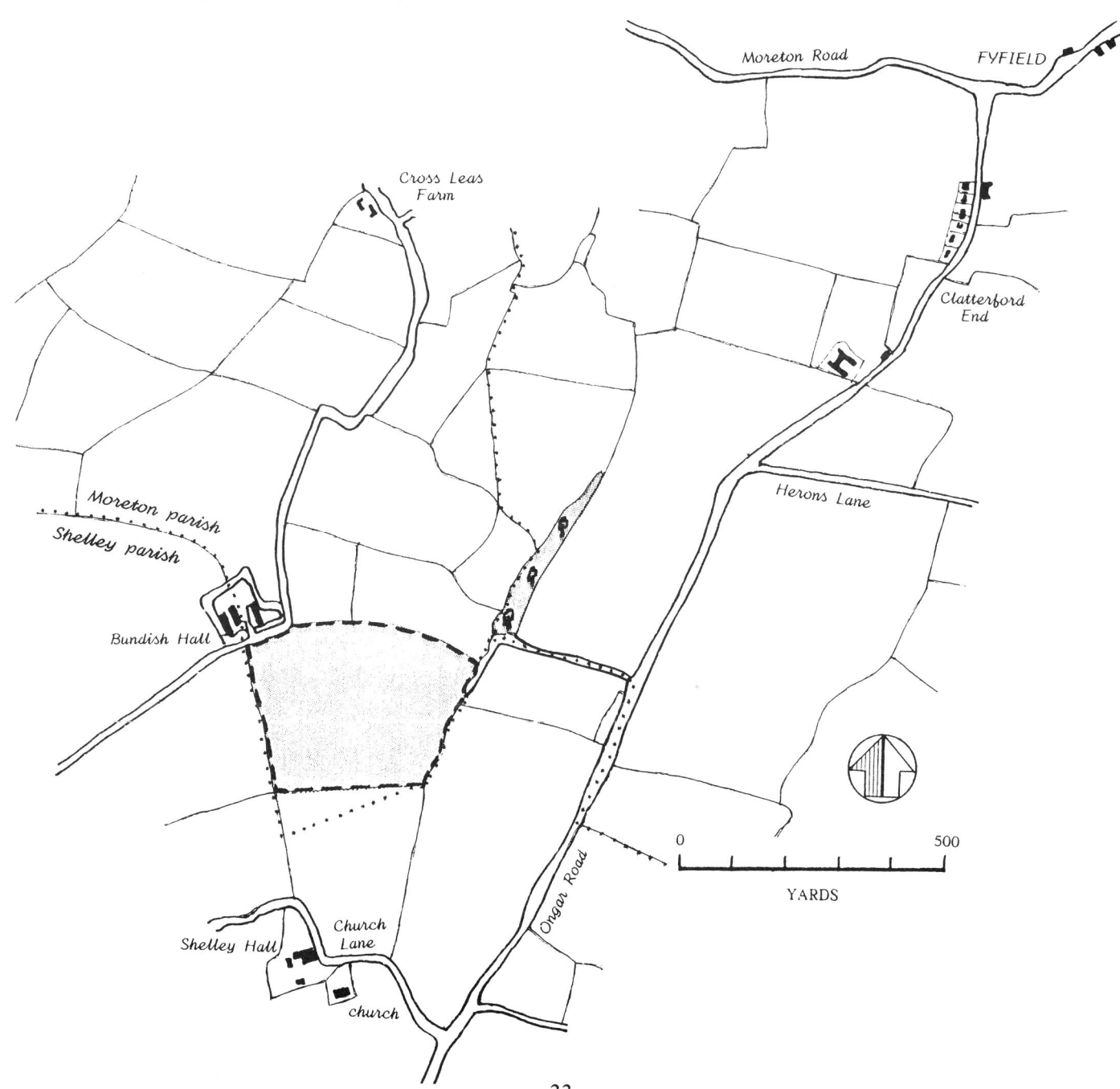

Main access to the landing ground was at Bundish Hall off the lane running from the north end of Shelley to Cross Lees farm, but a farm track put in from the Ongar-Fyfield road was also later used. Ground signals were displayed but no permanent structures of any sort were erected, the tents provided as wet weather shelter for the personnel setting up the landing flares being sited on the northern edge of the field to the east of Bundish Hall. Although it was lit up each night that fighter aircraft from Home Defence squadrons were operating and in the vicinity, the site saw little activity as a night landing ground.

On one occasion, the morning of 30 January 1918 after some 80 Home Defence sorties had been made the previous night, a Bristol Fighter of No. 39 Sqn was recorded as having made a forced landing. The aircraft, A7265, had been sent off from North Weald Bassett at 2202 as one of 8 Bristols and a B.E.2e that night, and was patrolling against a small force of four Giants attacking London but forced to land at Fyfield at 0040 when low on fuel. The crew, 2nd Lts W.B. Thomson and F.J.B.de S. La Terriere, were unhurt and the aircraft undamaged.

The site was kept active, and still 'on the books' of No. 39 Sqn, when the Royal Air Force came into existence in April 1918 but finally given up in December 1919 and returned to its former use with the land worked by tenant farmers.

During the Second World War Chipping Ongar airfield was built for the 8th Air Force in the parish of Willingale two miles due east. Apart from an unconfirmed reference of another American airstrip with the name of Moreton being considered for construction near Cross Lees farm half a mile to the north of the First World War landing ground, and centred on MR TL553062, the area has had no further aviation connections.

The entire Bundish Hall estate was purchased by the Lavender family in the early 1950s, and whilst in more recent times the farm access track has been relaid as a concrete road and the lane reverted to a footpath the single field which made up the landing ground has remained agricultural. Rumours that the base for a windsock mast still existed on the edge of the field have come to nothing despite extensive ground searches which failed to find any trace of it.

Fyfield NLG with Shelley church at bottom left and the Ongar–Fyfield road at bottom right. Between Bundish Hall and Cross Leas Farm is the site of the proposed Second World War USAF airstrip.

Goldhanger

This site, the only Flight Station with an area less than 100 acres, started life in August 1915 as a Home Defence night landing ground for the RNAS. Situated on the north bank of the River Blackwater 2½ miles east of Maldon the landing area of 77 acres comprising five fields in the ownership of George Dobson at Gardners and one belonging to Cobbs was unusual in that Gardners Farm was practically in the centre, only 200 yards south-west of the landing circle. Notwithstanding this slight handicap the RNAS remained in occupation until April 1916 when the aerodrome was re-assigned to the RFC as an advanced landing ground, but when 'C' Flight of No. 37 (HD) Sqn in 50th Wing, South East Area moved in with its B.E.12 aircraft in September 1916 the site changed to that of a 1st Class Home Defence Flight Station (night).

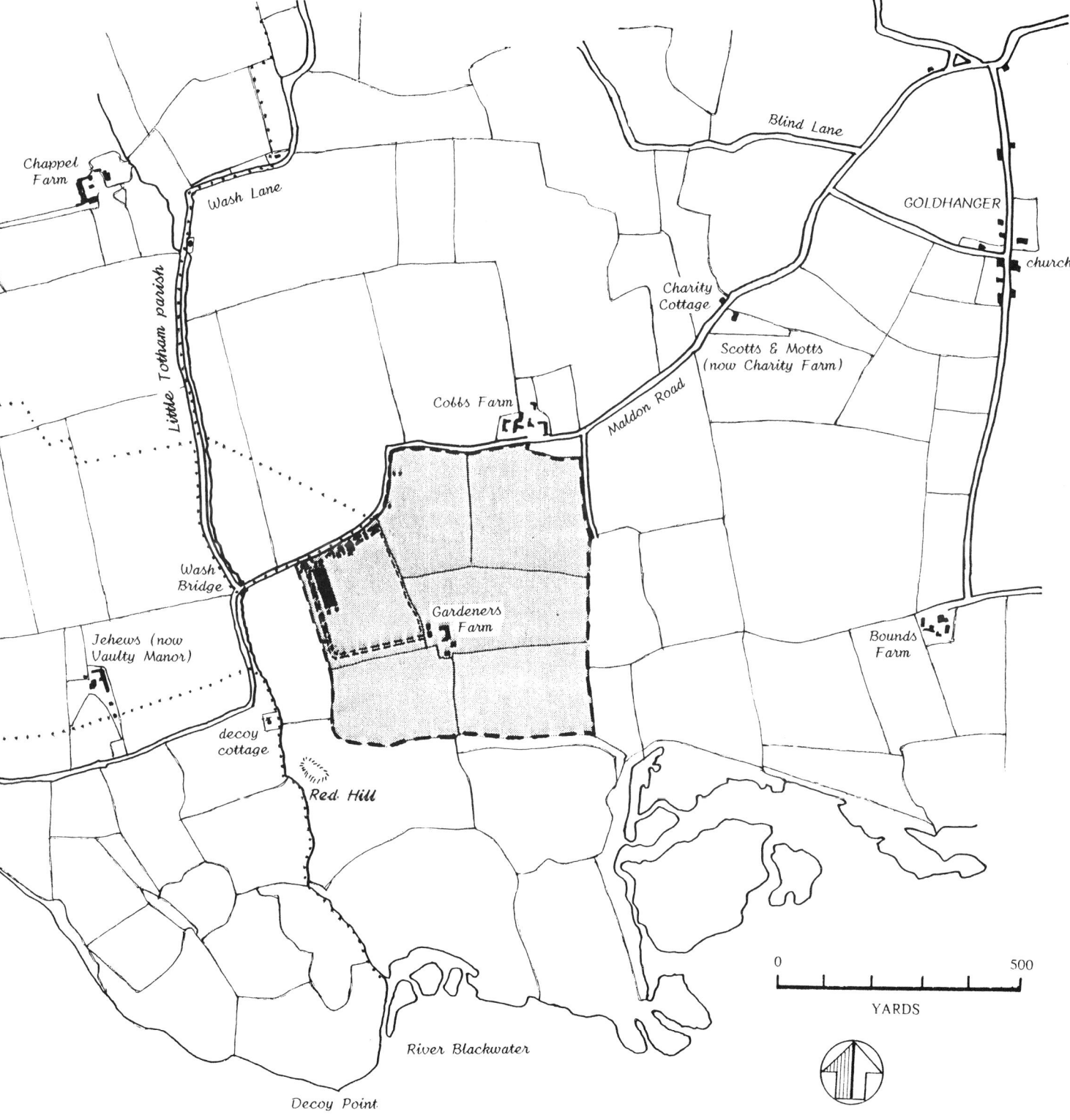

Building work started in earnest, with 24 structures sited on the western edge taking up 16 acres of the already cramped site. Four 90' x 60' aeroplane sheds were sited in pairs on the west boundary with a 75'0" wide apron in front, all built on the loamy soil overlaying the river gravels. At only 10' amsl the southern half of the landing ground was liable to flooding in winter. An existing track ran south from the Maldon Road to Gardners Farm which, as it went directly across the centre of the landing area, was considered a hazard and taken out to be replaced by a new approach built along the west boundary to reach the farm from that direction.

Landings onto the 600 x 600 yard square landing ground were generally good from all directions but it was necessary in February 1917 for the Commanding Officer of No. 37 (HD) Sqn to write to the farmer, George Dobson, a precautionary letter to the effect that "you are hereby required not to place any haystack or other obstruction of any description on the ground coloured red occupied by you without previous arrangement with O.C. No. 37 (HD) Sqn, RFC." (enclosed with this was a plan marked with certain areas to the north-east and south-west where the farmer had a habit of leaving large farm items!).

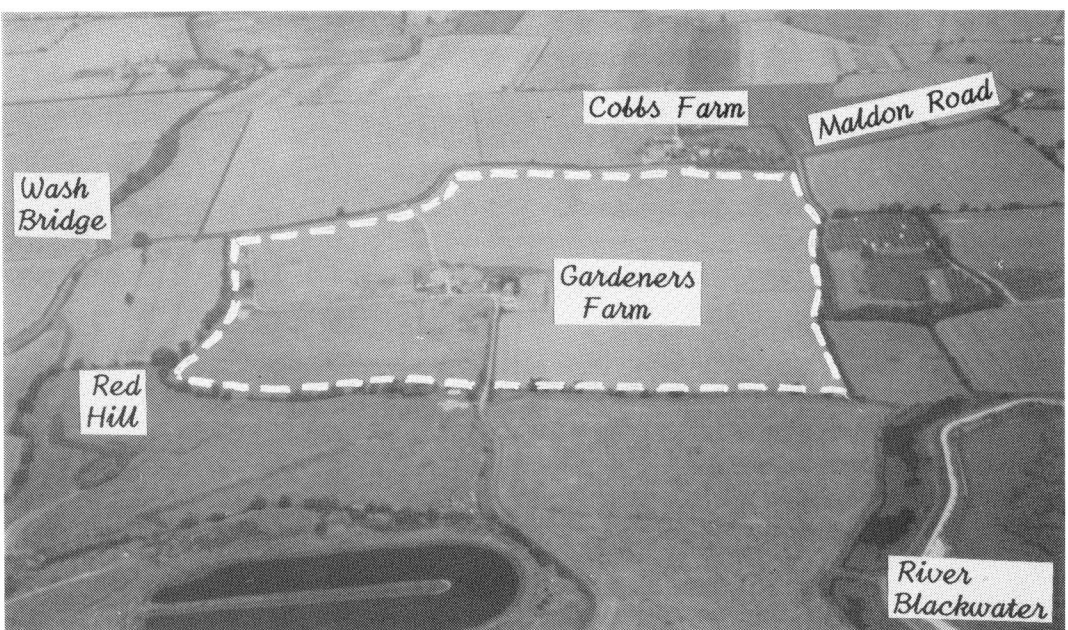

With all traces of buildings from the former Flight Station now gone Gardeners Farm is left as an 'oasis' in the middle of an historical site.

Anti-Zeppelin patrols became routine and often unsuccessful, a typical instance being on the night of 23/24 May 1917 when Captain William Sowrey (one of three brothers serving with the RFC, two being in 37 Sqn) was amongst seven aircraft up from Goldhanger against an armada of six airships bound for London. Whilst on his patrol line sooted-up plugs caused the engine of his B.E.12a to fail and he force-landed safely on the night landing ground at Easthorpe, his earlier flight that night in another B.E.12a having also been fruitless but on returning to Goldhanger his landing in bad visibility had resulted in him breaking both the propellor and lower port wing.

The most memorable patrol, as far as Goldhanger was concerned, occurred on 16/17 June when 2nd Lt L.P. Watkins took off in B.E.12 No. 6610 upon receipt of a Zeppelin raid on London being notified. The L48, captained by Kapitanleutnant Eichler, was one of four sent over that night and attacked by two pilots from Orfordness prior to Watkins arriving on the scene. He attacked and was credited with shooting down the airship, which fell at Holly Tree Farm, Theberton (Suffolk) as the last to fall on English soil. All on board perished, including Korvetten-kapitan Victor Schutze, commodore of the North Sea airship division, and were buried locally but in 1966 re-interred at the Soldatenfriedhof in Cannock Chase, Staffordshire, when the policy of bringing all German war dead together came into force.

Stragglers were also received. On 4 July, during sorties against 18 Gotha bombers which had raided Harwich and Felixstowe, Lt Cummings in Sopwith Pup A7319 of No. 40 (Training) Sqn from Croydon and Lt J.B. Jacques in D.H.4 A7508 of No. 2 AAP, Hendon, made safe emergency landings when low on fuel.

In October 1917, in order to open up the northern approaches to the field even further, the searchlight dynamo hut and two guard huts were removed to the searchlight station at Broad Street Green, Maldon, whilst by April 1918 the nearby Officers' huts had been sent first to squadron HQ at The Grange, Woodham Mortimer, then to RFC Stow Maries.

In March 1918 the station held a dance, booked via Stow Maries, at Maldon School for which the hire of the hall cost 5/- (25p)! At the end of the month No. 74 Sqn stayed for three days, this arising from a diversion due to bad weather encountered after leaving their London Colney station en route to duties in France with their SE5a aircraft.

Although Goldhanger was in the same status as other Flight Stations in the 37 Sqn 'clutch' personnel numbers were quite different to Rochford and Stow Maries, each of which also initially housed one flight of the squadron, the number of buildings also reflecting this.

A comparison with Stow Maries in December 1918 (when both stations were deemed to be complete) is given below:

Personnel	Goldhanger	Stow Maries
Officers	7	21
WOs and NCOs above Cpl	3	17
Corporals	2	16
Rank & file	43	150
Women	0	3
Women (household)	0	12
	55	219
Machines (Camels)	8	16
Buildings	29	44

The station closed down in March 1919 when the buildings were demolished and services taken out, the exception being the aeroplane sheds which were finally dismantled in 1922. A panoramic photograph of them in situ was taken by the farmer's son and printed in a 1978 issue of *Essex Countryside*, but the original has not been found since. After being purchased by May & Butcher of Maldon the outer walls from the northern pair went to the Crittal factory at Witham in 1925, being shipped in a convoy of horse-drawn 'whims' and re-erected with the roof and end walls from one shed to form a workshop and store. When the Crittal site was sold for housing the shed was finally demolished in 1992 and, having already been in use for some 74 years, acquired by the Brooklands Museum at Weybridge for possible further use in an aeronautical connection.

In the late-1920s a privately-owned biplane force-landed on the first fairway of the Maldon golf club, on the other side of the town from the WW1 landing ground. The identity of the pilot is not known, but he was attempting to visit Sir Claude de Crespigny at Champion Lodge in Broad Street Green and whose brother, H.V. Champion de Crespigny, became the Commanding Officer of No. 39 Sqn (previously a Home Defence unit) from March 1925 to April 1930. The aircraft was parked by the clubhouse until flown off the next day.

During the daily rounds of flying under the banner of his National Aviation Day displays Alan Cobham visited Maldon, not to the old landing ground at Gardners Farm but a site on the Mundon Road south of the town. The large field, known as Primrose Meadow, was closer to the town centre than the WW1 site and therefore a more lucrative location when the 'Astra' Show came on 8 July 1935. When he departed the following day for his next stop at Walton-on-the-Naze there were then no more aviation links with the area until part of the Mundon estate was selected as the location planned for one of eight new bomber airfields to serve the United States 8th Air Force in East

Anglia during the Second World War. The land was allocated in August 1942 and acquisition continued until October but construction was postponed indefinitely in the middle of December due to the need to complete existing sites which were behind schedule due to a season of bad weather.

Of the many devices, friendly or otherwise, which dropped into the small parish during the Second World War the most unwelcome 'visitor' was Big Ben 544, a German Army long-range rocket, which arrived on 16 January 1945. It fell in the river just south of Bounds Farm near the eastern boundary of the old landing ground, and while no casualties resulted the farm buildings were damaged by the effects of blast.

Today nothing is left of the WW1 Flight Station except the field itself, the shape of which has not changed in 80 years, with Gardners Farm still remaining in the centre and reached now also by a new road built on the line of the original track taken out in 1916.

Hainault Farm   TQ 468912

The site first occupied 60 acres of farmland in the ownership of Mr William Poulter when it opened in October 1914 as a day landing ground for the RNAS, the same year that the Woman's Suffragette Movement demonstrated in nearby Ilford. After a period of training courses the RNAS moved out in February 1915 when the RFC took over and classified it a 3rd Class night landing ground (no. 3) for Home Defence squadrons. By the middle of October further land to the north-east had been acquired to increase the area of the site to 100 acres and, with usable landing dimensions of 950 x 750 yards, it achieved the status of a 1st Class Flight Station (night).

The landing ground, which now straddled the parish boundaries of Ilford and Dagenham, sloped down from 140' amsl at the north to 95' amsl at the south with its undulating surface varying between moderate to rough. The clay soil sub-base became extremely wet in winter but the surroundings were fairly open with large fields close by, making for trouble-free forced landings after take-off.

Aircraft from various Home Defence units made use of it until it was allocated to No. 39 (HD) Sqn that formed there in April 1916 from No. 19 Reserve Aeroplane Squadron with B.E.2c aircraft as part of 49th Wing, South East Area. The building works programme required to bring it up to Squadron Station status then commenced, with some 12 acres of the site on the western boundary adjacent to Hainault Road eventually being taken up by four aeroplane sheds as well as the technical offices and regimental buildings, the estimated completion date for all these facilities being projected as 15 December 1918.

To serve the technical and regimental areas a separate sewage disposal works was built to the south-west on the other side of Hainault Road. Hainault Farm itself is very old, this being evident by the wall plaques having the year 1855 and 'VR' on, and being unoccupied in April 1916 led to it being taken up as the officers' billets with their Mess built just to the north.

By August 1916 No. 39 (HD) Sqn had split into three flights, with 'C' Flight remaining on site and 'A' & 'B' Flights dispersed to North Weald Bassett and Suttons Farm respectively, and from these stations pilots from the squadron brought down four German airships in the space of one month that year. In the early morning of 3 September 1916 Lt W. Leefe Robinson from Suttons Farm brought the wooden-hulled Zeppelin SL11 down at Cuffley. This was followed by 2nd Lt F. Sowrey, again from Suttons Farm, shooting down the L32 at Billericay on the morning of the 24th, and that same morning 2nd Lt A. de B. Brandon from Hainault Farm caused the damaged L33 to force-land at Little Wigborough. 2nd Lt W.J. Tempest, from North Weald Bassett, was the last of the four Zeppelin killers when he shot down the L31 at Potters Bar on 1 October.

Alfred de Bathe Brandon, a New Zealander, was airborne in a B.E.2c at 2333 hrs on 23 September for patrol and sighted the L33 just after midnight. He lost the airship but found it again and made two attacks, after which it descended slowly, coming to rest in Little Wigborough across the lane between New Hall Cottages and the church at 0120 hrs. The crew survived with only minor injuries and the commander, Kptlt Alouise Böcker, tried unsuccessfully to set the ship afire before mustering his men and making for the nearby cottages just 100 yards away. After failing to make the sleepy occupants understand his wish to surrender the entire crew proceeded along the road towards Peldon where they were met by Special PCs Edgar Nicholas and Elijaah Trailer. Special Sgt Ernest Edwards then arrived to take command until regular PC Charles Smith came to formally arrest them, they then continued to Mersea Island where they spent the rest of the night in West Mersea church hall before being transferred to Colchester and into captivity.

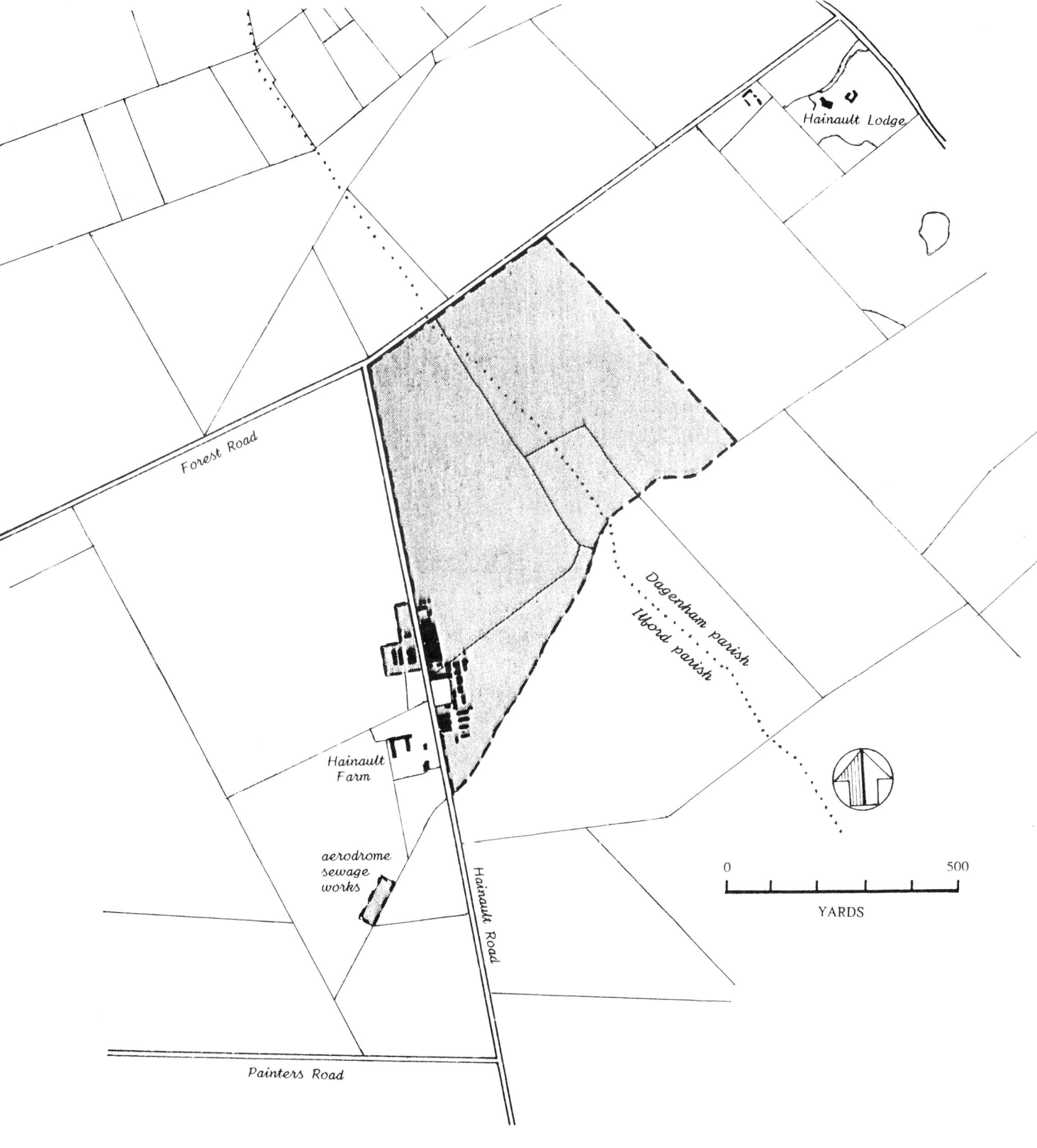

The remains of the L33 lay across the lane from Knapps to Glebe Fields for 14 weeks while engineers and draughtsmen from the Admiralty recorded precisely every detail of its construction, it was then dismantled and taken away. As a result of this the British airship programme produced the R33, which flew successfully from 1919 to 1927, the forward control cabin from which is at the Royal Air Force Museum, Hendon.

During the time the L33 lay across the road village life went on, with farming continuing around it and even extending to the extent of cutting a hole in the framework to allow parishioners, particularly those attending a funeral, to have access to the church. Although most of it was taken away parts of the airship still remain in St Stephens church at Great Wigborough, these taking the form of a large section of girder fixed to a tower wall, with both parish churches having pieces of framework forming a frame to an illustrated history of the events of that night. Twelve local people involved in the incident were honoured for their efforts with an inscribed watch presented by the Chairman of the Essex Standing Committee, this too is recorded on a separate brass plaque fixed in both the Wigborough churches. It was hoped to locate descendants of these notaries who might still have the family watch, but to date the author has only established that the one presented to Tom King still resides with his nephew at New Hall Cottages, whilst that awarded to PC Nicholas is displayed in the Essex Police museum at Chelmsford.

After flying many Home Defence sorties from Hainault Farm No. 39 (HD) Sqn left in October 1917 and went to North Weald Bassett, thence to the Western Front, but in the meantime No. 44 (HD) Sqn formed in the July with Sopwith 1½-Strutters as one of three extra day-fighter units set up specifically to deal with Gotha raiders.

No. 151 Sqn RAF, the first true night-fighter unit equipped with the Sopwith F1 Camel (the 'comic' conversion) formed in June 1918 from flights of Nos. 44, 78 and 112 Squadrons and was posted to France four days later. December 1918 saw the emergence on site of No. 153 Sqn RAF, this being the third true night-fighter unit equipped with F1 Camels, which remained until June 1919.

No. 44 Sqn left in July 1919 and no further flying took place, the

The former flying area is farmed whilst an industrial estate and gravel extraction works now occupy the technical and regimental sites next to Hainault Road.

flying field being handed back for agriculture in December 1919 and the buildings taken over for farm use until sold off as industrial units prior to the Second World War. Part of this area was then renamed The Hainault Works for a major manufacturer of tarpaulins.

The flying field was not used in the Second World War although from 1940 to 1941 it was set aside as an emergency landing ground for RAF Hornchurch. It has remained farmland to this day with the technical site area still an industrial estate, and whilst the remaining pair of aeroplane sheds has now been reclad in stone walling its former use is revealed by the inclined struts poking out of the gable walls. Other buildings in the technical area remain in fairly original condition and now serve as company offices, workshops for light and heavy engineering purposes or vehicle repairs.

Although nearby North Weald can lay claim to the usual Battle of Britain ghosts, of all the landing grounds in the county Hainault Farm has produced the greatest number of spectral sightings which seem to relate to the First World War period. Employees of companies based in the remaining aircraft shed pair, as well as those in the nearby newer buildings in the same area, report seeing on many occasions the same apparition in the form of a flyer dressed in 'old style' flying gear. Sightings normally occur late at night during overtime working (when the cold evening air sets the body cold?) and have involved the employee encountering the figure either walking towards them or seeing it on an upstairs level, but in all cases the figure has disappeared after a period of time. Even dogs brought into the buildings at these times have sensed something that has caused their owners to leave either for home or the pub. Whoever it is that inhabits the technical site area is determined to assert its presence for a long time yet.

Horndon-on-the-Hill   TQ 645835

This landing ground was one of two in Essex selected directly by the War Office for the Royal Flying Corps in March 1915 (the other being at Blackheath Common near Colchester) as part of a move to provide additional emergency facilities for Home Defence aircraft on night patrols, but was not put into use immediately.

Situated between Sticking Hill and Conway's Farm, 1½ miles north of the Cock Inn on the London-Southend road, the site was actually just in the parish of Orsett. The four grazing fields making up the 38½-acre landing ground had been owned by Mrs Jane Baker since at least 1839 and were occupied by the Hammers family as part of an area of some 200 acres called Moors-in-the-Clays that stretched south as far as Mount Baker House.

With usable landing dimensions of 525 x 425 yards on a level clay surface approaches to the site, part of which was known locally as Woodcock Field, were clear from all directions but whilst the surroundings were also fairly level the nature and number of obstructions in adjacent fields rendered them unusable for landings. A public bridleway starting at Golden Bridge cottages ran across the site from midway along the east boundary to the south-west corner, where access to the field was gained from the track running past the western edge.

It eventually opened in April 1916, coincidentally the same time as the site at nearby North Ockendon, and was similarly classified purely as a night landing ground in the emergency role. Only landing flares as befitted its night role were used, no ground signals for daytime use or a telephone were installed.

Intended for use by No. 39 (HD) Sqn from Suttons Farm as part of 49th Wing, South East Area during night operational periods it saw little or no use and duly closed in the autumn of 1916 when its role was taken over by Orsett, which became operational in October 1916. It returned to agriculture but received a Suttons Farm aircraft on 1 March 1917 when 24 HD sorties were flown against a single intruder attacking Broadstairs in daylight, children at the local school absconding to see the aircraft and being subsequently kept in detention afterwards. It was then re-requisitioned but saw no more activity, being finally given up early in 1918.

Aviation left the area until the 1930s when the Whitmore family at Orsett Hall (previously known as Mount Baker estate) established a private landing strip for their use and that of friends who were similarly aviation-minded.

In the Second World War a decoy aerodrome was set up some 1¼ miles to the north on pasture at Wick Place, Bulphan just south of Noke Hall on Doesgate Lane. Used from 1940 to 1942 it was manned by airmen from RAF Hornchurch who were taken there for their detailed shift and remembered it as a place 'generally full of sheep' (it still is! – author).

Its purpose was to draw German bombers away from the fighter airfield at Hornchurch and as such had dummy Hurricanes for day use as a 'K' site as well as lights at night when it took on the role of a 'Q' site.

During its period of use the decoy attracted Luftwaffe bombs as well as 'friendly' aircraft, such as Spitfire P9324 of 41 Sqn which arrived there on 15 September 1940 after being damaged in combat with a greater number of Bf 109s. In setting up for a force-landing on what was thought to be a normal aerodrome the aircraft struck telephone wires running over the decoy and crashed at the rear of Wick Place with P/O G.A. Langley being fatally injured during the resulting fire. This was the fate that befell so many pilots who mistook decoys for the real thing, as a result of which mishaps a red obstruction light was placed on the approach to warn pilots not to land. After the decoy closed down it was used late in the war as a gliding site by the Air Training Corps but is now (1997) home to the West Essex Model Flying Club.

The most noticeable change here is the growth of Gorwyn's Plantation at the south-east corner of what is now one field instead of four.

The First World War landing ground itself however has remained farmland ever since it was relinquished in 1918, the only differences being changes in the footpath line and new tree belts planted across the southern portion. Today, one mile to the north, another grass airstrip on the farm at Kings Hill plays host to a later breed of aeroplanes.

Little Clacton   TM 164202

Situated halfway between Little Clacton and Weeley Heath on the north side of the road junction known as Plough Corner, one mile south-west of Thorpe-le-Soken railway station, the site opened in October 1916 as a replacement landing ground for Beaumont. Six fields, three belonging to Miss Ann Freeman and three to Joseph Lott, were combined by hedge removal to make up a landing ground of 54 acres, the area immediately surrounding being generally open except for the presence of Weeleyhall Wood to the north-west, and due to this it was categorised as a 2nd Class night landing ground. At 85' amsl the site was lit at night and had ground signals provided, whilst the level surface of heavy clay soil provided useful landing dimensions of 650 x 420 yards.

All this was infinitely superior to the facilities available at Beaumont, additionally it was much closer to established lines of communication and transport. Allocated primarily to 'C' Flight of No. 37 (HD) Sqn, in the 50th Wing, South East Area it was made operational and given the telephone number of Clacton 100.

Although operations connected with the landing ground in its capacity as a 2nd Class site were conducted safely after it opened the later changes in aircraft type and operational requirements meant that, by January 1917, it had been re-designated as a landing ground in the 3rd Class category.

The landing ground remained a 3rd Class site primarily for the use of No. 37 (HD) Sqn until July 1919 when it was given up and returned to agriculture.

In his role as travelling aerial showman Alan Cobham made use of the site twice for his National Aviation Day displays, the first occasion being 26 July 1932 and the second when his No. 1 Tour visited on 28 May 1933.

TAKE NOTICE.

IN CASE OF INVASION.

You must have ready Blankets enough for your family, and food and drink for 48 hours.

Nothing more will be allowed.

You will be picked up by the waggons and carts of the district.

People with Bicycles & Horses and Carts are at once to proceed.

By Order of the

EMERGENCY COMMITTEE.

East Essex Printing Works, Ltd., Clacton.

Example of a leaflet distributed during the First World War, this one printed in Clacton was put out in Thorpe-le-Soken. (Mrs Eileen Church via Pearl Lonsdale)

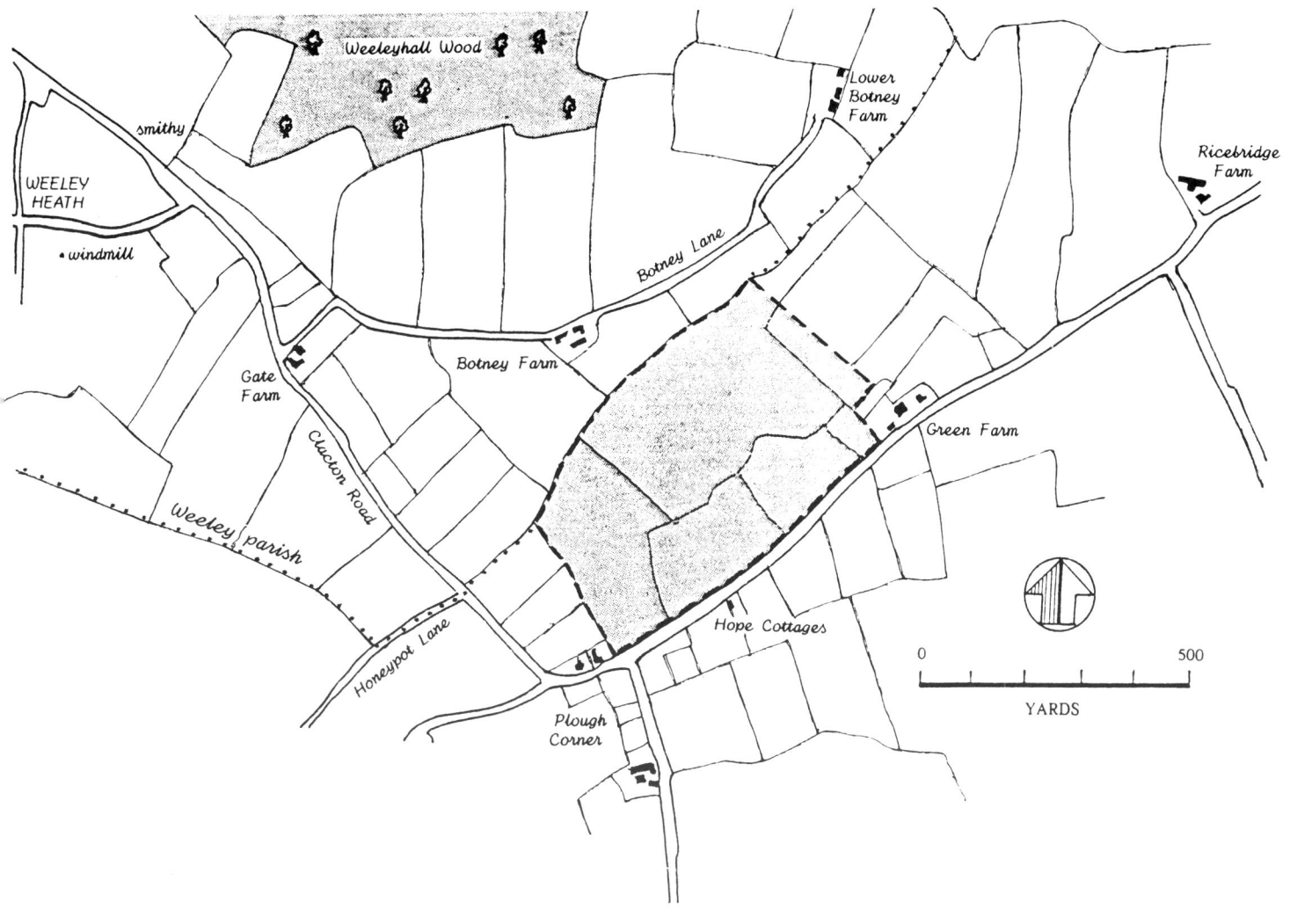

Throughout the Second World War the site was covered with many obstructions to prevent landings by enemy airborne forces. No use was made of it for any aviation purpose but the summer of 1942 saw the area immediately around, and including, the WW1 landing ground being surveyed by the Air Ministry as a possible location for a bomber airfield to serve the American 8th Air Force. Two local areas were investigated, Little Clacton and nearby Weeley Heath, but nothing further than land surveys and basic drawings were completed. Other proposed locations had detailed layouts prepared and were allocated a USAF Station number but Little Clacton and Weeley had none of these. Plans to build the sites were finally dropped by August 1942 due to airfield construction projects in East Anglia being critically behind schedule.

The area did receive a number of airborne 'visitors'. One such was Short Stirling W7564, an Austin Motors built Mk 1, which was hit by flak over Maastricht and lost three of its four engines before force-landing north of Weeleyhall Wood on 11 September 1942. The nearby Weeley railway bridge was the impact point for Big Ben 159, a German Army A4 rocket, which fell at 0108 hrs on 7 November 1944.

The agricultural use continued until the recreational and hobby needs of local residents took over, numerous football pitches and playing fields now covering much of the south-western half of the former landing ground which is still known as 'the flying field'. With a housing belt along the southern edge and many modern buildings housing such activities as youth club, light industrial units and the Essex County Council Training Centre occupying the south-western corner the Air Training Corps, in the form of No. 1830 (Tendring Hundred) Sqn, have also established themselves there as possibly the last flying(?) unit.

45

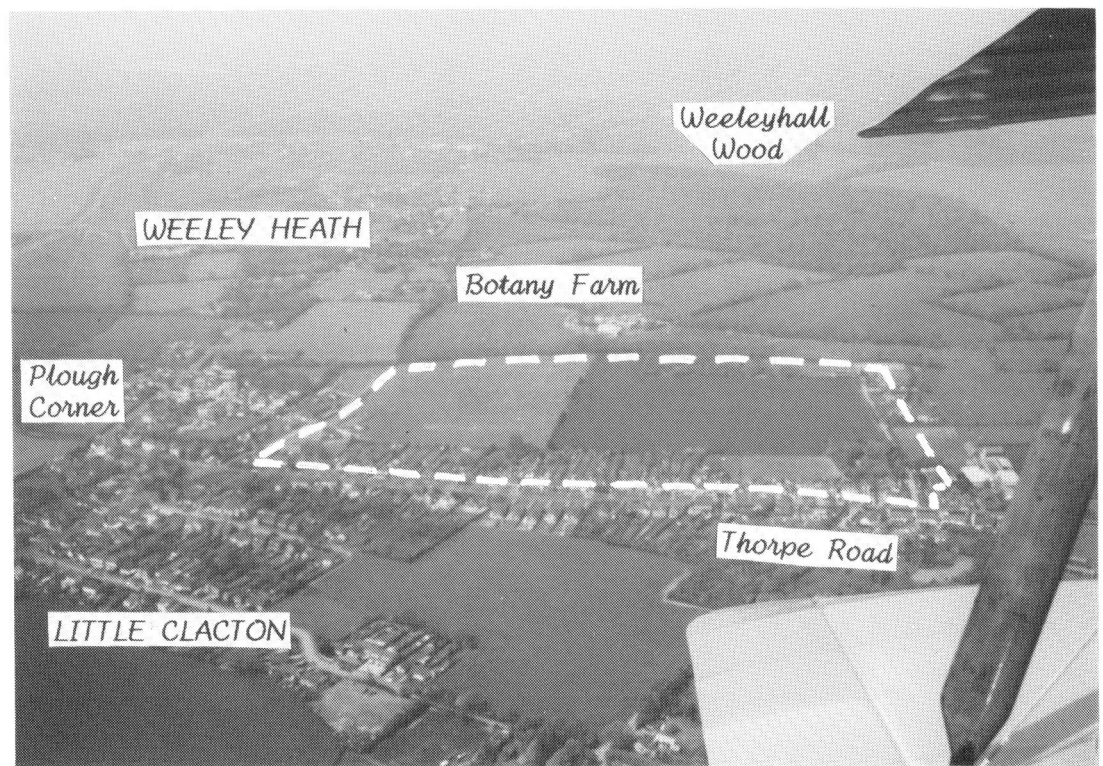

Seen from the south-east framed between the Jackeroo wingtips Little Clacton landing ground is bounded to the south by housing on the B1414 road. Plough Corner (the alternative name for the site) is at the left-hand edge with Botany Farm and Weeleyhall wood to the north. During the Second World War this wood contained the underground hideout for the Weeley patrol of the Auxiliary Units, the civilian-manned British Resistance movement who were to carry out sabotage against the occupying German army had invasion been successful.

Mountnessing   TL 646980

As the smallest night landing ground in the county, at only 21 acres, it was soon realised that a site that sloped steeply to the north, with a wood on one side and undulating fields that fell away in all directions on the other three sides, was not in keeping with the usual operational requirements for an emergency landing ground.

Established in April 1916, during the 'panic' period for night landing ground expansion, the land it occupied was owned by the Petre Estate at nearby Ingatestone Hall and lay between Lodge Wood to the west and the road to Bacons Farm on the east. The northern part of the site sloped down abruptly towards the River Wid which separated it from Heybridge village half a mile away on the Roman Road which ran from Brentwood to Chelmsford.

The need for the landing ground over-ruled any objections to its use arising from the topographical limitations, and it opened in the category of a 3rd Class night landing ground with usable dimensions of only 300 x 375 yards for No. 39 (HD) Sqn who were at the time stationed at North Weald Bassett as part of 49th Wing, South East Area. It cannot be confirmed what facilities were provided, but certainly the site did not have any ground signals placed on it. A telephone number for the site is also not known, but it would have had one in order to be able to receive orders to set landing flares.

After an inauspicious period of only nine months, with no record of landings of any kind being found to date, the landing ground closed in December 1916. The need for such a facility was then transferred to Palmers Farm, 2½ miles due west on the north side of the Roman Road, where better topographical features were found and Mountnessing returned to arable farming.

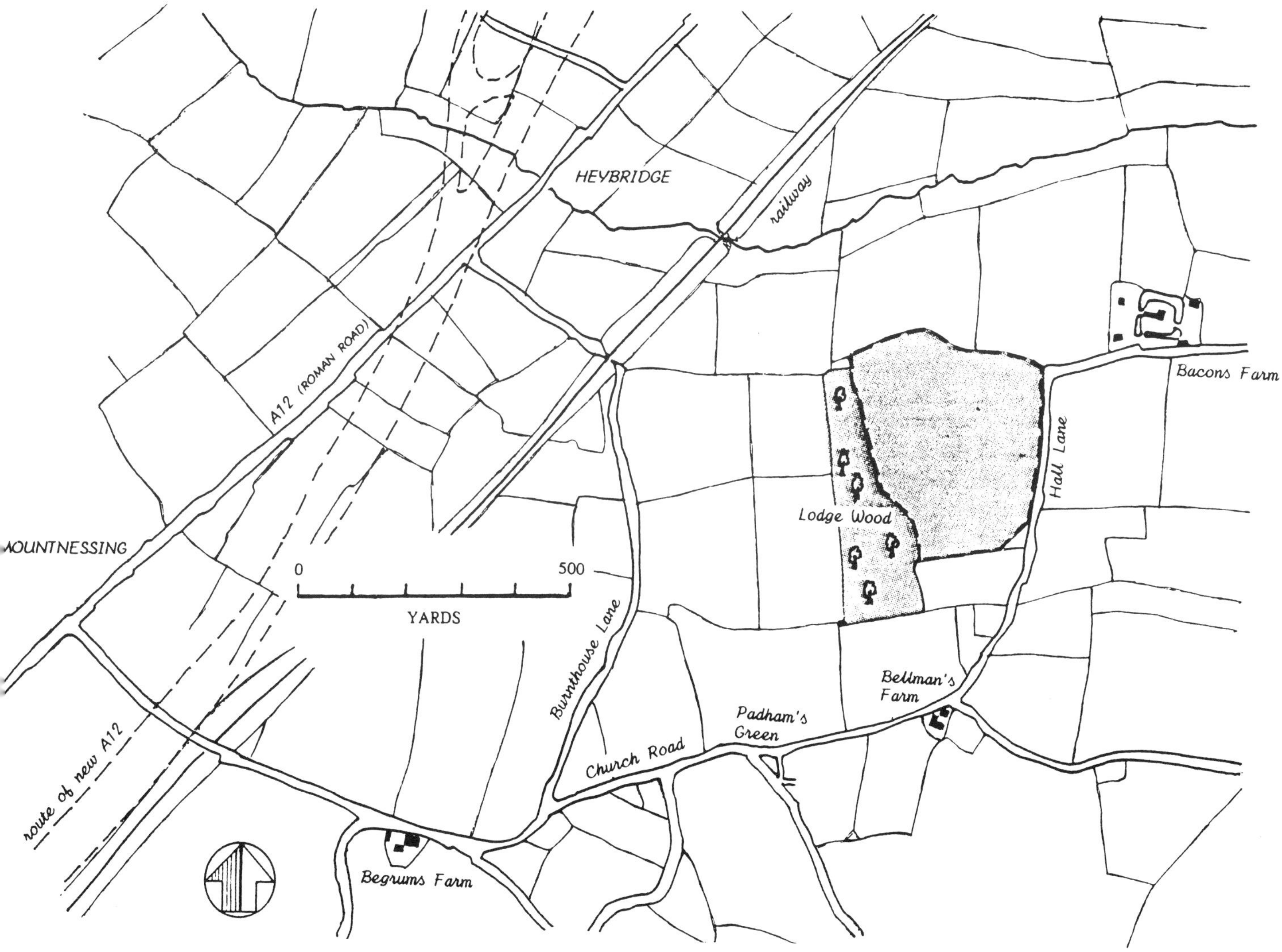

Located between Lodge Wood and the road to Bacons Farm, the landing ground looks quite usable. In reality it was a hazard to flying operations.

Of the 1,115 V2 rockets launched against the United Kingdom between September 1944 and March 1945 no less than four landed in the vicinity of the WW1 landing ground, which was lucky to escape the onslaught, with three falling in a straight line from the railway bridge near Begrums Farm half a mile to the south-west through to Bellmans Farm and Westlands to the south-east, and one in Ingatestone one mile to the north.

The site returned to arable farming 80 years ago and has continued in this role ever since.

North Benfleet   TQ 763880

In order to close the gap of some 21 miles which existed up to the start of 1916 between the flight stations of Rochford and Suttons Farm on the north bank of the River Thames, a permanent night landing ground for the RFC was proposed in the Pitsea area. Immediately adjacent to the river the land was low-lying and marshy, and liable to flooding, but further inland the higher ground proved more promising.

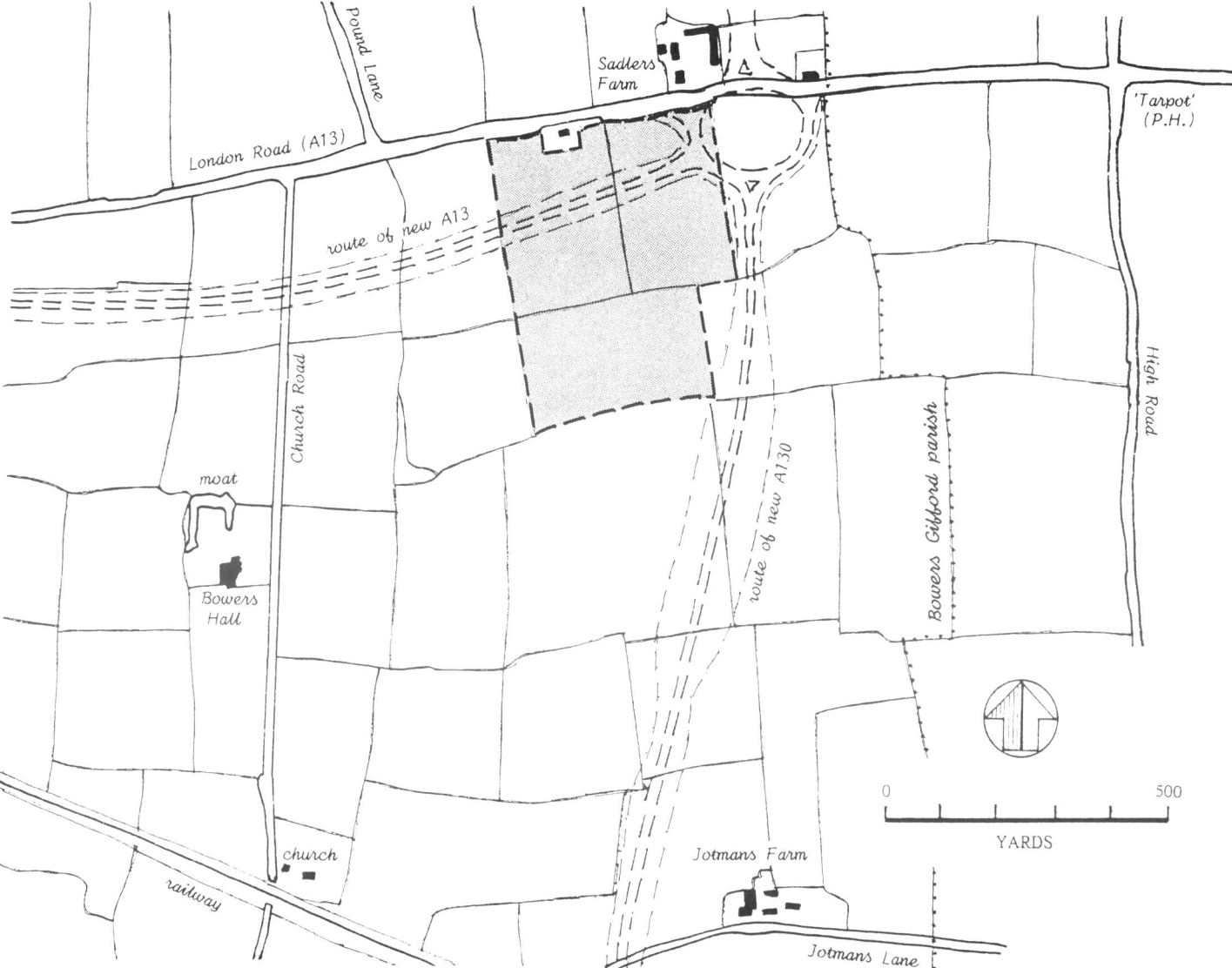

A site comprising three arable fields, two owned by Charles Bayley at Sadlers Farm and one by James Buckenham at Jotmans Hall, 1¾ miles from Pitsea railway station was thus selected. At 115' amsl the fields were combined by hedge and tree removal to produce a landing ground of 37 acres which had open surroundings and, although known as North Benfleet, was actually on the eastern edge of the parish of Bowers Gifford. Located to the south of the old Hadleigh Trust toll road, which had been authorised in 1793 by Parliament to run from Leigh to Grays, it was one mile north of the London-Southend railway line where it ran past the parish church of St Margaret's. The cottages housing workers from Sadlers Farm, the alternative name for the landing ground, were on the northern boundary next to the road.

Prior to its opening the site was noted as having bad ridge and furrows on a heavy clay soil, but it had useful landing dimensions of 300 x 550 yards and as such was categorised a 2nd Class site when it became operational in April 1916 with the telephone number of Southend on Sea 335. A windsock and wet weather shelter for the personnel manning the site were the only facilities provided, but ground arrow signals were also displayed.

The new A13 runs across what were two fields on the northern half of the former landing ground, whilst the roundabout on the extended A130 linking the A127 with Canvey Island intrudes on the east side.

In September 1916 the landing ground was allocated to No. 37 (HD) Sqn, the nearest part of which was 'A' Flight based at Rochford, but it was later noted for use by No. 61 (HD) Sqn which formed at Rochford in August 1917.

Only one instance of the site receiving an emergency has been found, this occurring on the night of 30 September 1917 when 37 Home Defence sorties were flown against eleven Gothas raiding London. From Suttons Farm No. 78 (HD) Sqn sent up five of its Sopwith 1½-Strutters on patrol of which B2593, crewed by Lt J.S. Castle and Airman 1st Class H. Daws, suffered engine problems and made a precautionary forced-landing at Sadlers Farm.

By October 1918 the landing ground had been allocated to other squadrons but little use was made of it, nevertheless it was held on the books of the Air Ministry until the end of March 1919, at which point in time it was decided not to retain it any longer and it passed back to its owners for farming to resume.

With the advent of the air circuses the locality was not overlooked as a venue. Burnt Mills Road, on the Nevendon side of Pitsea, saw the 'Ferry' show of Alan Cobham's National Aviation Day Display arrive on 26 August 1935, whilst Sadlers Farm hosted the British Empire Air Display in May 1936 when such aircraft types as the Avro 504, DH Fox Moth and Hawker Tomtit were present.

Although not used for aviation during the Second World War the site did receive one airborne visitor in the form of Big Ben 243, a German Army A4 long-range rocket which fell on the north-east corner at 2015 on 23 November 1944.

The site has changed considerably from the First World War period, with the new dual-carriageway A13 running across the northern two fields and horse paddocks occupying the area up to the old A13, but the southerly areas are still farmed. To the east a large road junction called Sadlers Farm roundabout, built to link both the old and new A13 with roads from the A127 and Canvey Island, intrudes on the north-east corner but the cottages and farm (now Sadlers Hall farm) off the northern edge of the site still remain.

North Ockendon   TQ 601846

A peculiar situation existed here for, at the same time as it was being set up to serve No. 39 (HD) Sqn at Suttons Farm five miles to the west, another landing ground for the same purpose was being established at Horndon-on-the-Hill only three miles away to the east.

Although the Ockendon site was nearer to the village of North Ockendon it lay south of that parish boundary and was actually in the parish of South Ockendon. Access to the landing ground was via the farm track which led off North Road at Groves Farm and ran to Middle Farm.

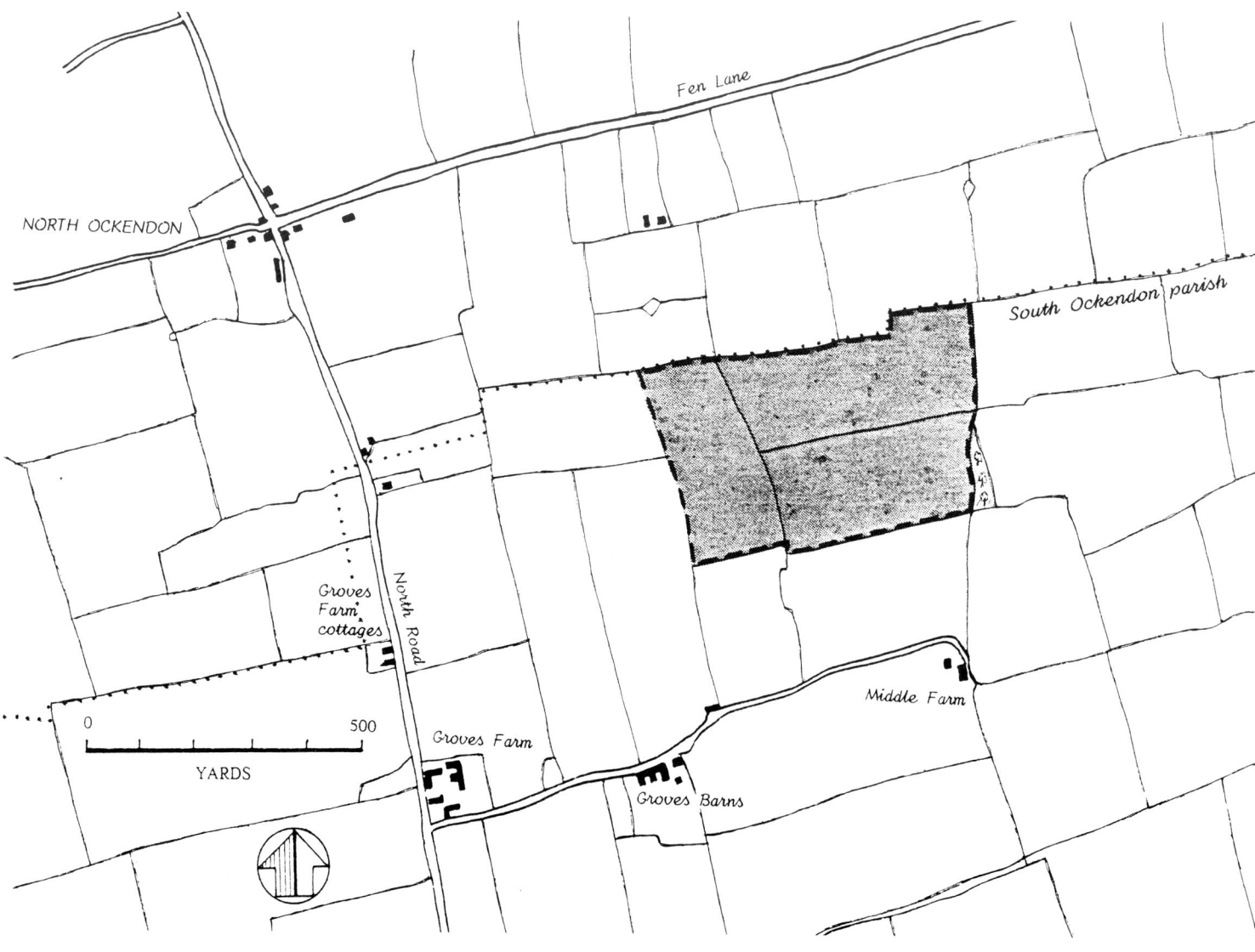

Comprising 39¾ acres of farmland on the John Henry Stewart estate the surface was firm clay overlying gravels. Whilst useful landing dimensions of 500 x 325 yards were attainable a seemingly un-noticed factor relating to the site was that the eastern boundary was at 50' amsl and the west at 100', and even higher ground rising to 133' amsl existed just north of Fen Lane. Whilst surroundings in all directions except to the west were open and fairly level the combination of this noticeable cross-fall and high ground on one side were not worthy of consideration as the landing ground was duly made ready for operations, and when opened in April 1916 was classified as a Home Defence night landing ground in the 3rd Class category.

Like its nearby neighbour the usual minimum of facilities were provided, and whilst it was also designated a 'lit' site for night use no telephone link with the outside world was provided nor were ground signals displayed.

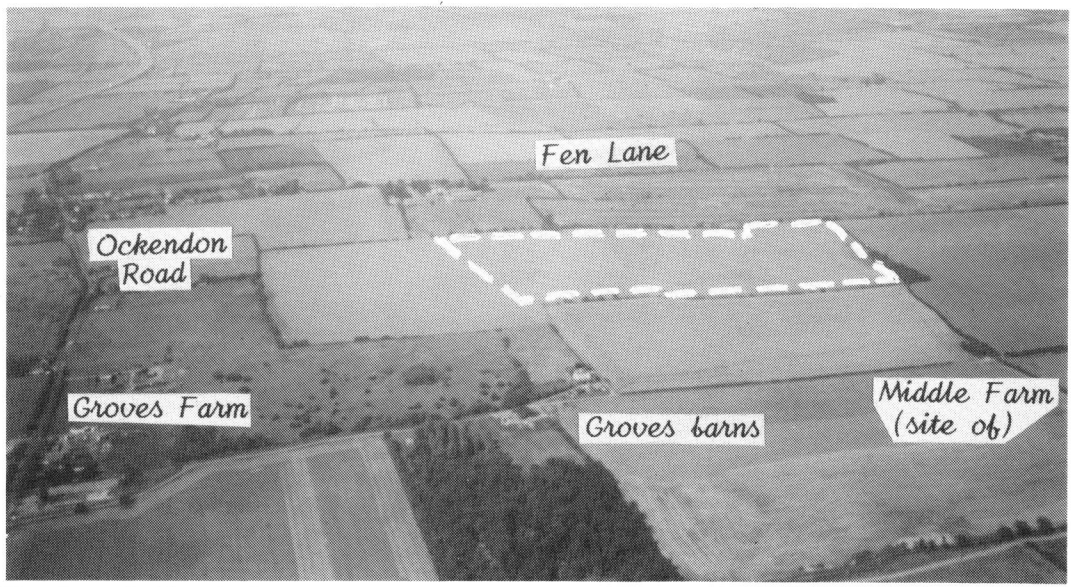

The three fields which made up the former landing ground are now one, with the remains of Groves Farm next to the Ockendon Road.

Little use was apparently made of the site and, like Horndon-on-the-Hill, it closed in October 1916 when the requirements for a night emergency landing ground were fulfilled by the much improved facilities at Orsett which opened that same month four miles to the south-east. It returned to farmland with part of the land to the west behind Groves Farm becaming an orchard. During the Second World War no aviation use was made of the site but in April 1944 the farm at Blankets, one mile to the east, housed a mobile radar set-up to enable the operators to be familiar with their equipment before the units moved over to Normandy as part of Operation Overlord.

Subsequent to the Second World War the western part of the site which had previously been an orchard was incorporated in a gravel pit for extraction of that material, this has now been backfilled whilst the remainder was returned to agriculture after being left fallow for many years.

North Weald Bassett TQ 489041

The site opened in April 1916 as a night landing ground for No. 39 (HD) Sqn in 49th Wing, South East Area. Covering 136 acres it had maximum landing dimensions of 900 x 850 yards but the clay surface became poor and very wet in winter. At 300' amsl a slight slope to the north did not restrict operations but the surroundings were enclosed, with the Epping-Ongar branch of the London North Eastern railway line and large woods to the south, and Epping Forest to the west. Fields outside the boundaries were noted as small.

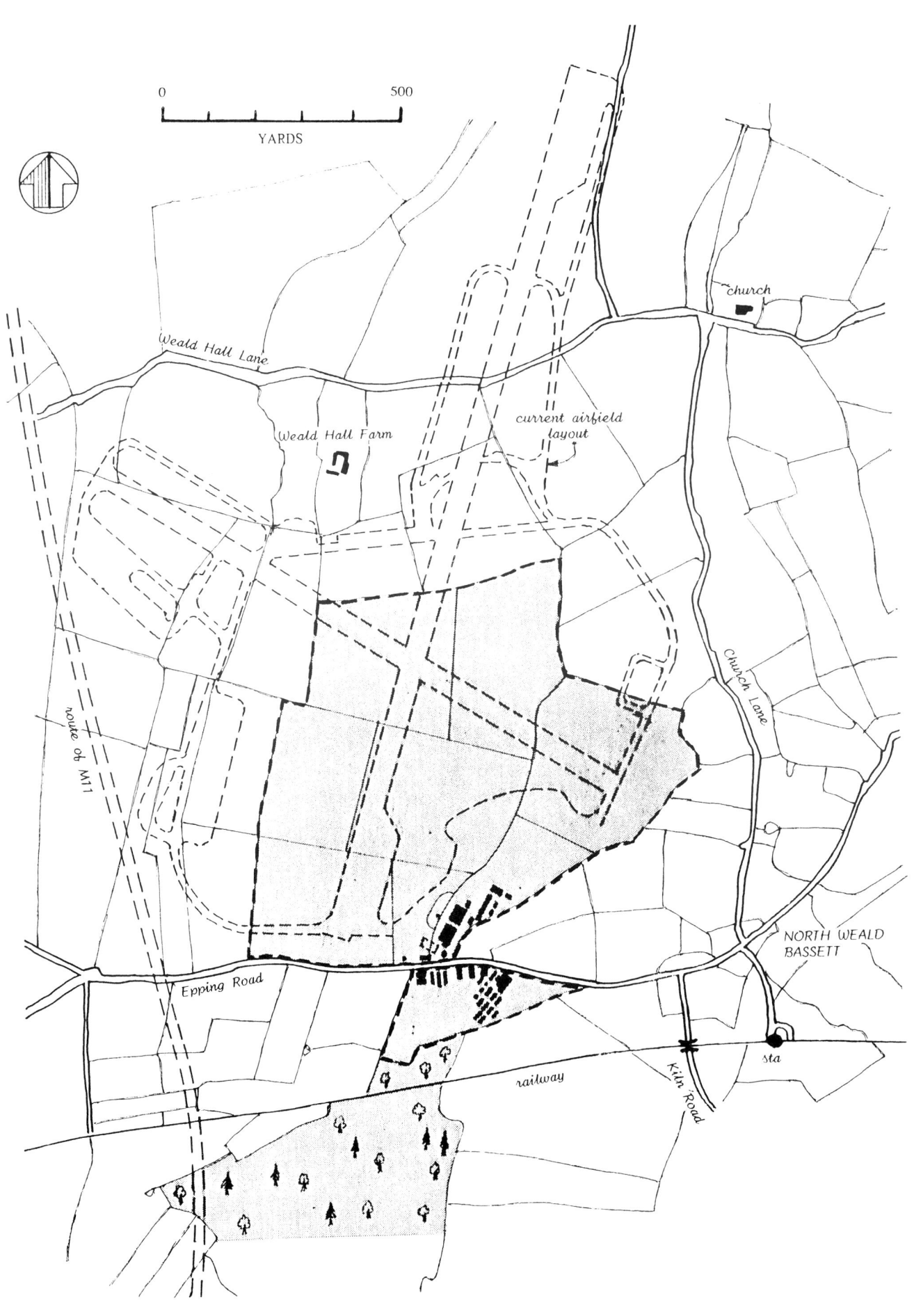

0   500
YARDS

Weald Hall Lane

Weald Hall Farm

current airfield layout

church

route of M11

Church Lane

Epping Road

NORTH WEALD BASSETT

railway

Kiln Road

sta

52

With the minimum of facilities, the landing ground was used until August 1916 when it was designated a Home Defence Flight Station (night) in the 1st Class category for 'A' Flight of No. 39 (HD) Sqn. Building works in keeping with its new role then started, with 18 taking up 15 acres on the southern boundary and a further 27 constructed in the regimental site to the south side of the Epping road which lay in the neighbouring parish of Theydon Garnon. The estimated date for completion of all buildings was 1 December 1918 but until the messing facilities were finished on the regimental site all personnel took their meals at the Kings Head inn in the village.

The detached flight operated successfully from the station until September 1917, the most notable sortie being that of 2nd Lieut Wulstan J. Tempest against the Navy Zeppelin L31 on the night of 1/2 October 1916. Tempest took off in B.E.2c, 4577, to patrol a line between Hainault and Joyce Green (Kent) and, just before midnight, saw a Zeppelin caught in the searchlights over Hertfordshire en route to bomb London. At high speed he made for it and carried out two attacks, the second of which set the airships' envelope afire, sending it crashing in flames into Oakmere Park, Potters Bar.

After two hours flying at great altitude and in horrific weather conditions Wulstan Tempest returned exhausted to North Weald Bassett but crashed on landing due to poor visibility, though luckily without injury to himself. All the airship's crew, including the experienced commander Kptlt Heinrich Mathy, perished and were initially buried locally in Mutton Lane cemetary but re-interred in the German War Cemetery (Soldatenfriedhof) at Cannock Chase in 1966.

For such an active station still in flying use little remains here from both the First and pre-Second World War periods.

Also stationed at North Weald Bassett was Captain T. Grant. In reality he was Jens Herman Tryggve Gran, a Norwegian who had been the skiing trainer to Robert Falcon Scott's party on the ill-fated 1910 expedition to the South Pole. In July 1914 he had flown an 80 h.p. Gnome Rhone-engined B.E.2 from Cruden Bay on the east coast of Scotland to Reevtangen in Norway in 4½ hours, the aircraft was then purchased by the Norwegian Ministry of Defence and Gran carried out coastal patrols in it.

In October 1916 Gran was attached to the Royal Flying Corps but, as Norway was neutral, had to take the name of Grant and give his nationality as Canadian. Based first at Northolt then Rochford Gran was sent to 39 (HD) Sqn at Suttons Farm and arrived at North Weald Bassett in December. Three sorties are recorded as having been flown by Gran from North Weald Bassett, the first on 24

May 1917 was uneventful and resulted in a forced-landing at Hamels Park, Ware when his B.E.12 ran out of fuel, that of 5 June also being without any success. The last on 13 June did bring some action if only by friendly forces, for after chasing a Gotha out to sea Gran was fired on by the AA gun battery at Shoeburyness and damage to the exhaust stacks of his B.E.12 caused him to force-land at Rochford. The following month Gran was ordered to Suttons Farm, then Hainault Farm where the flight there formed the nucleus of 44 (HD) Sqn.

In September 1917 'B' & 'C' Flights of No. 39 (HD) Sqn moved in, the whole squadron being based there until the end of October 1918 when it went to the Western Front.

On 1 November 1917 No. 39 Sqn, in common with others in the same operating role, lost its (HD) suffix when this was omitted from unit numbers on War Office orders.

In June 1918 'A' Flight of No. 75 Sqn moved onto the site from its Elmswell (Suffolk) base but, when the Armistice was signed in the November, all wartime operations ceased and the station went into a peacetime mode. The rest of No. 75 Sqn arrived in May 1919 but the unit only remained for another month before being disbanded on site, the station was then devoid of aircraft until No. 44 Sqn arrived in July for a five month stay.

The station closed down in December 1919 but in 1922 plans were laid to reconstruct it to house two single-seat fighter squadrons on a permanent basis. With the exception of a few structures on the technical site all the buildings to the north of the Epping road were demolished, the first of three new 125' x 256' aeroplane sheds being placed on the site of the two WW1 sheds. Only the outer two sheds 1 & 2 were completed; had there been all three they would have been within the boundary of the WW1 landing ground and formed a semi-circle typical of the later Expansion period aerodromes. Sadly only the No. 1 shed is still complete due to No. 2 having been lost to a fire in August 1996.

For the new layout the technical and accommodation areas of the aerodrome were extended to the east by land purchase and a new road system and buildings planned. The women's hostel was built here between two existing houses, one of which today houses the North Weald Airfield Museum, although the area of the hostel site has now been taken over by industrial units. One building however was 'second-hand', this being the Officers' Mess from Hainault Farm which was moved in on the closure of that station to serve as such until the Mess was built on the south side of the Epping Road. The Mess is now part of a council home for single parents but a plaque affixed in the porch recalls the birth of the station and its role in London's defence through two World Wars up to the time it closed.

The airfield re-opened in September 1927 and, with further improvements, again served in the forefront of London's defence in the Second World War. When the RAF entered the jet age it was apparent that restrictions would have to be placed on operations, and although the main runway was extended twice to cater for jet aircraft the station was put on Care & Maintainence in November 1958 leaving its two runways for use by the Essex Gliding Club which formed there in 1957. The airfield was transferred to the Army Department in 1966, the Queen's Regiment being the only active unit for that year, and gliding continued but in 1979 Epping Forest District Council purchased the entire site for leisure purposes. It now houses various sporting facilities, a hypermarket plus the now traditional weekend markets, and hosts the annual Fighter Meet.

The gliding club is still active along with other aviation-based organisations such as Aces High, who supply aircraft for film work and provided a hangar for the TV quiz 'Crystal Maze' to be filmed, and aircraft preservation groups on site.

Off what was the northern boundary of the WW1 site but is now the centre of the airfield two WW2 aircraft pens and other period buildings are used by the 'The Squadron', a flying club that provides a link with the airfield's past, the Harvard Formation Team having being formed there and where other 'warbirds' can be seen.

Orsett

In July 1916, to be more effective against Zeppelins raiding London, No. 39 (HD) Sqn was split into three flights located at North Weald Bassett (A Flt), Suttons Farm (B Flt) and Hainault Farm (C Flt). Soon afterwards emergency night landing grounds were sought out, with Orsett being one of a total of two 1st, two 2nd and six 3rd Class sites allocated to the squadron.

Situated south-east of the cottages next to the Cock Inn on the Grays-Stanford le Hope road two miles from the nearest railway station at Stanford le Hope the site comprised an irregular-shaped field on the northern half of Mucking Heath belonging to the estate of the Baker family. Main access was from Flight Hill to the north, where a track running from the Flight garage to Collingwood Farm formed the eastern boundary, whilst the southern edge of the field ran across the heath to include Mucking Heath Farm and finished at Old House Lane. Mucking Heath Farm was used as the station HQ but other facilities were of a temporary nature.

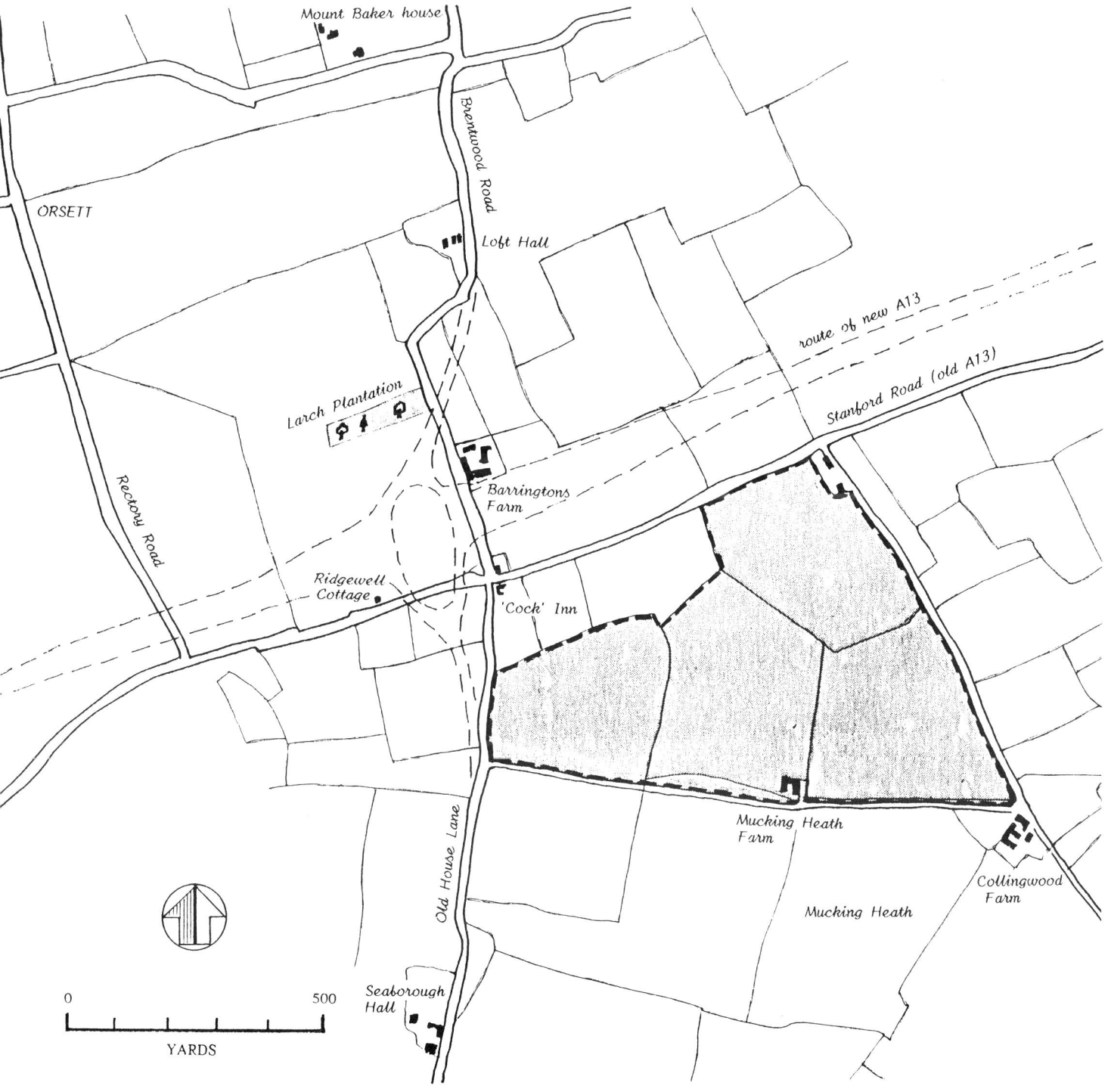

With usable landing dimensions of 650 x 520 yards on a level light loam surface, and open surroundings plus medium-sized fields nearby, the site was categorised as a 1st Class night landing ground which at 80 acres was greater in area than the flight station at Goldhanger. It opened in October 1916 with the telephone number of Orsett 9 as an advanced base for Suttons Farm and replaced North Ockendon and Horndon on the Hill, which duly closed at the same time.

Although landing flares and ground signals were displayed, and primarily for No. 39 (HD) Sqn, no use appears to have been made of it by that unit which held the site until October 1918. In July 1917 'B' Flight of No. 78 (HD) Sqn, also in 49th Wing, South East Area and based at Suttons Farm, was then allocated the site and used it in an emergency on at least three occasions.

On the night of 31 October/1 November 1917, having put up nine Sopwith 1½-Strutters as part of 50 defence sorties flown against 22 Gothas raiding London, Capt F. Billinge force-landed A5238 at Orsett. The type, one of three converted to single-seat configuration for night operations and known as 'Comics', made its debut that night.

16 February 1918 saw Lt I.M. Davies force-land Sopwith Camel C6716 on the site due to bad weather whilst patrolling against Giants attacking London, and Camel C1582 was force-landed by 2nd Lt T.L. Tebbitt on the morning of 20 May after suffering engine problems when flying against 28 Gothas raiding London.

At the close of the First World War the landing ground was retained for use by the RAF, but finally given up in December 1919 and returned to agriculture. The site was then re-activated during the Second World War as an emergency landing ground and, now known in part as Cock Meadow, received one of two Hurricanes that force-landed in the area on 5 December 1940 and Spitfire P8744, KH–P, of 403 Sqn which arrived on 19 August 1941.

Later in the war an AA battery was located on the eastern side and, during preparations for D-day in 1944, a camp to control road convoy traffic build-up, movement and forward concentration was set up on the west side. In connection with this many roads around the site were used as vehicle parks, one such park on the A13 to the north serving the docks at Tilbury started at Nevilles Farm, one mile to the west, and extended eastwards up to Hassenbrooke Hall at Stanford le Hope, a distance of 3½ miles.

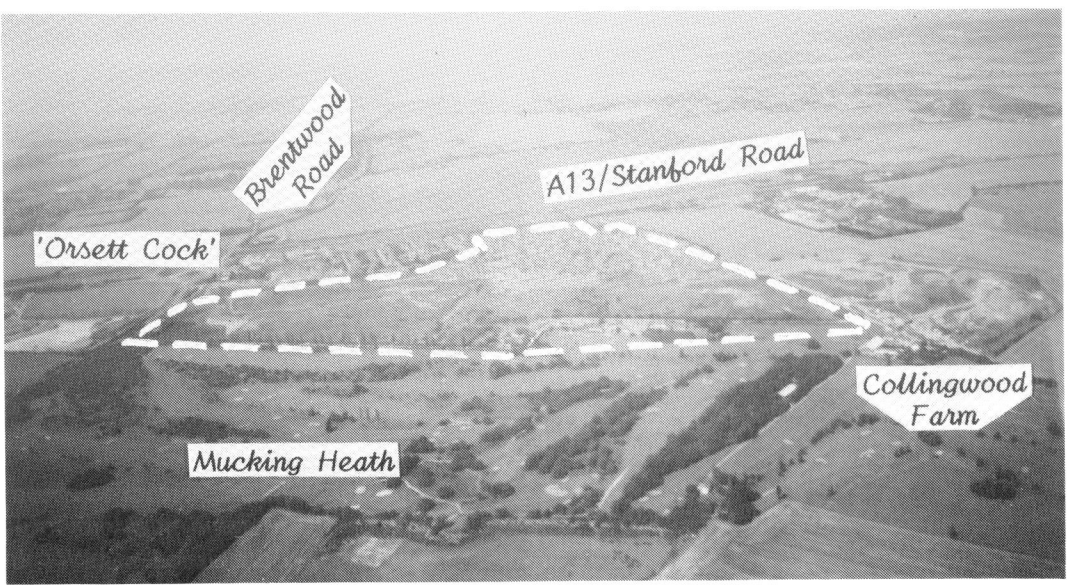

With Orsett Golf Club on Mucking Heath prominent in the foreground and the A13 to the north the site boundaries are still easy to find. The Brentwood Road runs past the Orsett Cock on the left-hand side and up to the wooded area at Horndon-on-the-Hill NLG.

Post-war a large depot for the Royal Army Service Corps was built on the southern half of the old landing ground but this has now gone, as has Mucking Heath Farm which changed its name to Old Kennels Farm. The new clubhouse of the Orsett Golf Club is next to the site, with the course itself on Mucking Heath to the south.

The eastern half of the WW1 landing ground now has housing built on it, with the western half a quarry for deep gravel extraction. Other changes include the Flight garage becoming the Red Lion Service Station, Flight Hill on the old A13 is now the Red Lion Hill stretch of the A1013, and Old House Lane has been renamed the Brentwood Road.

Rochford   TQ 869891

This flying ground, eventually to become the largest in the county and house the greatest number of units, came about in the autumn of 1914 when farmland between Westbarrow Hall and the Great Eastern railway line at Warners Bridge 2½ miles north of Southend Pier was acquired for RFC training purposes. Eastwoodbury Lane formed the southern boundary and from near St Lawrence & All Saints' church to the west a tributary of the River Roach and hedges ran northwards along the west side. The south and west sides also had 12'0" high poles with telephone wires strung between them but this was not considered too much of a hazard.

Relatively open country lay between the northern boundary and the church of St Andrew at Rochford Hall three-quarters of a mile to the north, whilst the east boundary stopped short of the railway line. At 40' amsl the level surface was a heavy loam soil which was moderate but wet in winter, maximum landing dimensions being 1000 x 800 yards with the surroundings fairly open with large fields. Initially marked during the day by a white strip the landing ground later had the usual luxury of a landing circle added.

Training continued until May 1915 when the site, known also as Eastwood, was taken over by the RNAS to become a Flight Station (night) in the fight against intruding Zeppelins. The camp area was set up in the south-west corner, near to the church, where a copse of trees existed. Only six defence sorties on five occasions were flown, the most effective being the night of 31 May/1 June when a total of 15 sorties were made by the RFC and RNAS. A Bleriot Parasol, 1546, piloted by Flt Sub-Lieut R.H. Mulock made the sole sighting of Army Zeppelin LZ38 but the pursuit was terminated abruptly when engine failure caused him to abandon the chase and force-land south of Rochford at Leigh on Sea.

After the last RNAS action from here on 26 April 1916 all personnel and stores went to Detling Air Station in Kent and on 4 June it became once again RFC Rochford. Initially it was defined as a Home Defence night landing ground but in September was reclassified as a Flight Station (night) in the 1st Class category. It was then allocated to 'A' Flight of No. 37 (HD) Sqn in 50th Wing, South East Area who moved in from the experimental station at Orfordness, Suffolk with their B.E.2 and B.E.12 aircraft.

A building programme had started in June for a planned completion date of 30 November 1918 and, with the site boundaries squared off to finally encompass an area of 168 acres, 73 structures eventually occupied 35 acres on the southern and western boundaries with a separate sewage disposal works a quarter of a mile to the south. However by the end of November 1916 on-site accommodation was still not finished such that the ground staff remained at billets in Rochford with aircrews at the Westcliffe Hotel in Southend town. On receipt of an alert, the first of which came on 28 November when only one defensive sortie was flown, the duty crews would be driven from the hotel to the aerodrome.

No. 11 Reserve (Night Training) Sqn arrived in January 1917 only to go through a series of name changes, becoming first No. 98 Depot Sqn in February then No. 198 Depot Sqn in June. Flying Avro 504s and Sopwith Camels it then became No. 198 (Night) Training Sqn in December and remained as such until disbanded on site in 1919.

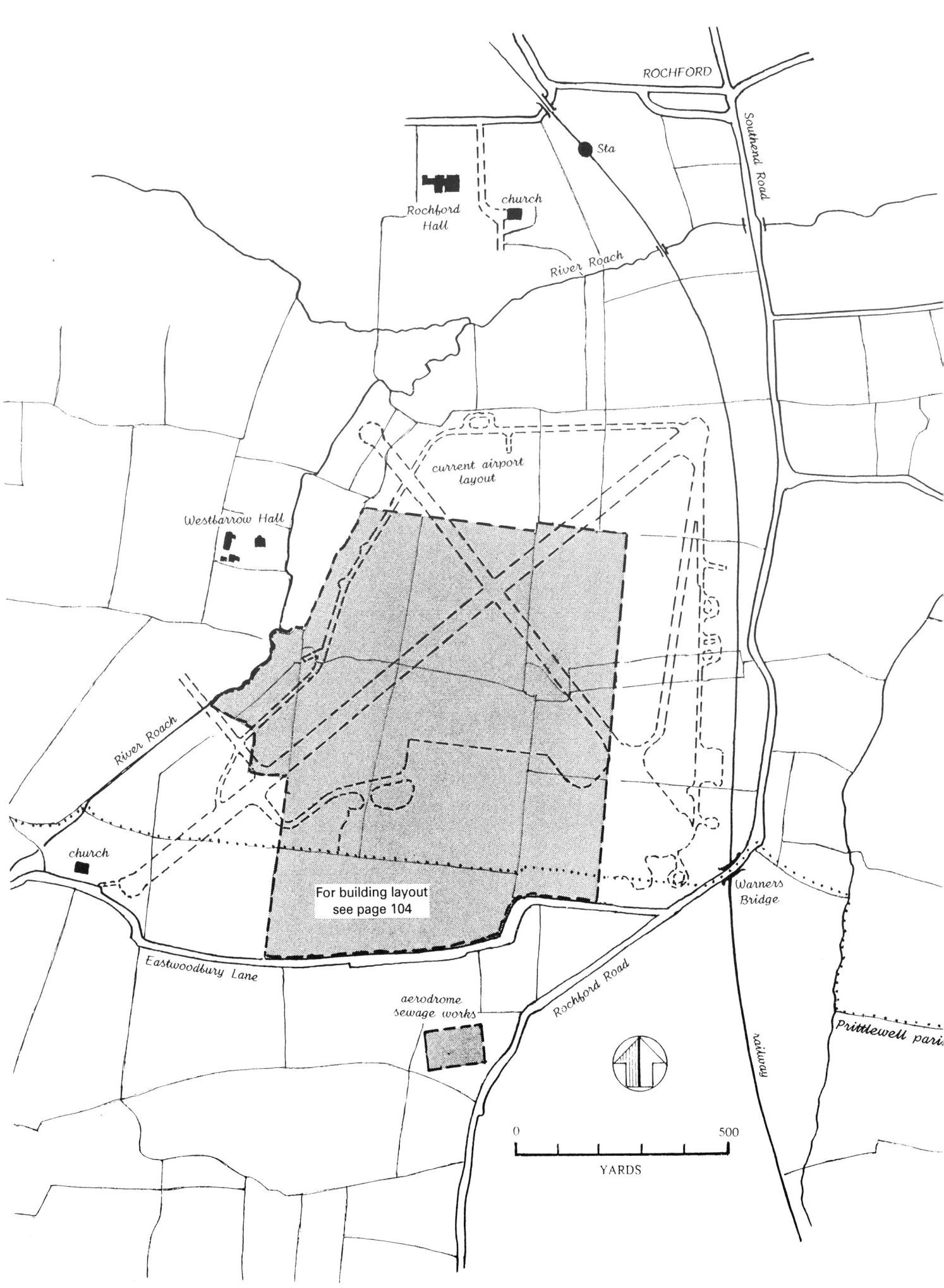

ROCHFORD

Sta

Rochford
Hall

church

River Roach

Southend Road

current airport
layout

Westbarrow Hall

River Roach

church

For building layout
see page 104

Warners
Bridge

Eastwoodbury Lane

aerodrome
sewage works

Rochford Road

railway

Prittlewell paris

0   500

YARDS

58

On 25 May 1917 when a Gotha raid on Folkestone was in progress a B.E.12 of No. 37 (HD) Sqn, flown by Lieut W.R.S. Humphries, took off for patrol but had to put into Stow Maries with throttle problems before force-landing at Goldhanger with a broken oil pipe, thus visiting all three of the squadron's flight stations in one day.

June saw a short visit by No. 99 Depot Sqn, with 'A' Flight of No. 56 Sqn arriving from France via Bekesbourne to stay for one month on temporary Home Defence duties whilst they traded in some of their S.E.5 aircraft for the S.E.5a variant.

During a 24-Gotha daylight raid to London on 7 July a Sopwith 1½-Strutter, A8271 from No. 37 (HD) Sqn, was flying a defensive sortie when it was shot down by AA fire and crashed in the sea near the Maplin light vessel. Tragically both 2nd Lt J.E.R. Young and his gunner, Airman C.C. Taylor, were killed. Later that month 'A' Flight of No. 37 (HD) Sqn moved to Stow Maries but before doing so spawned the birth of No. 61 (HD) Sqn on 2 August 1917 as an additional day-fighter unit with Sopwith Pups. Rochford was then designated a Home Defence station for that squadron.

No. 190 Depot Sqn was formed in September and promptly changed its name to No. 190 (Night) Training Sqn the next month, it remained on site until March 1918.

On 6 December 1917 a Gotha GV, 906/16 of Kagohl 3, was one of 16 attacking London when it was hit by AA fire from a Canvey site. Upon jettisoning its bombs it made for the aerodrome but had to force-land on the adjacent golf course after striking a tree on the approach, and was later unintentionally set on fire when a signal flare was ignited by an onlooker (landings similar to this occurred in the Second World War when a Dornier Do17Z-3 of 2/KG2 arrived on 26 August, closely followed by a Do17Z-2 of 9/KG3 on 2 September 1940).

On 1 January 1918 No. 141 Sqn formed from 'A' Flight of No. 61 Sqn with Sopwith Dolphins and moved to Biggin Hill the following month. The second true night-fighter unit, No. 152 (Single-Seat Fighter, night) Sqn, formed in October 1918 and moved to France the same month. Rochford was, by now, operating in the category of a Night Training Station.

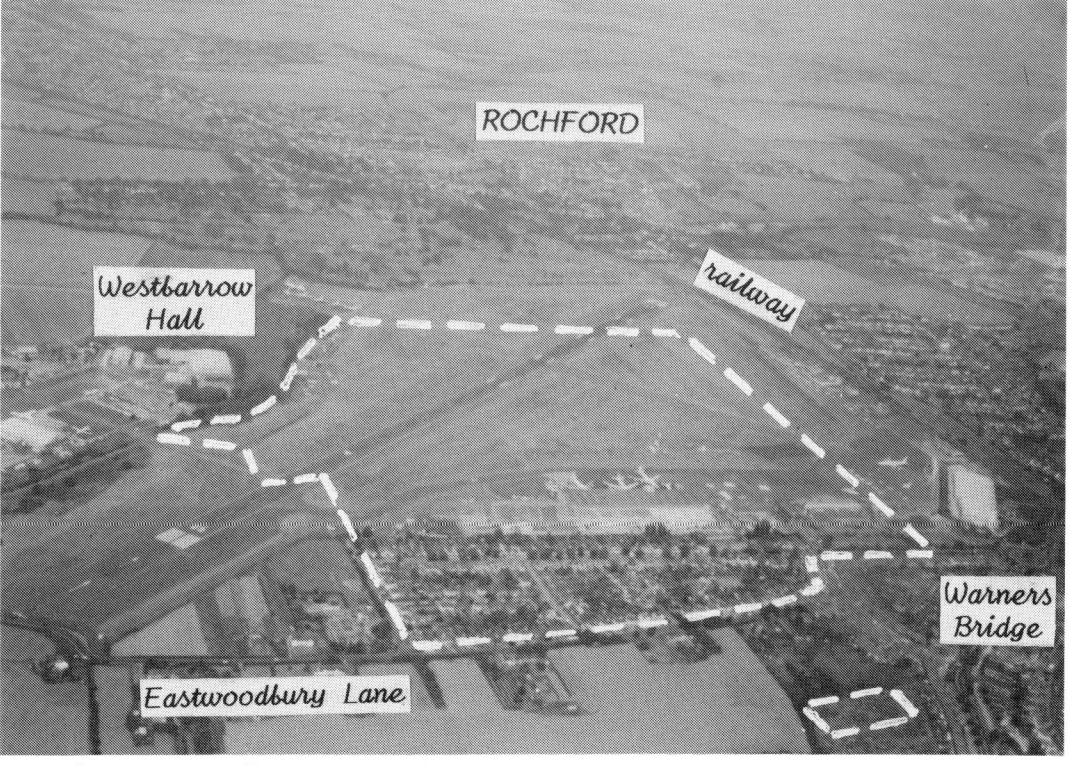

Apart from Eastwoodbury Lane to the south and the end of the houses at Avro Road very few 1918 boundaries remain, whilst the sewage works site next to the Rochford Road is on a parcel of waste ground.

Normal Home Defence duties continued until after the Armistice when a run-down of unit activities began, with No. 198 Sqn disbanding in May and No. 61 in June 1919. Except for the occasional civilian flights aviation lessened, even more so when the station closed in 1920 and the site returned to farmland. The whole of the southern technical site area was later developed for housing with roads having names such as Avro and Bristol being laid down to commemorate the aircraft types flown during the war just ended.

Early in 1933 Southend Corporation bought the aerodrome for a flying ground but prior to it opening, a site at Holt Farm on the Ashingdon Road to the north of Rochford, was used in the interim. With the aerodrome now firmly established Alan Cobham's National Aviation Day Displays visited, the No. 2 tour coming on 14/15 April and 22 August 1933 with their final visit on 28 August 1934.

On 18 September 1935 the flying ground became a municipal aerodrome, the opening being carried out by Sir Philip Sassoon, the Under Secretary of State for Air, who arrived in his DH85 Leopard Moth as one of the many aircraft to attend that day. Southend Flying Club, Crilly Airways and Southend on Sea Flying Services Ltd were in residence, along with a RAF Volunteer Reserve unit which was based here along with No. 34 E & RFTS until the outbreak of the Second World War when the civil aerodrome closed on 1 September 1939.

Taken over by the RAF it became a satellite of Hornchurch as RAF Rochford in No. 11 Group, Fighter Command but was renamed Southend in October 1940. By March 1943 the war had passed it by and in 1944 it became part of the V1 balloon barrage network. In May 1946 it closed and was handed back to Southend Corporation for civil flying to be resumed. From 1948 it was the main base for Aviation Traders Ltd who, for many years as the resident aircraft company, carried out the conversions and servicing of Handley Page Halifax/Halton aircraft and other types working on the Berlin Airlift.

Cross-channel car and passenger ferry services were operated by Air Charter and Channel Airways using the Bristol Freighter Mk 31, then in 1956 two asphalt runways were laid inside the WW2 concrete perimeter track to replace the grass surface. Further airlines then took advantage of the airport location for both internal and cross-channel services and it became a busy terminal for flights of all types to the Continent and beyond.

In 1957 Aviation Traders (Engineering) Ltd were tasked to design and build for Freddie Laker the 'Accountant', a DC3 replacement which did not progress past the sole prototype, which was followed in 1960 by the ATL 98 'Carvair', a conversion of the Douglas DC4/C54 design. This accommodated the flight crew in a cockpit elevated above a new opening nose door and allowed five cars plus up to 22 passengers to be carried, the 21 aircraft produced between October 1960 and July 1968 being a vast improvement over the long-nosed Mk 32 Freighter in terms of range and carrying capacity. Carvairs operated in the cross-channel car ferry role until 1975 when the trade declined, the carriage of freight then took over both the type and the airport's role, and although private aviation has increased to date the air freight companies still struggle to survive.

Runwell   TQ 746948

Although shown on the list of landing grounds proposed at the end of May 1915 the site was not made ready for operations until August 1917, when it was allocated to No. 61 (HD) Sqn which had formed at Rochford from 'A' Flight of No. 37 (HD) Sqn as part of 50th Wing, South East Area on day-fighter defence duties.

Located three-quarters of a mile due north of Wickford railway station and occupying 32 acres on part of Church End Farm belonging to Thomas Kemble, Lord of the manor at Runwell Hall, the site was fairly level and had open surroundings all round except to the north where it started to rise at its northern end. Sited to the north-east of Swan Lane, where it finished at Wantz Corner, the southern boundary was formed by Church End Lane with the road from Wantz Corner to Brock Hill running northwards past the western edge but separated from the site by a small strip of land. This 400 yard long strip was actually part of two of Kemble's fields known as The Wants and Ox Eyes but, due to a local peculiarity known as the Runwell 'islands' which left odd fingers of land in adjacent parishes, fell into the parish of South Hanningfield and was not taken up as part of the landing ground.

The flying surface, on a clay soil sub-stratum at 36' amsl, had usable landing dimensions of 400 x 500 yards but due to woodland and higher ground at 230' amsl one mile to the north at Brock Hill, Downham it was categorised as a 2nd Class landing ground. Whilst ground signals were displayed on site the facility of a telephone was not provided, instead two or three despatch riders were on hand to take messages to and from the Flight Station at Rochford.

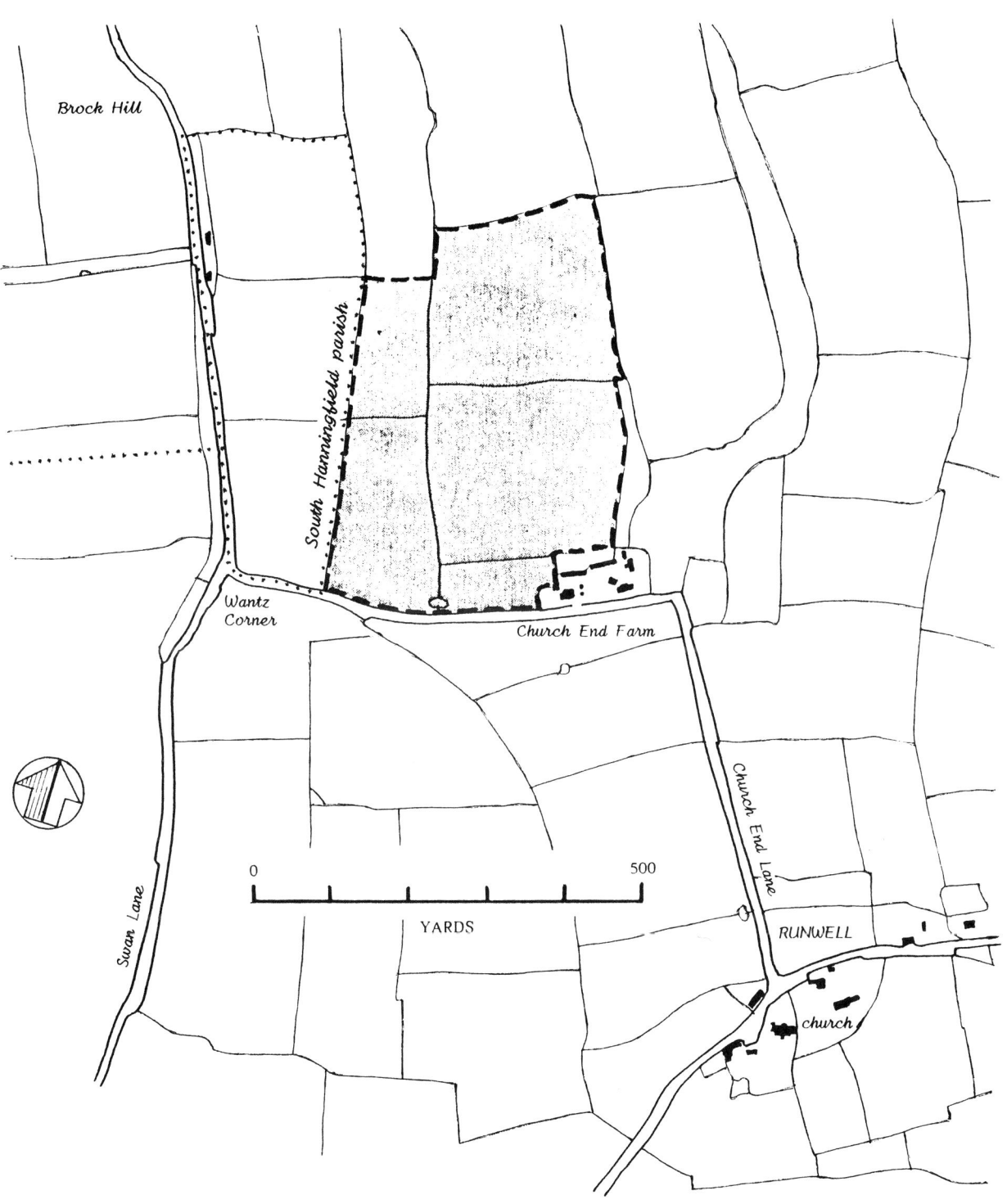

Runwell was unusual in that personnel manning the site had accommodation of a more permanent nature than that normally found at other landing grounds, namely a bungalow situated just off the southern edge of the field in a plot of land belonging to Church End Farm known as Garden Mead. This black-painted timber building survived until the late-1970s when it was demolished upon a change of use for the site. Access to the site was gained from Church End Lane near to the farm buildings.

In October 1917 the landing ground was also allocated to 'A' & 'B' Flights of No. 37 (HD) Sqn at Stow Maries as an emergency night landing ground, but although both Nos. 37 and 61 Sqns were still notionally using it up to October 1918 no record of any emergency landings having taken place there has come to light. The site was kept on the books of the Air Ministry until March 1919, it being finally given up in March 1920 and returned to agriculture.

Aviation returned briefly in 1923 when W.G. Pudney, the remaining partner in the Essex Aviation Company, operated an Avro 504K on pleasure flights from the 'Swan Lane' flying ground as it was known. This enterprise was short-lived, suffering both financially and as a result of one of the ground staff losing an arm whilst prop-swinging.

No use was made of the site subsequently but in the Second World War flying was carried out a half mile to the south-west on the Barn Hall estate near the London - Southend railway line. During the Battle of Britain period ditches and hedges in fields here were grubbed up, and replaced by false hedges, with four single-engined fighters (precise type and unit not known) dispersed under the tree canopy around the edges. Servicemen were on hand to roll up the 'hedges' in daylight hours to allow the aircraft to be flown off then roll them out until they returned, when they were rolled back to give a clear run for landings. With the aircraft safely hidden away at the end of the day they were once more rolled out to give the illusion of farm fields, but since then real hedges have grown back on these fields. It may seem a strange tale but not the first the author has come across, a previous one gave a similar situation at Castle Green school playing fields near Ripple Road in Barking where four Spitfires and two Hurricanes were hidden under false haystacks and flown off daily.

This shot had to be taken from over Brock Hill to the north due to housing south of the site. To the right is Swan Lane running to Wickford town centre whilst on the left Church End Lane leads to Runwell church.

One of many enemy aircraft to fall in the area during the Second World War was a Messerschmitt Bf 110D/O shot down at Swan Lane on 7 September 1940 during a bomber escort to London. Both crew were killed in the crash, which resulted from a joint effort by S/L Douglas Bader and Sub Lt Dickie Cork from 242 Sqn at Coltishall. Cork was one of the 'irregulars' from other flying branches serving with the RAF, as a Royal Navy officer he had been seconded to the service to help make up the critical shortfall in pilot numbers during the Battle of Britain.

The area once occupied by the WW1 landing ground is now owned by the Jessup family and split up for horse grazing, with the boundaries lined by tree belts, whilst Church End Farm itself has been replaced by modern housing.

Shenfield

TQ 603971

This landing ground came about by necessity. It opened in September 1916 to replace Mountnessing, considered unsuitable by reasons of size and terrain, and was on prime dairy land owned by the Langdon family at Palmers Farm some 2½ miles from Brentwood railway station. The area available comprised eight fields making up a total of 60 acres but, as it was split by a stream running part way across the northern portion from the east, the area to the south of 40 acres was deemed usable even though it sloped gradually down to the southern boundary.

When taken over for the duration of hostilities the fields, on a clay sub-base at 240' amsl, had surroundings which were noted as being 'rather wooded' as well as many trees on and around the boundaries themselves which had to be cut down to provide better landing approaches. Facilities in keeping with its purpose of a night landing ground were minimal, with only wet weather shelter in the form of tents for the few personnel on site to man the landing flares and ground signals, and the obligatory windsock.

When the landing ground became operational for No. 39 (HD) Sqn in 49th Wing, South East Area, it had usable dimensions of 500 x 400 yards and was given the classification of a 3rd Class site with the telephone number of Brentwood 143.

No. 39 (HD) Sqn however made no use of the landing ground in an emergency capacity before its flights were concentrated at North Weald Bassett in September 1917 and it was left to No. 44 (HD) Sqn, formed at the Flight Station of Hainault Farm in July 1917 for Home Defence duties, to avail themselves of its facilities. On the night of 25 September 1917, when fourteen out of fifteen Gothas attacked London and twenty Home Defence sorties were flown against them, Captain C.J.Q. Brand safely force-landed his Sopwith Camel at Palmers Farm due to Hainault Farm being fog-bound. Quentin Brand eventually rose to command No. 10 Group of Fighter Command during the Battle of Britain in 1940.

In February 1919 the RAF gave up the use of the landing ground and it returned not to dairy but arable farming, and in this use it has continued ever since.

During the Second World War the whole of Thoby Wood, one mile to the north-east, was removed as part of the preparatory works involved in building a bomber airfield. The new station, which would have been called RAF Ingatestone, was to have been used by the U.S. Eighth Air Force and had land allocated for it on 10 August 1942. This was confirmed the following month but, after acquisition notices had been served and work duly started in the Thoby Priory area, construction was postponed indefinitely on 16 December 1942 due to the need to complete other airfields already in progress where works at these locations had slowed due to bad weather that autumn. In January 1943 a letter to John R. Cotton, of Swallows Cross Farm to the north, from the Essex War Agricultural Executive Committee advised that the Air Ministry had decided not to proceed with the use of part of his land at that time. Whilst he was assured that farming plans could go ahead he was reminded that the Air Ministry might review the proposal at some later date – luckily they did not, but many farmers received similar worrying correspondence during this period.

Whilst no use was made of the landing ground at Palmers Farm for flying purposes in the Second World War it was 'bracketed' by two German V2 rockets during the early part of 1945. Launched by the Army the official British designation was the A4 although the name 'Big Ben' was used for Civil Defence purposes. Big Ben 429 landed just outside the western site boundary on 21 January and 780 in a field to the south on 16 February.

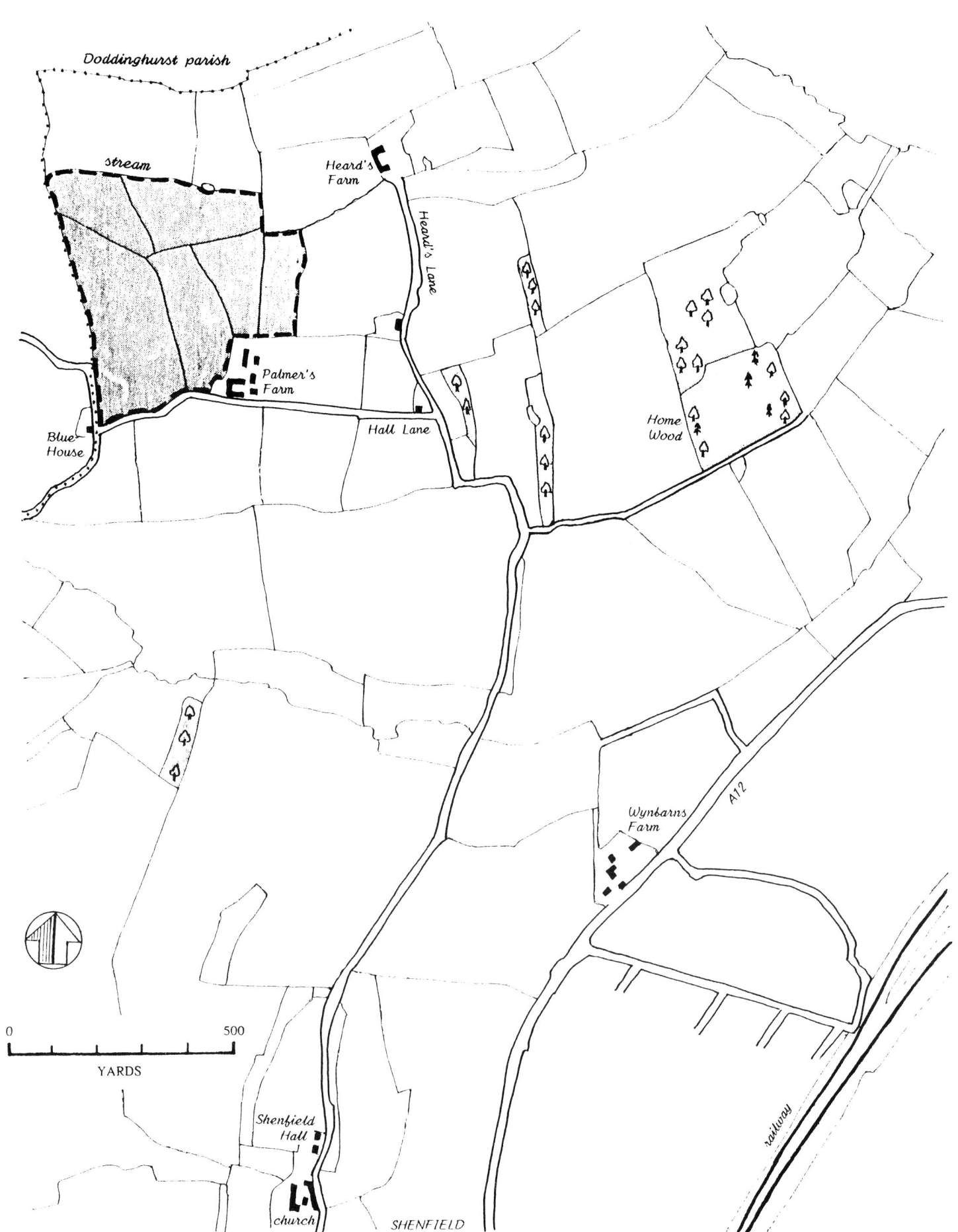

Doddinghurst parish

stream

Heard's Farm

Heard's Lane

Palmer's Farm

Hall Lane

Blue House

Home Wood

0   500

YARDS

Wynbarns Farm

A12

railway

Shenfield Hall

church   SHENFIELD

64

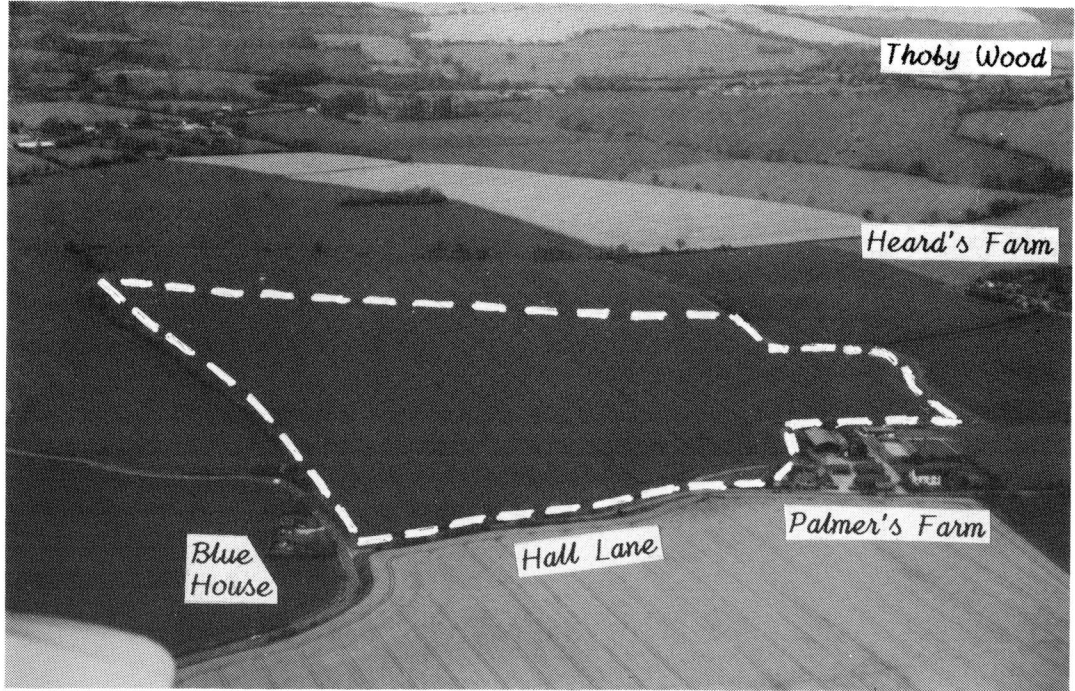

With Palmers Farm at bottom right of the landing ground, and Doddinghurst Road winding northwards from Blue House on the west side, the site looks just as it was 80 years ago.

It has been said that a large pit once existed on the north edge of the old landing ground and contained remnants of landing flare holders dumped there after the First World War, but as this has been slowly filled in with farm soil and other refuse over many years now the chances of unearthing any 'treasures' are remote. The land is currently owned and farmed by the McCheyne family, who also have interests in land at Noke Farm, Bulphan, adjacent to the WW2 decoy site for RAF Hornchurch.

Sible Hedingham   TL 763316

Another of the sites 'borrowed' for the RFC, the 38 acres of farmland on heavy clay soil 2½ miles from Sible Hedingham railway station and farmed by George Lewis on the Liston Hall Farm estate became a night landing ground in April 1916 with the telephone number of Sible Hedingham 8. The most southerly two acres of the landing ground and Liston Hall Farm itself were in the parish of Gosfield, due to the parish boundary running across the southern edge of the site.

At an altitude of 280' amsl the usable landing area of 600 x 400 yds was edged on the south by a public road with steeply-sloping meadows on the other side, which made forced landings dangerous, and to the north-west by trees which were duly felled to create better approaches from that direction. After the necessary tree removal, when it was noted as having 'fairly open' surroundings, the landing ground only managed to achieve a 2nd Class rating in May when it was allocated to the 47th Wing, South Midland Area for use by 'A' Flight of No. 51 (HD) Sqn based at their Flight Station of Harling Road in Norfolk.

Tenancy of the site by 51 (HD) Sqn lasted until 29 December when it was taken over by the 50th Wing, South East Area and the NLG redesignated a 3rd Class site for 'B' Flight of No. 37 (HD) Sqn at Stow Maries as an alternative to Easthorpe. On 31 March 1917 it was once more raised to the category of a 2nd Class NLG and allocated also to 'C' Flight of No. 75 (HD) Sqn at Therfield, Hertfordshire. By October 1918 both squadrons were still notionally allocated to the site and it remained a designated landing ground for them and others until June 1919 when it was returned to agriculture.

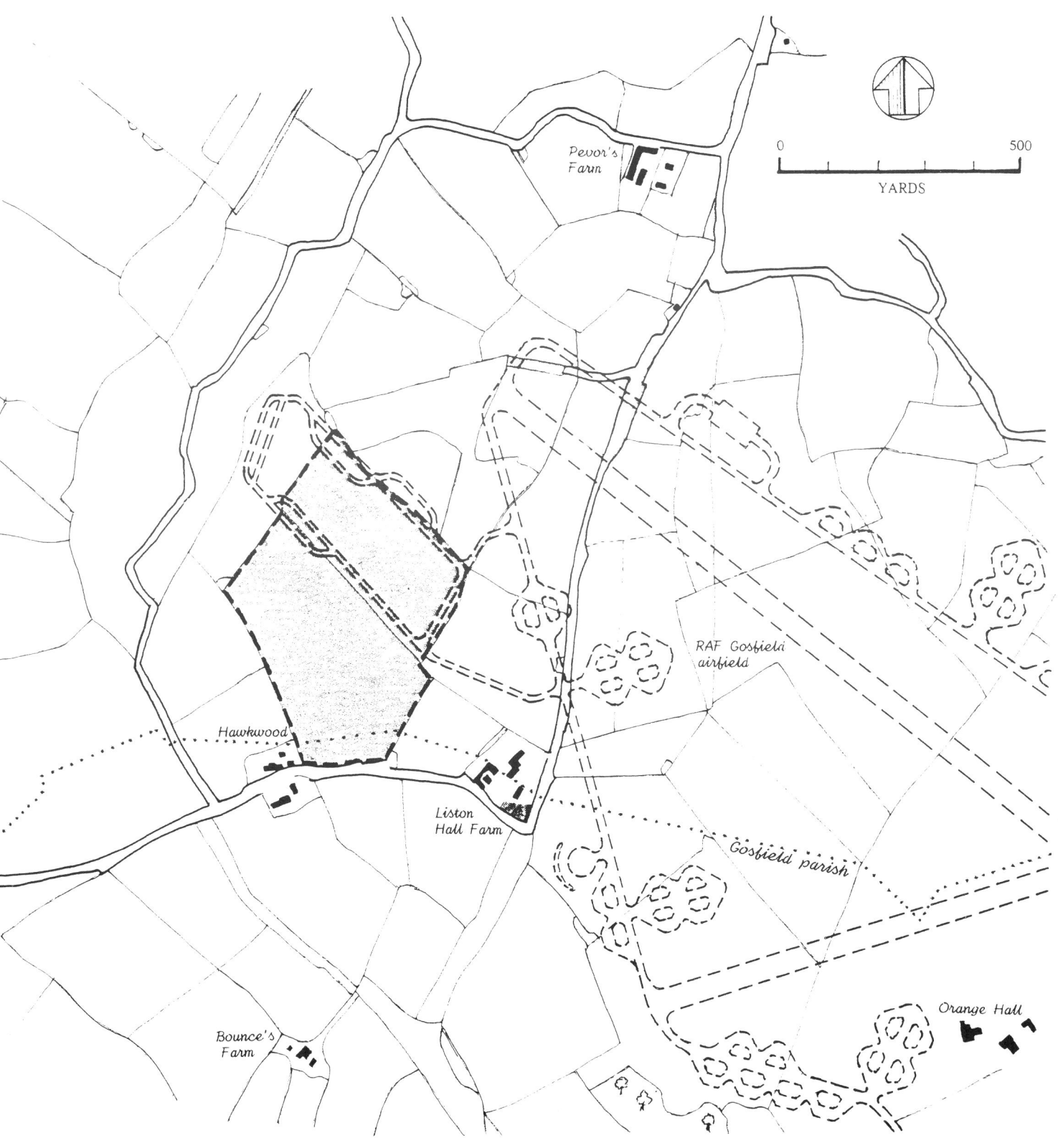

From 1943 during the Second World War, the bomb storage area laid down to serve RAF Gosfield
was sited between Pevors and Liston Hall Farms and ran across the top edge of the landing ground
from its northern extremity to the eastern corner. USAAF Station 154, as Gosfield was known, was
built just to the east adjacent to the A131 as one of the many airfields for the United States 8th Air
Force in Essex. Although the WW2 flying field did not include the WW1 site it is noted that the
runways laid down in 1943 followed the same general landing directions as used on the WW1
landing ground.

RAF Gosfield ceased operations with the Rhine crossing in March 1945, thereafter it was used as a collecting point for recovered Horsa gliders. These were repaired under an Air Ministry contract on one part of the airfield before being towed in a finished condition to another and handed over to a contractor who scrapped them under a different contract, but even now the odd Horsa parts such as wheels still turn up to be used by the farmers on farm implements. Safeguarding of the site by the RAF was finally relinquished in May 1956, when most of the hutted sites and concrete roadways started to be cleared and the fields returned to agriculture again in the hands of the Lewis family, but even in recent correspondence between both the farmers and the Ministry of Agriculture the area of the WW1 landing ground is still referred to as 'the flying field'.

Taken from the south-east, this shot shows the close proximity of the Second World War RAF Gosfield and particularly its bomb dump which occupied the north-eastern half of the landing ground.

The area of the landing ground crossed by the Second World War bomb storage area had mole-drains installed in 1962 due to it being very wet in the winter months, whilst the oak trees felled in WW1 to permit landing approaches from the north-west still lay in the field ditches until 1988 when they were finally cleared in order to open up the old (pre-1916) watercourses. Of the many Nissen huts used during WW2 as bomb fusing points only two now remain and have been reclad, these remain on a portion of the bomb storage area road system that follows the line of a footpath which once lay next to a field boundary running across the centre of the landing ground from north-west to south-east. It would be nice to imagine that the old gateway on the southern edge was the access to the First World War landing ground but this cannot be confirmed.

Stow Maries   TL 822002

Situated in farmland on a plateau at 174' amsl and first surveyed in August 1916 the site took in a total of twelve fields belonging to Edwins Hall and Old Whitmans farms, three-quarters of a mile to the north-west of the village that was itself located two miles north of the River Crouch. The locals knew it as Stow St Mary, after the parish church of St Mary & St Margaret, although the name 'Maries' came from a marshy area of the parish by the river. Occupying some 118 acres of land in the hands of Frederick Todd, farm bailiff to Strutt & Parker, it gave a useful landing area of 850 x 650 yards with open surroundings but for a few small woods.

No activity occurred until 15 September 1916 when 'B' Flight of No. 37 (HD) Sqn moved in from Orfordness, Suffolk. The unit had been based there whilst on attachment to the experimental establishment but now as a squadron in 50th Wing, South East Area it was dispersed, 'A' and 'C' Flights being sent to Rochford and Goldhanger respectively, and the squadron HQ established at The Grange, Woodham Mortimer, a large house at that time owned by Charles Bentall.

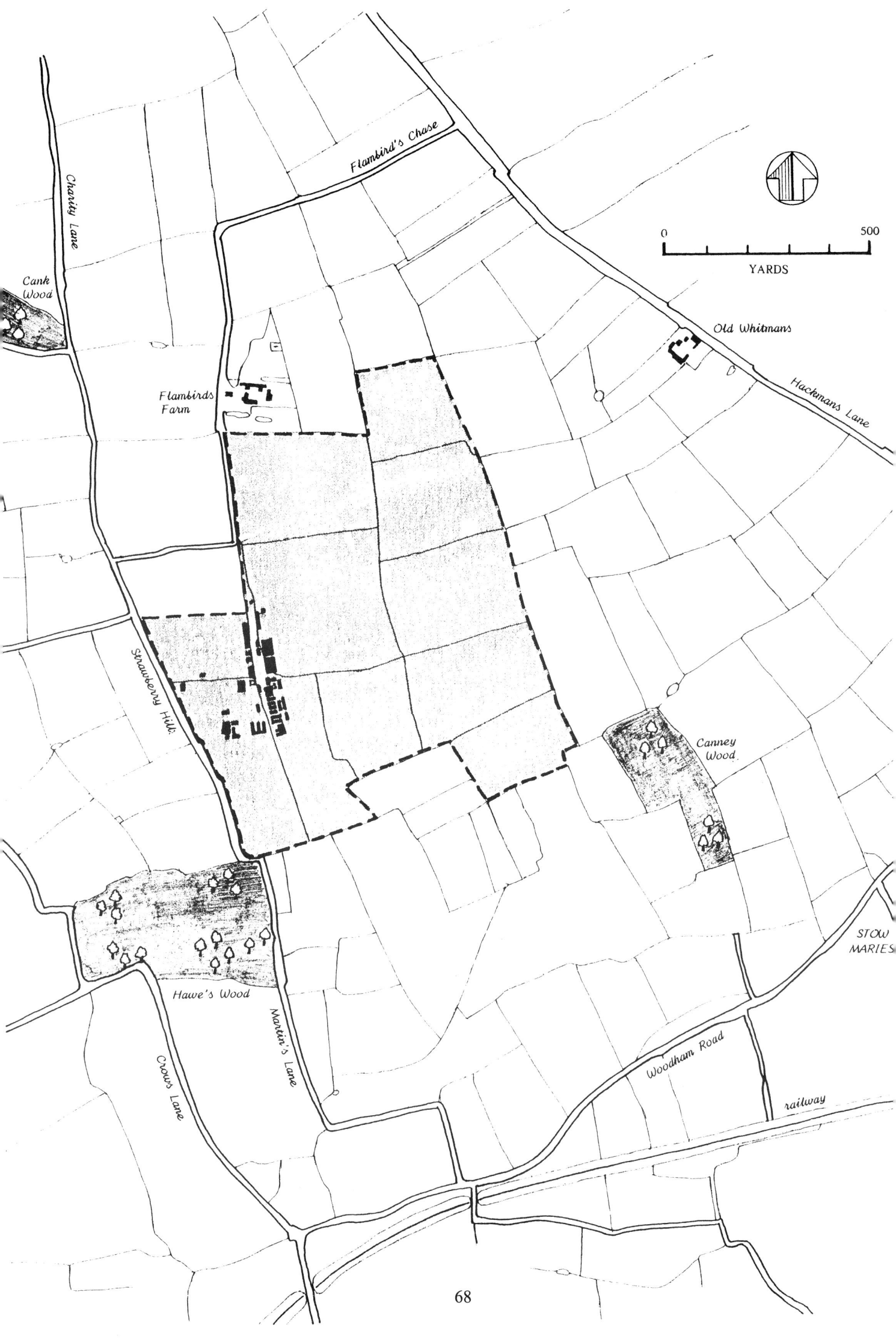

Charity Lane

Flambird's Chase

Cank Wood

Old Whitmans

Hackmans Lane

Flambirds Farm

Strawberry Hill

Canney Wood

Hawe's Wood

Martin's Lane

STOW MARIES

Crows Lane

Woodham Road

railway

0   500
YARDS

68

Building works started but the landing surface, although moderate, had to be improved in order to achieve 1st Class Flight Station status. Indeed such was the rate of deterioration of the surface due mainly to weathering that remedial works by the 'works and bricks' section using the station steamroller were carried on throughout the operational life of this flight station.

Ostensibly to be used as a base for HD aircraft operating at night no facilities for night flying were initially provided, the first official sorties of this type carried out on 23 May 1917 by two B.E.12a aircraft being uneventful although later operations fared better.

On 4 July 1917 Lt J.W. Potts in Spad A8804 of No. 56 (Training) Sqn from London Colney in Hertfordshire landed low on fuel after a long defensive sortie against 18 Gothas raiding Harwich and Felixstowe. That same month 'A' Flight of No. 37 (HD) Sqn moved in from Rochford but the presence of two flights, with a greater utilisation of aircraft of varying types, soon caused the landing ground to be put out of use for periods of repair due to the heavy clay soil becoming extremely rutted.

In 1918 re-equipment with Sopwith Pups and 1½-Strutters preceded Camels as the more advanced types appeared, and in June the squadron HQ moved onto the site in anticipation of all the flights operating from there. By December of 1918 a batch of Sopwith Snipes had arrived, which also coincided with the end of the programmed building phase for the station. All the completed buildings were retained for use whilst the other unfinished structures making up a total of 44 on the 15-acre technical site area were demolished down to foundation level and building works then ceased.

In February 1919 'C' Flight arrived from Goldhanger, this then being the only instance in the squadron's WW1 history when its three flights operated from one site, but a move for the unit to Biggin Hill the next month brought about its disbandment by renumbering as No. 39 Sqn.

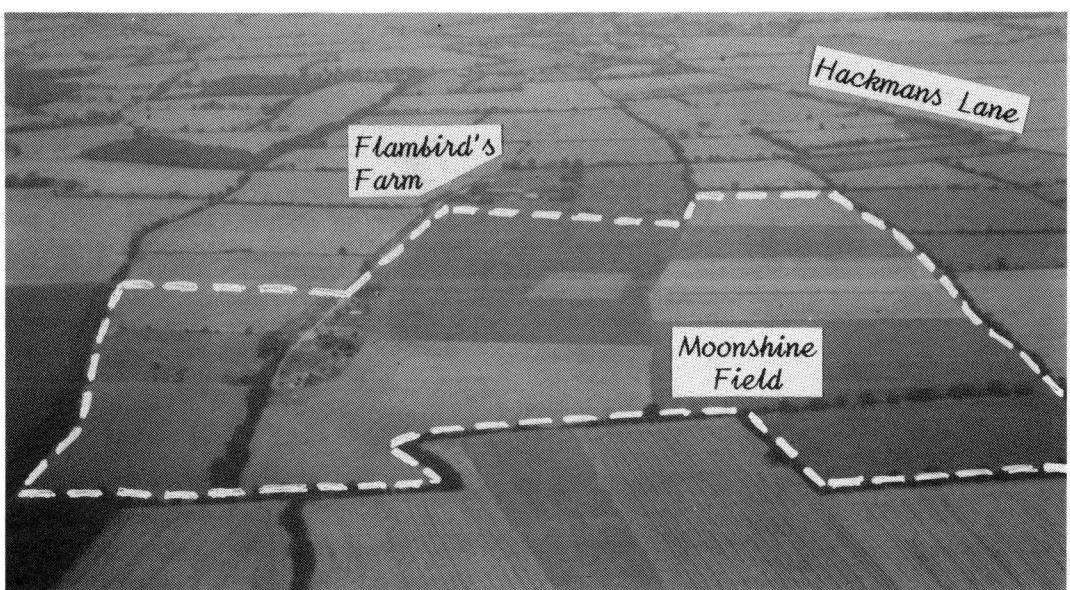

Restored to the original field lines the site is still unchanged, even to the extent of the 24 buildings on the west side. From the air it is still just possible to see traces of the cinder tracks which led onto the flying area from the aeroplane shed locations whilst one noticeable addition is the Anglia Model Flying Club 'square' in the very centre of the old flying area.

Stow Maries closed down on 17th March 1919 and the site reverted back to its original owners and, with Harry Turner at Edwins Hall making no attempt to remove any of the completed buildings, agriculture and grazing took over the flying field. All the draining was left in situ and remains to this day but, whilst traces of the cinder tracks leading away from the aeroplane sheds can be seen from the air, one thing noticeably absent from the southern part of the site is the silhouette of a Gotha cut out of the turf and filled with whitened stones for use in firing practices.

In the 1930s point-to-point steeplechases were held on the site, frequently by the Essex Farmers Hunt Club, with the venue reported in the press as 'Stow St Mary Aerodrome'.

Prior to the Second World War surveyors from the Air Ministry inspected the site to see if it could be re-opened but it was decided instead to upgrade Rochford, some 8 miles to the south-east. No attempt was made to demolish the aeroplane sheds or other buildings, or to obstruct and camouflage the landing ground, as a result of which it still resembled an operational station and attracted a number of Luftwaffe bombs as well as Hurricane P3715, LE-D of 242 Sqn, which force-landed there with radiator damage as a result of combat on 7 September 1940. A pair of parachute mines dropped near to Flambirds Farm on 20 April 1941 partially demolished the northern aircraft shed but they were not all taken down, as the only post-WW1 removals, until 1946.

After seeing no more action the site was again surveyed in 1942, this time as the proposed location for a bomber station to serve the expanding American Eighth Air Force in East Anglia. Allocated the USAF Station number 163 it would have had the name of RAF Cold Norton, this being a reversion to 1843 when the airfield site had been completely in that parish. The new airfield would have taken in most of the WW1 flight station, but due to the need to finish other airfields already in progress the land requisitioned and surveyed in September was given up in December when the project was shelved. The site remained as agricultural and grazing land, and 26 WW1 Flight Station buildings were left in place, some being used post-war to house Italian farm workers.

In the mid-60s a nearby resident, Katherine Peyton, had the idea of writing a novel based on the exploits of the RFC in the First World War, taking as the title 'Flambards', a slight variation on the name of 'Flambirds', a farm to the north seen when buying horse fodder there. After the book was finished she made another visit to the farm by a different route and saw the decaying aerodrome buildings that remained. On being told what they had been she was amazed that her book had been written without any knowledge of this historic site only two miles from her home.

To finally dispel any myths, the books were not based on the activities of No. 37 (HD) Sqn based here, nor was the Yorkshire TV series 'Flambards' filmed in the locality, any such references have grown up with the locals. The radio-controlled aircraft models, used during location filming at Finningley, now reside at the Muckleburgh Collection in Norfolk.

In 1966 flying returned to the site in the form of the Anglia Model Flying Club, who were ousted from their Great Baddow flying ground by housing development and continue the aviation link

At peace. Thoroughbreds graze beneath the illuminated cross atop the spire of St Mary and St Margaret, Stow Maries. *(Photo courtesy Mike Marsh)*

started on the site 50 years before they moved in. A threat to their existence came about in 1992 when an application was made to the Civil Aviation Authority for fields on the adjoining Old Whitmans Farm to be used as a strip for glider operations. The site was promptly included on the 1995 air charts **before** the application was over-ruled, but as no flying takes place there the model flyers are safe to carry on.

Of all the sites in the county Stow Maries is the most completely preserved example of a WW1 Flight Station, let alone landing ground, due mainly to the inaccessibility of the site. Short of a change of use for the land it looks set to last another 50 years.

Suttons Farm   TQ 533847

The name means 'South town', originally it was a tenement of the Royal Manor of Havering until Henry II granted land worth £25 a year to the Canons of St Nicholas and St Bernard at Montjoux, Savoy, and this grant became known as Suttons Manor.

In 1915 90 acres of farmland having root crops on it was acquired from Tom Crawford at Suttons Farm, Rainham, two miles east of Dagenham, and use of the site for flying agreed. A further 15 acres were added to accommodate the majority of the station buildings which were positioned south of the farm. The first structures built were two canvas RE5 hangars, eventually rising to four, and with two pairs of aeroplane sheds next to them the rest of the buildings filled the north-eastern corner of the site. Two locations outside the flying ground were a women's hostel, built to the north of the farm, and some gravel pits to the south-east which were used for live firing practices.

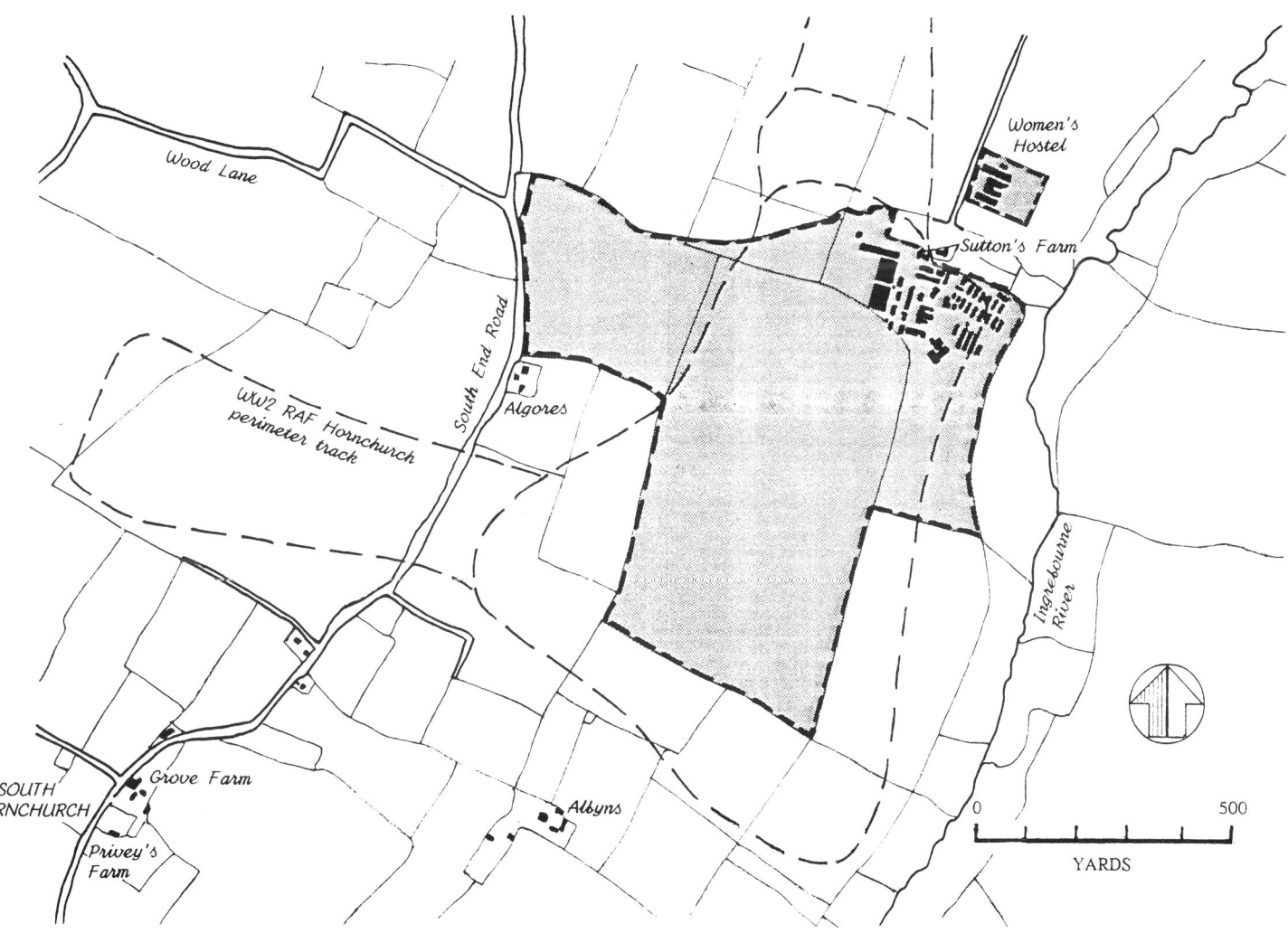

The T-shaped flying field as laid out to the south of the station buildings was, at 30' amsl, good and level with a loam surface showing traces of clay (although at this time nobody knew that the underlying ground was rich in gravel deposits) and the surroundings were quite open. The agricultural land nearby was noted to have rather small fields, which made forced-landings interesting, but when Captain Arthur T. Harris (later to become Commander-in-Chief of Bomber Command in the Second World War) was posted there with 'B' Flight of No. 39 (HD) Sqn he commented that the site itself was 'one large field full of sheep'.

In October 1915 the site lost its designation of Landing Ground no 2. when it was classified a Flight Station (Night) and used by detachments from Gosport, Beddington (Croydon) and Hounslow until April 1916. It then achieved the status of a 1st Class Home Defence Flight Station (Night) and 'B' Flight of No. 39 (HD) Sqn moved in, staying until September 1917.

No. 39 Sqn became known as a crack unit after squadron members brought down four airships in the space of one month. The first to strike was Lt W. Leefe Robinson, airborne from Suttons in a B.E.2c, who shot down the wooden-hulled Army SL11 on Castle Farm, Cuffley in the early hours of 3 September 1916. The crew of 16 died when the airship came down behind the Plough Inn in a hilltop beet field next to the old tin church of St Andrew at 0220 hrs. For this action Robinson was awarded the Victoria Cross, and later a memorial to his bravery was erected nearby on the Ridgeway, but he died two years after this action as a result of influenza contracted whilst in captivity after being shot down in April 1918.

Exactly three weeks later 2nd Lt F. Sowrey, again in a B.E.2c from Suttons, brought the Navy Zeppelin L32 down at Snails Hall Farm, Billericay on the morning of the 24th. Whilst the crash was next to Jacksons Lane (now renamed Greens Farm Lane) the elevators and rudder were found in woodland a quarter of a mile away with a propellor hub and gearbox some three miles distant. The 22 dead crewmen were first put into a barn on the crash field then buried in the graveyard at St Mary Magdalene church, Great Burstead, until 1962 when they were re-interred at the Soldatenfriedhof in Cannock Chase, Staffordshire. Sowrey is today Air Marshal Sir Frederick Sowrey, KCB, CBE, AFC and currently president of the Cross and Cockade Society International (UK), the First World War historians. The other successful squadron 'Zeppelin-killers' that month operated out of Hainault Farm and North Weald Bassett.

In July 1917 No. 46 Sqn returned from France for a month with its Sopwith Pups to counter the menace of the Gotha GII bomber, and 'B' Flight of No. 78 (HD) Sqn moved in for the same purpose equipped with Sopwith Camels. When No. 39 Sqn moved away in September the aerodrome became a Home Defence Squadron Station for No. 78 Sqn who were to stay until December 1919 as the last flying unit. A night training unit, No. 189 Sqn equipped with Avros and Camels, then arrived in April 1918 and continued in this role on site until March 1919, by which time the site was now classified as a Squadron Station in the Night Training role.

By November 1918 all the buildings were complete, ahead of the estimated completion date of 31 December, but at the Armistice it was decided that these and their drainage were to be demolished and the grass areas reinstated within one year. However strange this may seem the RAF were still intent on staying, for in May 1919 No. 51 Sqn arrived for a one-month detachment.

On 24 November 1922 however, just as the last vestiges of WW1 roadways were being removed, the site was reinspected for re-use as a permanent airfield. In May 1924, only after it was stated that no aircraft would operate any closer to his farmhouse than 300 yards, Tom Crawford once again gave up his land, this time to a compulsory purchase.

With the flying field now positioned well to the south the aerodrome reopened in April 1928 and was subsequently developed up to 1929 when it was renamed RAF Hornchurch and once again provided defence for London in the Second World War. Transferred to Training Command in 1945 the station became an Aircrew Selection Centre in 1952 before finally closing in June 1962. Auctioned off on 27 February 1963 a buyer's Cessna 310 landed for the sale, the very last aircraft movement.

The WW2 technical site on the western side of the airfield was subsequently demolished to be replaced by housing whilst the airfield itself became a quarry for gravels extraction. By 1980 the quarry had become exhausted and as the infilled area could not be developed for housing it was turned over to leisure and renamed Hornchurch Country Park.

Both Suttons Farm and the later RAF Hornchurch have now disappeared completely due to housing development but the connection with aviation is remembered by pilots' names given to estate roads situated on what was the western end of the WW2 E-W runway. The Officers' Mess from WW2 remains on the western side of South End Road (its name in 1918), with a memorial to the site erected inside the grounds of the local school opposite having been unveiled by Air Chief Marshal Sir Harry Broadhurst (a former WW2 Station Commander) in July 1983. The nearby Good Intent public house also has an aeronautical inn sign in the form of a Spitfire, plus an unexploded bomb as a memento in its foyer, and Hornchurch Public Library has the station badge featured in a permanent display, so the aerodrome is very well remembered in the locality.

With housing having taken over the west and north edges the only good reference point, apart from South End Road to the west, is Albyns Farm lying off the southern boundary.

Thaxted   TL 628320

Located 1½ miles north-east of Thaxted station at the end of the Elsenham-Thaxted branch of the Great Eastern railway the site occupied 47 acres of arable land then owned by the Franklin family at Terriers Farm in Boyton End to the north-west. The landing ground itself was at the end of Copthall Lane near to Bluebarn Cottage, with the parish boundary to Little Sampford running along its north-eastern edge. At 360' amsl it was the highest point in the area and although bounded on its eastern edges by two woods, Blunts and Highgates, usable landing dimensions of 450 x 400 yards were available.

The clay soil surface overlaying gravels sloped noticeably down to the south and the surroundings were otherwise open with nearby fields fairly small, but it was classified as a 2nd Class night landing ground when opened in January 1917. Subsequent alterations to the site involved the removal of Blunts Wood, as well as existing hedge and ditch lines, but this did not improve the status of the landing ground which remained in the 2nd Class category.

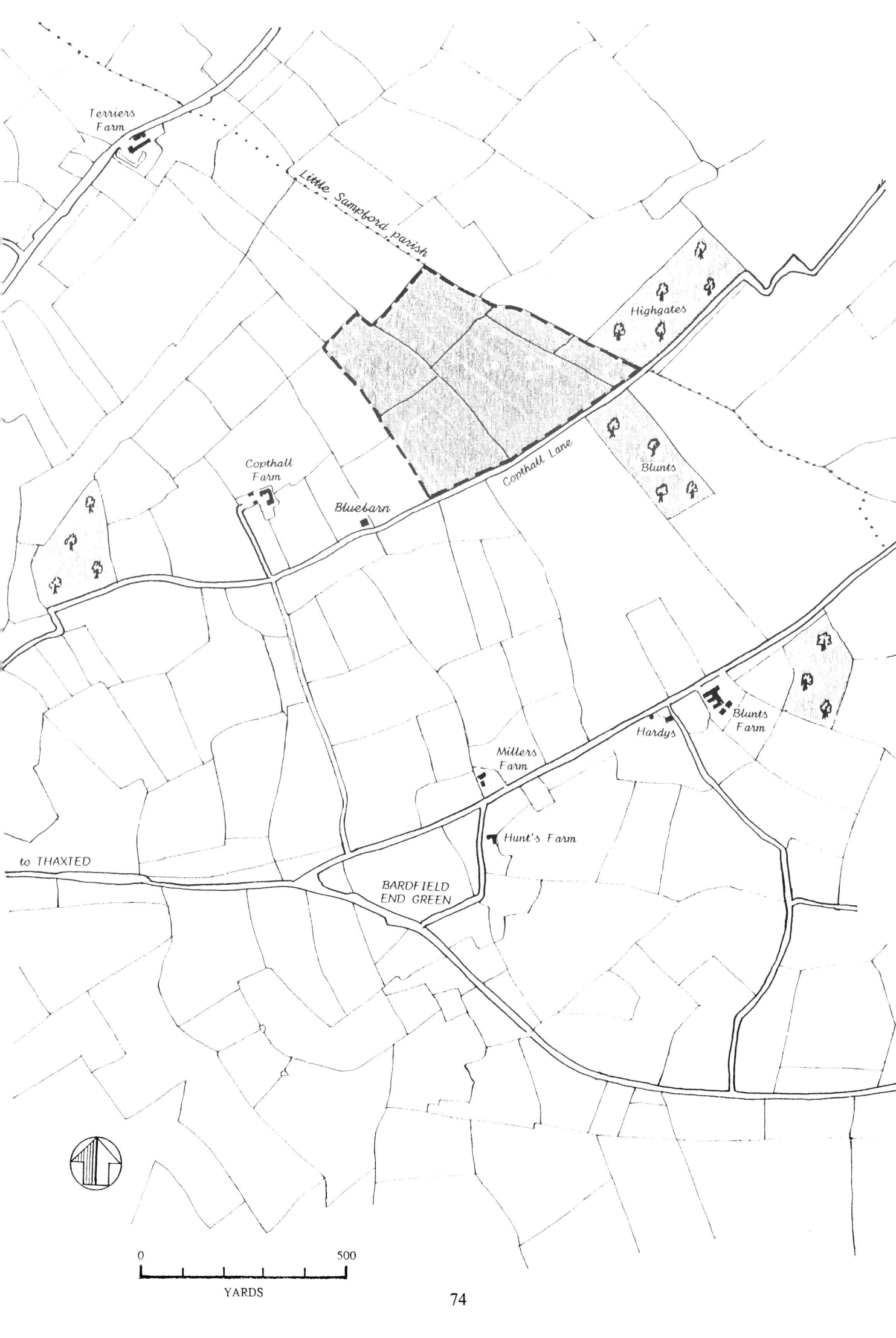

Terriers
Farm

Little Sampford parish

Highgates

Copthall Farm

Bluebarn

Copthall Lane

Blunts

Blunts
Farm

Hardys

Millers
Farm

Hunt's Farm

to THAXTED

BARDFIELD
END GREEN

0   500

YARDS

74

The only unit allocated to the site was 'A' Flight of No. 75 (HD) Sqn based at Yelling near St Neots, the squadron having formed the previous October at Therfield near Baldock in Hertfordshire with Avro 504 NF (night fighter) and B.E.2c aircraft. The squadron later received the B.E.12 but no use of the site has been recorded by aircraft from this or any other unit.

The landing ground remained open until the summer of 1918 when it was returned to its owners, and with No. 75 Sqn moving to North Weald Bassett for disbanding in June 1919 no further use was made of the site. The nearest that aviation next came to the area was when RAF Great Sampford opened in 1942 two miles to the north as a satellite to the fighter station at Debden.

Both Copthall Farm and Bluebarn have gone now, whilst Blunts Wood has grown back and is known by locals as Dewberry Field where pheasant shooting can be had in season.

Of all the sites in the county Thaxted was the only one where an oblique photograph was not possible, this being due to the photo ship having been built so many years before the introduction of the transponder equipment required for entry into the controlled airspace around Stansted airport. This Special Rules Zone extends north just far enough to overlap the Little Sampford boundary by three-quarters of a mile(!).

Widford   TL 691057

When the German air offensive against England opened early in 1915 it was not with mass formations of airships but individual sorties by small floatplanes. In anticipation Widford was chosen on 27 December 1914 to operate landplanes as one of five 'branch stations' of the RNAS, the others being Burnham-on-Crouch and Chingford, as well as Maidstone and Ramsgate in Kent. The Admiralty, being responsible for defence of London, decided that advanced bases from which to despatch aircraft to form a screen against airships from Northern Germany and bombers from Belgian bases were needed and, except at Chingford which had four, these branch stations were allocated two aircraft each from either Hendon or Eastchurch. The strange thing about Widford however, is that the few records available relating to operations carried out from here by the RNAS show they only ever referred to it as 'Chelmsford'.

Situated 1¼ miles south-west of Chelmsford railway station and a quarter of a mile north of Widford Hall the site occupied 23 acres of arable land worked by the Hammond family. At 110' amsl the two fields taken over by the RNAS sloped slightly down to the River Wid, which formed the western boundary, and the surroundings were open with large fields nearby. With an alluvium subsoil useful landing dimensions of 425 x 300 yards were available but no permanent buildings of any kind were erected on the site during its period of use.

The only obstructions to flying would possibly have been farm traffic using Widford Hall Lane on the eastern boundary but an elderly resident of Widford, George Bewers, recalls that as a seven year-old in 1914 he and his friends used to sit in the hedges on the eastern edge of the field next to the Lane and watch the aeroplanes fly over and alight without problems on the landing ground.

Whilst no defensive patrols were carried out immediately after being established the landing ground received its first straggler on 6 January 1915 when a Vickers Gunbus F.B.4, of 'C' Flight, No. 7 Sqn RFC made a forced landing due to encountering very strong head winds whilst flying from the RNAS station at Great Yarmouth to Joyce Green in Kent. Although it was misty and had taken 2 hrs 20 mins to travel from Yarmouth the two-man crew landed safely and when conditions improved two days later left to continue to Joyce Green.

Then, seemingly at variance with the defence plans previously implemented, the Admiralty changed tactics and decided to provide purely night emergency landing grounds around London for use by those patrolling fighters. These plans changed almost overnight such that the idea of basing aircraft at the site was re-introduced, the arrangements coming into effect in March 1915 included the sites previously selected at Chingford, Maidstone and Widford which were duly improved by the provision of basic flarepath lighting for aircraft based there or landing after a patrol.

Sorties were flown by the detached aircraft on various occasions but no successes were recorded. On 3 July 1915, whilst flying one of the three Widford-based Caudron G.3s on a defence sortie, Flt Sub-Lieut E.V. Reid meandered around for 45 minutes and included landings at St Osyth and on the golf course at Felixstowe, as well as flying out to sea before returning to Widford having seen nothing.

The night of 17/18 August also brought no successes but saw some drama. Two Caudrons which received the order to take off after the German Navy Zeppelin L10 had passed both crashed on landing after this uneventful sortie, one being blown up by its load of Hale bombs and both pilots seriously injured.

On 11 September 1915 flights that night by the two replacement Caudrons against the Army Zeppelin LZ77 were uneventful, as were similar excursions by the RFC from nearby Writtle.

One important point to be noted was that by the end of September 1915 very few RNAS pilots were night-trained, Widford having only one so rated out of a total of just sixteen distributed around the eight RNAS stations concerned with the defence of London. There was therefore little chance of a pilot effecting a successful interception when he was more concerned with being able to control his machine in unfamiliar conditions.

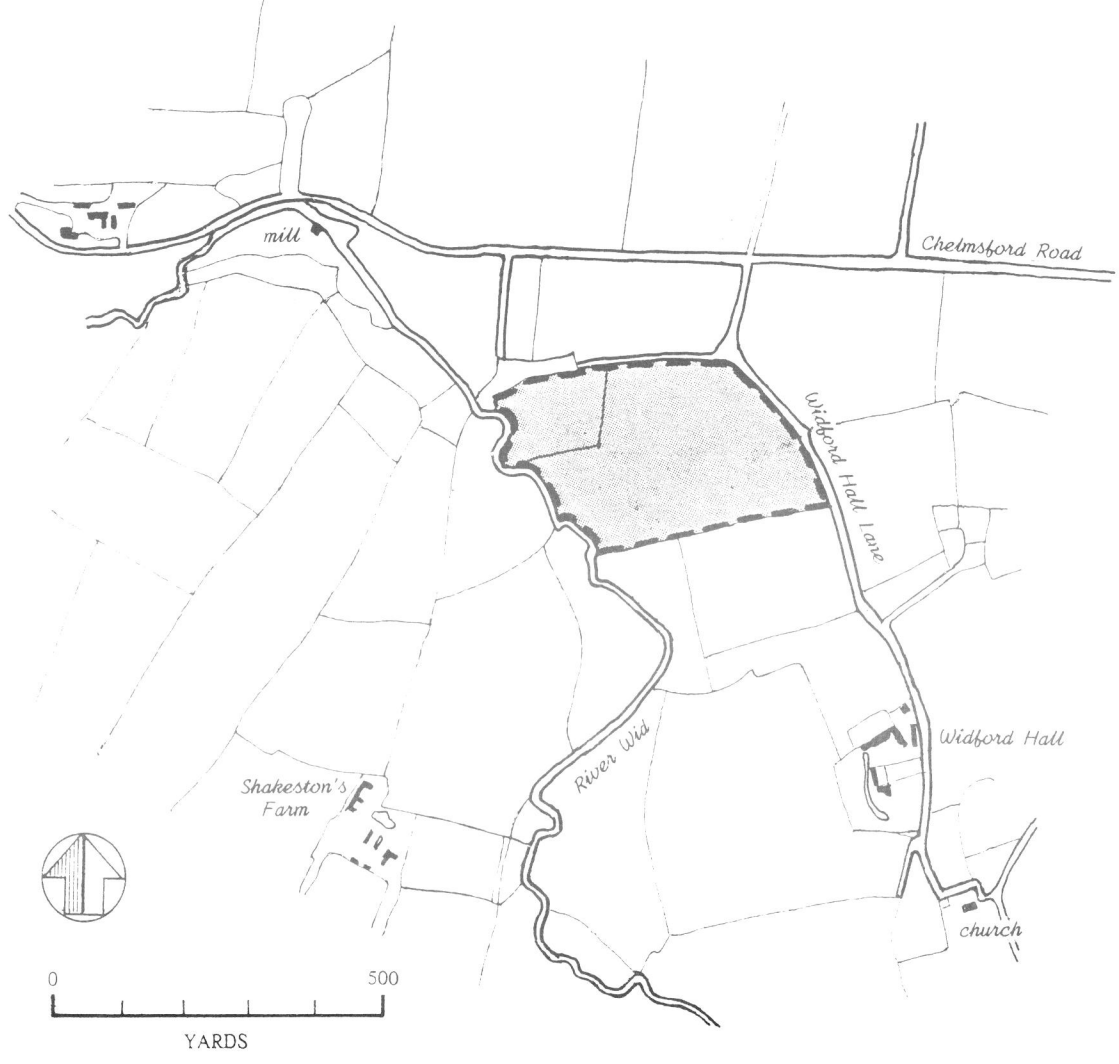

The RNAS moved out of Widford at the end of September 1915, whilst the RFC remained at nearby Writtle for another year. After the RNAS left no more flying took place on the site until, yes you've guessed it, a visit from an air pageant. When the calendar of daily displays for the British Empire Air Display brought it to Chelmsford on 1 July 1936 the Widford site was used as the venue. A total of 38 joy-rides were had that day at a cost of 5/- (25p) when the team of visiting pilots included many from the British Hospitals Air Pageant organisation of 1933. The air pageant left the following day for its next display at Barton near Cambridge.

The site returned to arable land and, although the buildings at Shakestons Farm and part of the landing ground remains, the premises of Messrs Cundalls built in the mid-1960s on the Widford Industrial Estate encroach on the eastern half. Widford Hall is now inside the trading estate and next to a modern bowling alley.

Now mostly taken over by the Widford Industrial Estate only a small portion remains next to the River Wid. Note the close proximity of RFC Writtle.

Wormingford   TL 930302

Situated only one mile south of the village but three miles from the railway station at Bures it was also known by the latter when it came into use in December 1916. To make matters even more complicated the parish boundary between Wormingford and Fordham ran across the site from east to west. Located on the Robert Everard estate it was slightly lower than its immediate surroundings and both the nearby manor house of Rotchfords and Jenkins Farm. These lay outside the eastern edge of the field on the opposite side of the public road running south to Fordham village upon which the site entrance was situated.

The surface of the landing ground was given as heavy clay with bad ridge and furrow when the land was taken over, but at 200' amsl with a total size of 78 acres and usable landing runs of 750 x 450 yards it was categorised as a 1st Class site (the third pure night landing ground to achieve this status in the county – the others being Burnham-on-Crouch, Orsett and Blackheath). With the telephone number of Colchester 222 it opened as a night landing ground for 'C' Flight of No. 37 (HD) Sqn at Goldhanger as part of 50th Wing, South Eastern Area.

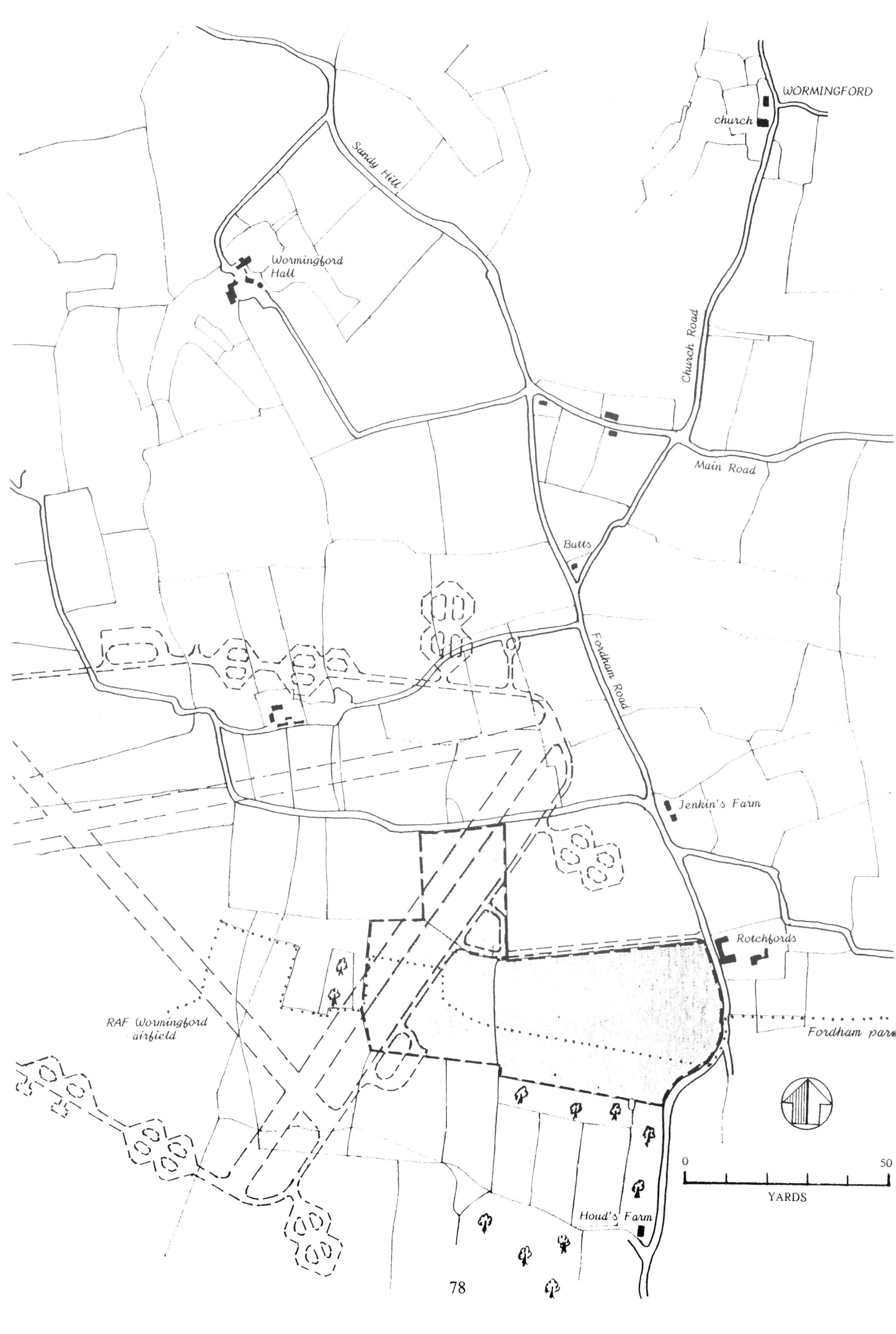

WORMINGFORD

church

Sandy Hill

Wormingford
Hall

Church Road

Main Road

Butts

Fordham Road

Jenkin's Farm

Rotchfords

RAF Wormingford
airfield

Fordham par

Houd's Farm

0   50

YARDS

78

Early in 1918 No. 75 Sqn was allocated to the site and in March No. 37 Sqn ceased to make use of it. By October 1918 it was then available for use by any unit with its prime allocation to No. 75 Sqn continuing but by June 1919, with no record of use by any unit, the land was returned to its owners and farming resumed.

The old landing ground is still three fields, with the western two crossed by remains of the Second World War RAF Wormingford airfield NE–SW runway and perimeter track.

In 1942 the whole site became swallowed up by the construction of RAF Wormingford, or USAF Station 159 as it was known to that Air Force when they moved in. A baseball field and administrative site were laid out on the easternmost portion of the WW1 LG, with the WW2 airfield technical site and its NE-SW runway and parallel perimeter track crossing its western section. Although intended as a bomber base it was, surprisingly in view of the need for this type of airfield, declared surplus to requirements and allocated instead to the 362nd FG of the 9th Air Force in November 1943 then to the 55th FG of the 8th Air Force in April 1944.

The 55th FG left in July 1945 and in October Wormingford was transferred to the RAF but given up in January 1947 for use as a store by H.M. Government. The site was finally disposed of in 1962 and returned to farmland, with most of the runway widths removed by the St Ives Sand and Gravel company for use in building new sections of the A12 trunk road. The perimeter track remains in situ, and crosses the fields once used for the WW1 landing ground. In 1992 a memorial was dedicated to the WW2 occupancy of the airfield by the 362nd FG, situated on the roadside opposite Rotchfords and next to what had been the edge of the WW1 landing ground it is now overflown by gliders from the Essex & Suffolk gliding club which operates from the site.

Writtle   TL 680065

In October 1914 aircraft from No. 1 Reserve Aeroplane Squadron, RFC, at Farnborough were ordered to be sent to a new temporary landing ground here to assist the RNAS in countering the anticipated threat due from Zeppelin incursions over East Anglia. This was to be in addition to their prime function of anti-invasion duties in which they would be operating under the direct control of local army commanders.

The move was not incepted immediately, which was just as well for the intrusions did not start until January 1915 and then only by single raiders, nevertheless the RFC decided to provide cover over the Christmas period and between 19-22 December the first of these aircraft, a B.E.2b and Maurice Farman Longhorn from No. 1 RAS were positioned here.

Situated just north of the village 1½ miles west of Chelmsford railway station the site was to the west of Lower Ford Lane. The land sloped down to the lane and, whilst the site was close to the village with its high church tower, its surroundings to the north and east were fairly open, the fields in this quadrant deemed to be more than suitable for forced landings after take-off if the need arose.

The two fields making up the landing ground, Hop Garden and Loam Pit Fields, were on the site of a Napoleanic camp and gave an area of 22 acres with landing dimensions of 425 x 325 yards. At 100' amsl the arable ground had a head clay stratum and tended to be wet in winter, and as an added bonus a sewage works lay in the adjacent field to the east.

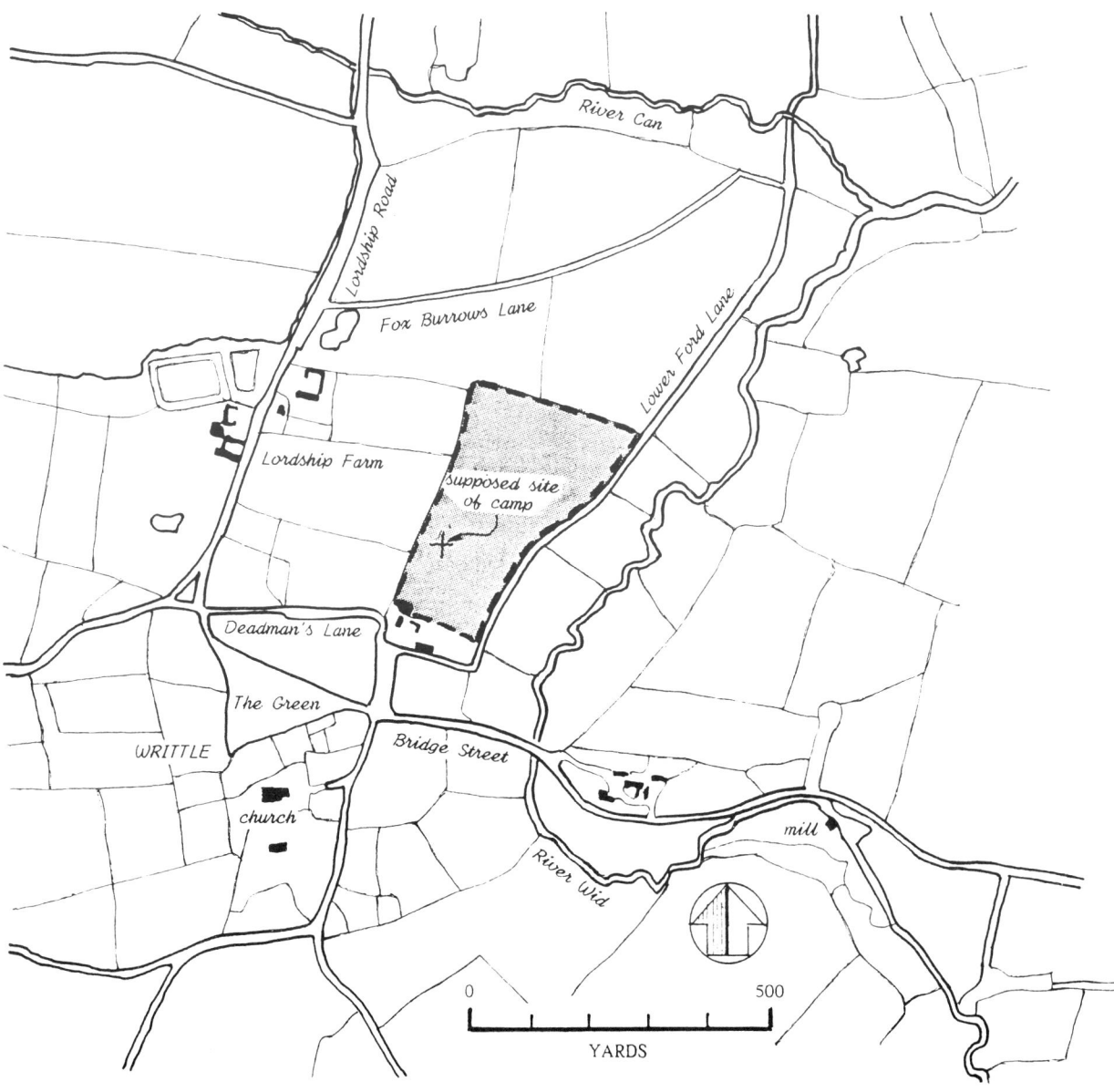

Although ground personnel numbers that December were fairly minimal the aircrews were nevertheless provided with a comprehensive arsenal of weapons for each pair of aircraft to carry during the execution of their tasks, namely – 3 carbines, 50 flaming bullets, 10 HE bombs, 10 petrol bombs and a Fiery Grapnel.

No defensive sorties were flown from the site in the early part of 1915, the aircraft and personnel being duly sent back to Farnborough, but after numerous night airship raids on London had occurred a B.E.2c from No. 5 Wing RFC was sent to Writtle on 9 September 1915 under direct orders from the War Office. Only one defence sortie by the aircraft is recorded, this being two nights later when a 60-minute attempt against the Army Zeppelin LZ77 proved uneventful.

The RFC remained the sole users of the site, with sorties being flown infrequently over the following months, until it closed down in November 1916. Its duties were then taken over by the more suitable night landing ground at Broomfield Court which had been opened the previous month some four miles to the north.

A tree belt and orchards belonging to Writtle Agricultural College cross the northern half of the former landing ground whilst the sewage works remain to the east. New housing on the Marconi site is named erroneously after Dame Nellie Melba, who sang not from here but the main offices of the company in Chelmsford in the early days of radio broadcasting.

When the RFC left no more military flying took place on the site, but three years later on an adjacent field a company arrived which eventually was to change the world of aviation. In 1919 the Marconi Company sent engineers from its headquarters at Chelmsford to Writtle in order for them to have a more relaxed location to carry on the vital work in the early days of wireless broadcasting. In due course thoughts turned to putting wireless sets into aircraft and, with the benefit of a well-tried landing ground next door, the team soon had the use of a company Avro 504 aircraft (G–EBAJ) for their trials.

Based in an old army hut on the 5½ acre field to the east known as First Hazell, between the River Wid and Lower Ford Lane, research continued into the Second World War. By this time Marconi had expanded their work in the field of airborne radio and for this purpose a complete Avro Lancaster fuselage was brought onto the site for equipment trials. In time more modern offices were built on the land to replace the army hutting, the work continuing until the 1980s when the site was sold off for housing.

The connection with aviation continued in an architectural fashion a short distance away to the west when the Writtle College of Agriculture had hangars placed on its land during the Second World War for distribution of foodstuffs and equipment. To the eastern side of Lordship Road, in what is now Writtle College garden centre but was the buffer depot at Lordship Farm, one shed still survives to this day.

Surviving First World War buildings

With the advent of the construction period known as the Expansion Scheme, commenced in 1935, the majority of the buildings that remained from the First World War on airfields designated for improvement were finally swept away. Agreements made during that conflict stipulated that when sites were deemed to be no longer required afterwards all buildings on them, particularly those temporary structures, had to be removed or put up for sale prior to the land they occupied being offered back to its original owners. In most cases this was so, such that when landing grounds selected for further development were reopened in the mid-1920s the construction companies generally found nothing but fields when they were given possession of land upon which new buildings and services had to be built.

In the county a few notable exceptions to this rule occurred, namely at Stow Maries, Hainault Farm and North Weald Bassett. The first was left complete and untouched, the next only used as a designated ELG for a short period in the Second World War, whilst the latter site had a number of WW1 structures remaining in the technical area that were incorporated in the 1925 reconstruction as a fighter station.

The plan for North Weald (sic) shows the technical site area where at least eight WW1 buildings remained until the late-1960s. In 1924 the base of the timber aeroplane sheds and their apron became the position for the new aeroplane shed No. 1. When the main camp entrance was relocated 150 yards to the east the 1918 guardroom was demolished, to be replaced by one built on the new road system. The road layout shown was built to serve the enlarged technical area planned for the reopening of the station in 1927 and remained, with later revisions, until the early 1980s when the WW2 technical site here was removed for a hypermarket. The house 'Brockley', used as the Station Commander's residence, now houses the North Weald Airfield Museum.

Part of the Other Ranks' canteen at Stow Maries. Note the multi-pane, top swivelling metal windows and the condition of the roof structure which, considering the age of all buildings at this location, is remarkably good.

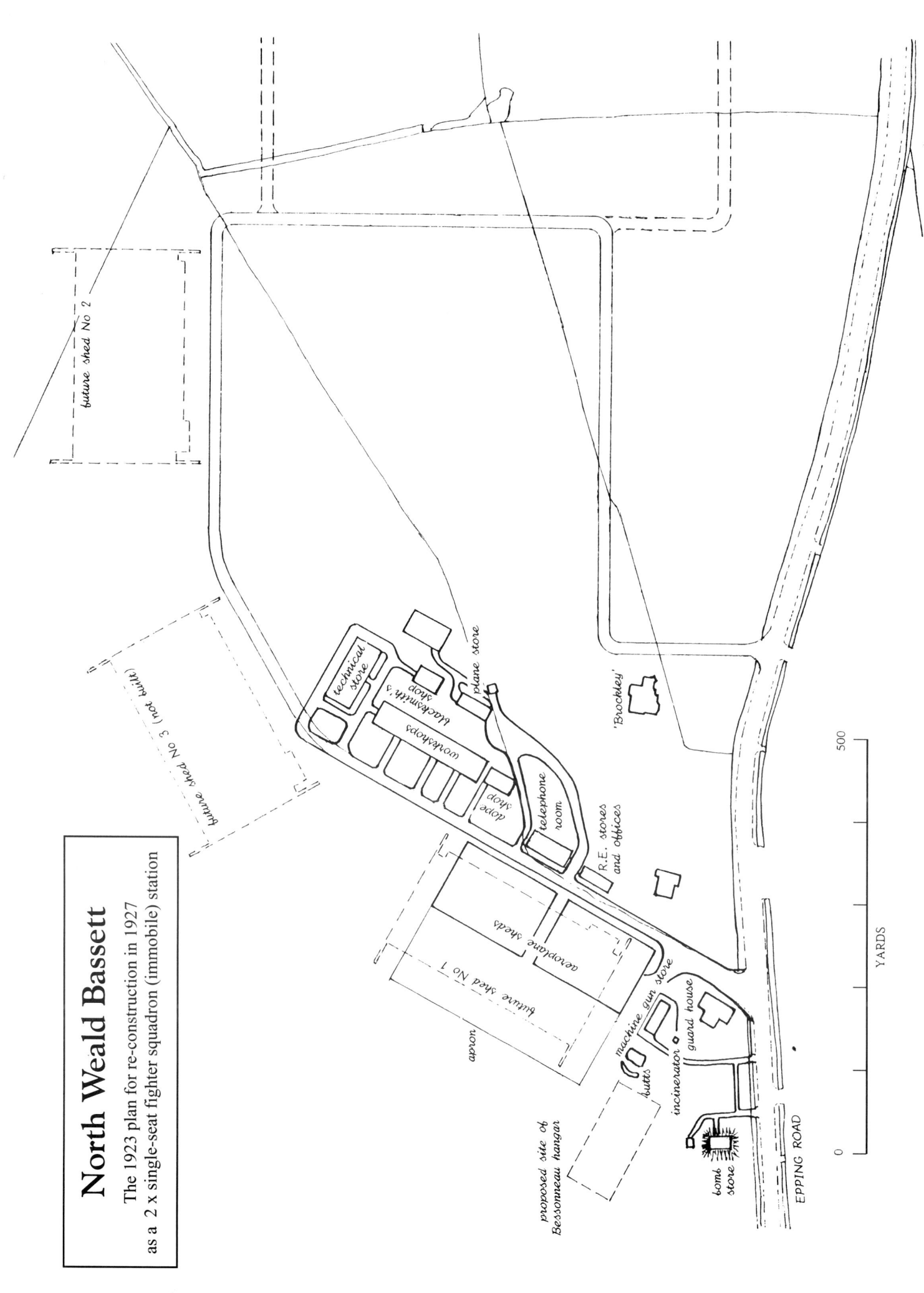

North Weald Bassett

The 1923 plan for re-construction in 1927
as a 2 x single-seat fighter squadron (immobile) station

future shed No 2

future shed No 3 (not built)

technical store

blacksmith's shop

workshops

plane store

dope shop

telephone room

R.E. stores and offices

'Brockley'

aeroplane sheds

future shed No 1

apron

proposed site of Bessonneau hangar

butts

machine gun store

incinerator

guard house

bomb store

EPPING ROAD

YARDS

0   500

83

Above: Typical of the hutting to be found on First World War Flight Stations is this example at Sparrow Wyke Farm just east of Stow Maries. Half of the second side panel has been brushed by bushes, indicating that the hut has been dismantled for moving at some time during its lifetime.

Left: A cast-iron water boiler in place still at Stow Maries.

The 12-bay brick-built Motorised Transport shed at Stow Maries with, attached to it in the left background, the timber stables for what horses were on site.

As the title page picture shows, Stow Maries has by far the greatest number of WW1 buildings still remaining in situ, and mainly in an un-modified state. Of all the structures to have been completed at this Flight Station only two are missing, namely the four 95' x 60' aeroplane twin sheds, one pair having been destroyed by an aerial mine in April 1941 with the remains of both taken down in 1946 and the timbers sold off locally, but amazingly 24 other buildings from the 1918 period remain out of 43 originally started on the technical and regimental sites. Whilst little maintenance has been carried out to keep the buildings sound those such as the water tower and barrack areas are still most prominent, whilst the Officers' Mess still has its kitchen servery hatches, lounge fireplace of Dutch bricks and the main washrooms (sadly though the latter has been damaged by vandals). The trussed rafter roofs in most buildings are in extremely good condition, and original corner fireplaces still remain in most billets and offices. For those with an architectural leaning Stow Maries is definitely the place to be.

The aeroplane sheds from Goldhanger lasted a bit longer than those of Stow Maries, one 90' x 120' pair being moved in 1925 on horse-drawn whims to the Crittal window factory in Witham. Re-assembled as a single 90' x 60' shed using the end and outer walls it served the manufacturers as a workshop until that part of the site was closed down in 1990 and sold off for housing development. After being offered to the IWM at Duxford, Mosquito Aircraft Museum at London Colney and The Squadron at North Weald, it was acquired by the Brooklands Museum in Surrey, where the remains lie in a dismantled state.

Happily one half of another twin shed remains in extremely good condition quite close to where it was originally erected between 1917–18. Flying from North Weald Bassett ceased in 1919 and after the site had lain dormant for four years the aeroplane sheds and other timber buildings were put up for sale by tender. In nearby Moreton village the Matthews family had a farm threshing business and bid for what they had thought was one shed pair to keep their steam engines in, however when the sale was closed it was found they had bought **all** the sheds. Due to the need to move their property off site as soon as possible they were taken down and moved to a field just outside the airfield next to the regimental site where they were again put up for auction. The shed retained was re-erected in 1925 as a 60' x 60' unit in Moreton village and for many years housed steam engines and other

Half of an ex-North Weald Bassett aeroplane shed, still at nearby Moreton in use as a garage and apparently in better condition than the later side addition.

The London Playing Fields pavilion at Fairlop today. In 1917 this building on the Fairlop Oak Playing Field was taken over as the RNAS Officers' Mess. Note the word 'CAFE' on the roof, a throw-back to the 1930s when places of refreshment with landable grass fields nearby were advertised thus to passing aviators.

The guard room at Hainault Farm, one of the original buildings remaining and now used as offices by a vehicle company. The window shutters and bollards are new, but the Hainault Road still runs past the right background.

One pair of the twelve bungalows still extant at Fairlop which, apart from modern glazing and vehicles, remain as they were when built as officer accommodation in the First World War.

implements. When the farm was sold and a petrol garage opened on the site it was used as the workshop in which use it continues today.

In complete contrast a pair of similar pattern but 90' x 60' in size still remain to this day at Hainault Farm alongside the Hainault Road. Again two pairs were originally built, of which one has survived, but for durability and security in these modern times timbering to the external elevations has been replaced by Ashlar block walling and sturdy end doors are fitted. The internal stanchions and roof construction are unchanged and motorists speeding past will only realise the historical importance of the buildings if they take time to view the flying buttresses projecting through the roadside end walls.

To end the subject of timber aeroplane sheds constructed on Flight Stations in the county during the First World War it should be realised that a total of 30 in varying sizes were eventually built. Chingford had eight large sheds, North Weald Bassett two, and Rochford four with the other four Flight Stations having four each erected as twin sheds, but only two remain in place with another at a new location, and the remains of a further shed outside the county. Considering their great size it is surprising that more have not survived, to be found still on factory or farm sites providing shelter for today's breed of machines.

Also at Hainault Farm are still a number of the technical and regimental buildings, now in use as offices or workshops for the companies based on the trading estate known as the Hainault Works which occupies this part of the former Flight Station. One building from here, the Officers' Mess, was dismantled after the First World War and moved from its original location on the west side of Hainault Road to North Weald Bassett.

A half-mile west of Hainault Farm lies the site of the Training Depot Station at Fairlop and here too, remarkably, buildings from the First World War period of occupancy by the RFC and RAF still remain tucked away just out of immediate view from Forest Road. To the western end of what was the landing ground most residents of the properties now called 'The Bungalows' are unaware that they live in dwellings put up for Air Force officers who were resident there some 80 years previous. Whatever the design life was for these single-storey structures it must surely have been exceeded many times over, for all twelve of the buildings still retain their original construction except for the modern additions of double glazing and central heating.

A short distance along Forest Road to the east can be found the pavilion which served as the officers dining room and now once again is a pavilion for the London Playing Fields Society, whilst next door amongst factory buildings of the Hampshire Engineering Works slab bases for three airmen's huts can still just be made out.

Further to the east the southside approach road which served the rear of the nine canvas hangars sited along Forest Road is barely recognisable now but remains as an access road to the sports field car parks here.

Two more non-military structures, included to illustrate other buildings used by the RFC, are The Grange, Woodham Mortimer and the Royal Forest Hotel, Chingford.

The Grange was requisitioned from its owner, Charles Bentall, in September 1916 as the headquarters for No. 37 (Home Defence) Squadron when it was allocated its 'clutch' of Flight Stations at Rochford, Stow Maries and Goldhanger and served as such until June 1918 when the SHQ was relocated on Stow Maries aerodrome. In private ownership once again it still has, adjacent to the main house, the barn built by the RFC to service aircraft engines in the First World War.

The Royal Forest Hotel was used as the HQ for No. 7 Balloon Wing of South East Area, No. 1 Training Group which controlled 11 balloon aprons in Essex and Kent as part of the London defence network. No changes were made to the building during its period of use by the military, and it is now a popular public house and restaurant

The timbered barn at The Grange, Woodham Mortimer, used for servicing aircraft engines from 'B' Flight of 37 (HD) Sqn at Stow Maries and those of 'C' Flight at Goldhanger. On the left is the house itself which was requisitioned as headquarters for the squadron from September 1916 to June 1918.

The Royal Forest Hotel, Chingford which was the headquarters for No. 7 Balloon Wing of South East Area, No. 1 Training Group.

First World War aviation memorials in the county

Whilst the Second World War has been widely remembered across the county relatively few memorials relating specifically to First World War aviation exist.

The few memorials that do exist to the RFC or RAF have been erected either by a grateful parish, and include the fallen aviators alongside the soldiers and sailors of the district, or are headstones on isolated or family graves and this chapter can only illustrate some of these. Those erected by families of the serviceman tend to be an insignificant headstone or cross form in the churchyard, whilst those placed by the Commonwealth War Graves Commission are more prominent due to the stark white Botticino limestone used. Set on a headstone beam for rigidity and absolute verticality the latter are more long-lasting and easily recognisable, whether placed singly or grouped such as in a War Graves plot around the Cross of Sacrifice.

A mix of headstones exists at the church of St Mary and St Margaret, Stow Maries, where four pilots of 37 Sqn are buried. These comprise Celtic cross, plain stone and the CWGC pattern but also inside the church are various plaques to Claude Ridley who was a Flight Commander at Stow Maries with 37 (HD) Sqn. He so loved the area that he supported the church over many years and, when he died of cancer in 1942 as a Wing Commander in the RAF, was buried there as was his wife later. On the church spire an illuminated cross, paid for and maintained under a covenant, is known locally as 'Ridley's beacon'.

A poignant pair of graves can be found at St Peter's church, Goldhanger. 2nd Lt Sydney Armstrong, previously of the Royal Field Artillery, died when his 37 Sqn B.E.12 suffered engine failure, crashed and caught fire at Tolleshunt Major in February 1918. Armstrong's replacement, 2nd Lt Frederick Augustus Crowley, crashed his Camel behind the 'Chequers' inn in Goldhanger village just one week later and is buried next to him.

The Commonwealth War Graves Commission headstones in Goldhanger churchyard to Frederick Crowley (front) and Sydney Armstrong, both of No. 37 Squadron, RFC.

One significantly different pair of memorials still just exist alongside the London-Southend railway line at Dollymans Farm, Shotgate. The phrase 'just' is used as the isolated site has suffered many times at the hands of vandals over the years and the original decorations desecrated despite frequent repairs. Two grave-type plots were placed in open fields, one topped by a three-bladed wooden propeller, in memory of two RFC pilots who collided during a patrol against Giants raiding London in 1918. On the night of 7/8 March Capt A.B. Kynoch of 37 Sqn took off from Stow Maries at almost the same time as Capt H.C. Stroud of 61 Sqn left Rochford. The reason for Kynoch being so far south of his allotted patrol line has never been established, it may be that he was in pursuit of a Giant seen some distance away, but his B.E.12 collided with Stroud's S.E.5a in cloudy conditions and the two aircraft fell in neighbouring fields.

Each crash site 'grave' has a memorial stone, but vandals have repeatedly desecrated both plots such that the two-bladed Fairey-Reed propeller currently on Stroud's has this time been securely bolted on by the Blake Hall Aircraft Museum who have taken on the task of renovating the site. In recent years proposals by Basildon Council to have them taken away and the pilots remembered instead by memorials in the town centre have been defeated by petitions from local residents which have so far halted these proposals on the grounds that the memorials should stay where they are.

Alexander Bruce Kynoch was laid to rest in Golders Green, London with Henry Clifford Stroud buried at St Andrew's church, Rochford near to his Flight Station. Stroud's grave has on it a round plaque with RFC wings and also once had a stone propeller (but this has now disappeared) whilst around him are the CWGC headstones of four other Rochford pilots who lost their lives in training accidents, 2nd Lt G.C. Malcolm (Kings Own Yorkshire Light Infantry, but attached to the RFC) and Lt A.S. Talbot who collided on 27 September 1917, Lt H.E. Davis MC who crashed on 19 June and Lt J.W. Sheridan on 27 September 1918. John Wilton Sheridan is also remembered in the church on a propeller which carries his name on a plate affixed to it.

Most photos show the propeller memorial to Clifford Stroud as it is visible from the railway line, but we must not forget the pilot with whom he collided before crashing on Dollymans Farm, Shotgate. The author's children at Bruce Kynoch's plot on a cold March 1996 day. The inscription reads:

'Sacred to the memory of Captain Alexander Bruce Kynoch who was killed in action here on the night of March 7th 1918. Aged 24 years'. 'RAF' has been added beneath his name, wrongly, for that title did not come into being for another month.

Between the electricity pylons in the background is Stroud's plot, this having been the subject of much repair work by the Blake Hall Aircraft Museum.

Henry Clifford Stroud's grave in the churchyard of St Andrew, Rochford when it had a propeller at the west end and the round plaque was at the east end. Although not visible in this shot there are, at each corner of Stroud's grave, headstones of the CWGC pattern to four other WW1 pilots who lost their lives flying from Rochford, that visible in this photograph being to 2nd Lt G.C. Malcolm.

The church of St John the Baptist with Our Lady and St Laurence at Thaxted has, affixed to the tower base near to the font, an individual wall plaque to Flight Sub Lieut C.R.W. Hodges, RN. He was shot down near Dixmude (France) on 18 August 1917 after an aerial action which took place at an altitude of 12000' against a superior German force. Aged just 19½ at the time of his death he is also remembered on a framed picture in the nave which shows 48 other Thaxted heroes from all services of the Great War.

The attendance en masse by the general public at airship crash sites was such that it has resulted in quite a few 'trophies' still remaining in family possession. At the time so many youngsters managed to pick up fragments of wreckage from the scene that an appeal today for memento details will result in a bulging postbag, typical of these being wall plaques or letter openers and clock or mirror surrounds, all fashioned from pieces of the airship's metal framework. Visible signs are also to be found where the airships fell in the county, such as the list in rank order of the crew from the L32 originally buried in the churchyard of St Mary Magdalene church, Great Burstead and given in the original burial register still kept there. The remains have since been re-interred in the Soldatenfriedhof at Cannock Chase, Staffordshire in 1962. A larger remnant in the form of a portion of girder from the L33 is displayed in the church of St Nicholas at Little Wigborough, and both St Nicholas' and St Stephens' church in Great Wigborough have vivid accounts of the night's events framed in fuselage latticework.

A 'living' memorial to the Zeppelin raids is represented by an Essex octogenarian, Mrs Z. Williams of Great Totham. Born into the Clarke household at Abbotts Hall Cottages, Great Wigborough on the night of 24 September 1916 as the L33 was coming down just one mile to the east, she was given the Christian name of 'Zeppelina' in remembrance of the event.

Outside the county memorials exist by way of that at Cuffley in Hertfordshire to Lt Leefe-Robinson from 39 (HD) Sqn at Suttons Farm for downing the SL11 there (the observation car from which is on display at the Imperial War Museum, Lambeth), and at Potters Bar to the L31 downed by 2nd Lt Tempest from 39 (HD) Sqn at North Weald Bassett where he is also remembered by the road name 'Tempest Avenue'. At Theberton in Suffolk pieces from the L48 shot down there and accredited to 2nd Lt Watkins from 37 (HD) Sqn at Goldhanger are in the church tower.

Two examples of Zeppelin memorabilia, the upper being a portion of metal framework from the L31 brought down at Potters Bar on 2 October 1916 ('not the Cuffley one', says the label – rightly so, as this was the wooden SL11) and the lower a piece of flat panel from the L32 at Billericay fashioned into an unlikely propeller shape.   *Tony Dyer photo*

Above: A piece of structural girder from the L33 which force-landed at Little Wigborough on 24 September 1916 is still affixed to the church tower there, whilst in both Wigborough churches the story of that night's event is displayed within elaborately crafted surrounds (below) made from the airship framework. Considering that the airship was dismantled on site by Admiralty engineers why does so much still exist in the area, and elsewhere?

DAILY SKETCH.

GUARANTEED DAILY NETT SALE MORE THAN 1,000,000 COPIES.

No. 2,372.   LONDON, SATURDAY, OCTOBER 14, 1916.   [Registered as a Newspaper.]   ONE HALFPENNY.

ZEP. WRECKERS THREE: Potters Bar Hero Gets The D.S.O.

The name of the airman who brought down the Zeppelin at Potters Bar is now officially announced. He is Lieut. Wulstan J. Tempest, R.F.C. The new hero of the air is seen arm-in-arm with Lieut. Robinson, (the Cuffley Zep. V.C. (on left), and Lieut. Sowrey, one of the Foxes Zep. D.S.O.s (on right).

Lieut. Wulstan Tempest, with his brothers—Major W. N. Tempest (seated), who was killed in the same day the air hero won the D.S.O.; Lieut. Achrol, who was a sergeant when this photograph was taken, and Lieut. E. R., who is also in the Air Service. (Photograph by Maud.)

Newspaper article of Saturday, 14 October 1916 depicting three of the pilots from 39 (HD) Sqn who became 'Zeppelin-killers' whilst flying the fragile B.E.2c on night operations. At left is Lt Leefe-Robinson (the SL11 at Cuffley) with Lt Tempest (the L31 at Potters Bar) centre and Lt Sowrey (the L32 at Billericay) on the right. Wulstan Tempest is seen in the lower picture surrounded by his brothers, all being serving officers. No contemporary picture is available of Lt Brandon who brought the L33 down at Little Wigborough to make it four in the space of one month.

95

Glossary of terms

Aeroplane sheds	vertical-sided, pitched-roofed timber hangars normally erected in pairs
Aeroplane lights	searchlights shone vertically from known positions near Flight Stations to enable returning fighters to locate their base in adverse conditions
Armstrong hut	tarred felt-covered wooden hut used as bad weather shelter on ELGs
'Archie'	pilots' nickname for anti-aircraft fire, also known as Ack-Ack. Today it is known as AAA, or anti-aircraft artillery, and includes missiles along with conventional gun rounds
B.R.	Bentley Rotary (engine type)
Bessonneau hangar	sloping-sided, curved-roofed timber hangar covered in canvas (other types more akin to tents were the 'RAF' and 'RE7' hangars)
Big Ben	Civil Defence code name for the German Army A4 long-range rocket impacts during the latter part of the Second World War
B.E.	Bleriot Experimental (aeroplane type)
BG	Bomb Group (USAAF – Second World War)
Brock & Pomeroy	incendiary gun ammunition used against airship envelopes
Comic conversion	Sopwith 1½-Strutters and Camels equipped for night-flying by fitting navigation lights and brackets for landing flares. Fabric on the top plane centre-section was also removed to improve upward vision
DLG	landing ground for use during daylight hours
ELG	emergency landing ground for general use, mostly at night
F.E.	Farman Experimental (aircraft type)
Fiery grapnel	resembling a 4-fluked anchor it was dangled beneath the fighter on a line until it entangled with an airships envelope, whereupon an explosive charge was set off to ignite leaking hydrogen. Normally carried in pairs beneath a fighter's fuselage between the undercarriage legs
FG	Fighter Group (USAAF – Second World War)
Giant	type name for the German Zeppelin Staaken multi-engined bomber
goose-neck flare	watering can-shaped container filled with paraffin or tar for night use
Gotha GIII/IV	twin-engined German bomber
Holt flares	parachute flares ignited electrically and released from fighter wing-tips to light the ground for night landings
(HD) Sq	(Home Defence) – RFC fighter units for defence of mainland Britain; on 1 November 1917 the term 'HD' was dropped from squadron titles
L or LZ	prefix to serial number for Zeppelin airships (Note – LZ also prefixed the construction number for airships; the L31 being c/no LZ72, L32 was c/no LZ74 and L33 c/no LZ76)
Le Prieur rockets	a 5-rocket battery fitted to a fighters' outer interplane struts and fired electrically for use against observation balloon or airship envelopes
Money flare	a wire cage filled with paraffin-soaked asbestos for night flarepath use
NFE store	(night flying equipment) building for storage and maintenance of the aerodrome lighting systems necessary to operate aircraft at night
NLG	night landing ground – for use by patrolling fighters in an emergency
Rankin darts	three-finned metal missile weighing 1lb, dropped in batches of up to 24 and designed to enter an airships envelope before detonating inside
R.E.	Reconnaissance Experimental (aircraft type)
S.E.	Santos (later Scout) Experimental (aircraft type)
SL	abbreviation for Schütte-Lanz series of German wooden-hulled airships
Soldatenfriedhof	central cemetery for German servicemen killed in Great Britain during both World Wars and located in Cannock Chase, Staffordshire
state board	frame with 'tote board' graphics placed (generally) between two pairs of aeroplane sheds to instruct pilots when to start a defensive patrol, with the stages of readiness for aircraft to fly the patrol being shown
timber whim	farm cart with axles and spine only, for moving felled trees to the mill
V.F.B.	Vickers Fighting Biplane (as in Vickers Gunbus F.B.4)
wind sleeve	another name for the windsock, the traditional wind indicator

Appendix 1

Patrol Lines

Standing patrol lines were,

at January 1916	37 (HD) Sqn	Rochford - Farningham - Biggin Hill - Esher, and All Hallows - Rochford - Goldhanger - Easthorpe.
	39 (HD) Sqn	North Weald Bassett - Farningham.
	50 (HD) Sqn	Rye - Pluckley - Herne Bay, and Dover - Margate, and Rochford - Herne Bay - Throwley.
	78 (HD) Sqn	Telscombe Cliffs - Rye
at November 1917	37 Sqn	London northern approaches from Goldhanger to Leigh-on-Sea
	50 Sqn	South of Thames between Nore lightship and Swingfield
	39, 44 & 78 Sqns	Shared an arc from Enfield to Grove Park
Night aeroplane patrol areas		B Chingford - Enfield C Chingford - Woodford D Woodford - Goodmayes E Goodmayes - Dagenham F Dagenham - Eltham Park G Eltham Park - Grove Park

at May 1918

	Patrol Line	*Sqn*	*Base*	*Aircraft*
B	Balls Park, Hertford - North Weald Bassett - Crabtree Hill, Hainault	39	North Weald Bassett	Bristol Fighter
C	Greenstead Farm, Havering - Suttons Farm	44	Hainault Farm	Sopwith Camel
D	South Weald - Tilbury	78	Suttons Farm	Sopwith Camel
E	Joyce Green - South Ash - Biggin Hill	141	Biggin Hill	Bristol Fighter
F	Northey Island - Tiptree	37	Goldhanger (C flt)	B.E.12/12a
J	Hatfield Peverel - Stow Maries	37	Stow Maries (A & B)	B.E.12/12a/12b
G	Stow Maries - Leigh on Sea - Yantlet Creek	61	Rochford	S.E.5a
H	Throwley - Faversham - Warden Point	112	Throwley	Sopwith Camel
K	Wingham - Margate sands	50	Bekesbourne	S.E.5a, B.E.12/12b
M	Detling - Marden	143	Detling	S.E.5a

Marham

Mattishall Norwich

Great Yarmouth

Hingham Burgh Castle

Upwood Harling Road

Covehithe

Thetford

Cambridge Elmswell

Newmarket

Martlesham
Heath

Hadleigh Orfordness

Ipswich

Wormingford

Felixstowe

Hertford Colchester

Goldhanger Clacton On Sea

London Colney North Weald
Bassett

Stow Maries

Hendon Hainault
Farm

Chingford Havering Rochford

Northolt LONDON Suttons
Farm RIVER THAMES

Southend

Isle of Grain

Hounslow Eastchurch Westgate

Joyce
Green

Wimbledon Chatham Manston

Croydon Farningham Detling Canterbury

Frinsted

Kenley Biggin Hill Throwley Bekesbourne

Maidstone Walmer

Wye Dover

Penshurst

Pluckley Lympne

Folkestone

Rye

● Aerodrome
• Patrol reference point

Brighton Telscombe
Cliffs Eastbourne

Patrol Lines Map

98

Appendix 2

Operational periods for landing grounds

Site and Function	1914	1915	1916	1917	1918	1919
Beaumont NLG			rfc			
Blackheath Common NLG				rfc		
Bournes Green DLG				army		
Braintree NLG				rfc		
Broomfield Court NLG			rfc			
Burnham-on-Crouch FS		rnas				
NLG			rfc			
Chingford FTS	rnas/raf				/	
MS					raf	
Clacton ASB		rnas				
East Hanningfield NLG			rfc			
Easthorpe NLG			rfc			
Fairlop FTS			rnas/raf		/	
Fyfield NLG			rfc			
Goldhanger NLG		rnas/rfc	/			
FS			rfc			
Hainault Farm DG	rnas					
NLG		rfc				
FS			rfc			
Horndon on the Hill NLG			rfc			
Little Clacton NLG			rfc			
Mountnessing NLG			rfc			
North Benfleet NLG			rfc			
North Ockendon NLG			rfc			
North Weald Bassett NLG			rfc			
FS			rfc			
Orsett NLG			rfc			
Rochford FTS	rfc					
FS		rnas	rfc			
NLG			rfc			
Runwell NLG				rfc		
Shenfield NLG			rfc			
Sible Hedingham NLG			rfc			
Stow Maries FS			rfc			
Suttons Farm FS		rfc				
Thaxted NLG				rfc		
Widford FS		rnas				
Wormingford NLG				rfc		
Writtle NLG	rfc					

Abbreviations

ASB	advanced seaplane base	FTS	flight training station	raf	Royal Air Force
DLG	day landing ground	MS	mobilisation station	rfc	Royal Flying Corps
FS	flight station	NLG	night landing ground	rnas	Royal Naval Air Service

N.B. 1. Where 'rfc' is shown on the chart it has not been changed to 'raf' if the site was still active after 1 April 1918 (i.e. when the Royal Air Force came into being).

2. The only sites to survive as airfields into the 1930s were the larger flight stations with road and rail access adjacent or close to, namely North Weald Bassett, Rochford and Suttons Farm.

Ultimate organisation of H.D. wings and squadrons

No. 46 Wing   Formed at York 6/3/17

No. 36 Sqn	Bases	Newcastle (HQ), Ashington, Cramlington, Hylton/Usworth, Seaton Carew
	Aircraft	B.E.2c, B.E.12, Bristol Scout, F.E.2b, F.E.2d, Sopwith Pup, Bristol Fighter
No. 76 Sqn	Bases	Ripon (HQ), Catterick, Copmanthorpe, Helperby
	Aircraft	B.E.2c, B.E.2e, B.E.12, B.E.12a, B.E.12b, Bristol Fighter, Avro 504k
No. 77 Sqn	Bases	Turnhouse (HQ), New Haggerston, Penston, Whiteburn
	Aircraft	B.E.2c, B.E.2e, B.E.12, B.E.12b, Avro 504k

No. 47 Wing   Formed at Adastral House, London 17/10/17, Cambridge 10/11/17

No. 51 Sqn	Bases	Thetford (HQ), Roudham/Harling Road, Hingham, Marham, Mattishall, Tydd St Mary
	Aircraft	F.E.2b, F.E.2d

No. 48 Wing   Formed at Gainsborough 1/2/18

No. 33 Sqn	Bases:	Filton, Tadcaster, Gainsborough, Kirton-Lindsey (HQs). Beverley, Bramham Moor, Coal Aston, Elsham, Scampton
No. 90 Sqn	Bases:	Buckminster, Leadenham, Stamford
	Aircraft:	Avro 504k

No. 49 Wing   Formed at Upminster 24/9/17

No. 39 Sqn	Bases:	Hounslow, Woodford (HQs), Biggin Hill, Hainault Farm, North Weald Bassett, Suttons Farm
	Aircraft:	B.E.2c, B.E.2e, B.E.12, B.E.12a, S.E.5, Sopwith Camel, Armstrong Whitworth F.K.8, Bristol Fighter
No. 44 Sqn	Base:	Hainault Farm
	Aircraft:	Sopwith 1½-Strutter, Sopwith Camel
No. 78 Sqn	Bases:	Hove, Harrietsham (HQs), Telscombe Cliffs, Gosport, Biggin Hill, Chiddingstone Causeway/Penshurst, Suttons Farm
	Aircraft:	B.E.2e, B.E.12, B.E.12a, B.E.12b, F.E.2d, Sopwith Camel
No. 141 Sqn	Bases:	Rochford, Biggin Hill
	Aircraft:	B.E.12, B.E.12a, B.E.12b, Sopwith Dolphin, Bristol Fighter

No. 50 Wing   Formed at Adastral House, London 28/8/17, Great Baddow 26/3/18

No. 37 Sqn	Bases:	Woodham Mortimer (HQ), Goldhanger, Rochford, Stow Maries
	Aircraft:	B.E.2d, B.E.2e, B.E.12, B.E.12a, B.E.12b, R.E.7, Sopwith 1½-Strutter, Sopwith Pup, S.E.5a, Sopwith Camel
No. 61 Sqn	Base:	Rochford
	Aircraft:	Sopwith Pup, S.E.5a, Sopwith Camel
No. 75 Sqn	Bases:	Goldington (HQ), Therfield, St Neots, Thrapston, Elmswell, Hadleigh, Harling Road
	Aircraft:	B.E.2c, B.E.2e, B.E.12, B.E.12b, Avro 504k

No. 53 Wing   Formed at Harrietsham 11/3/18

No. 50 Sqn	Bases:	Dover, Harrietsham (HQs), Bekesbourne, Detling, Throwley
	Aircraft:	B.E.2c, B.E.2e, B.E.12, B.E.12a, B.E.12b, Sopwith Camel, Armstrong Whitworth F.K.8, S.E.5a
No. 112 Sqn	Base:	Throwley
	Aircraft:	Sopwith Pup, Sopwith Camel
No. 143 Sqn	Base:	Detling
	Aircraft:	Armstrong Whitworth F.K.8, S.E.5a, Sopwith Camel

Appendix 4

Ground Signals

ELG Landing Flare Layout

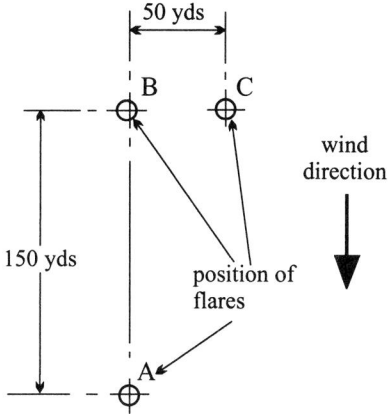

Ground Arrow

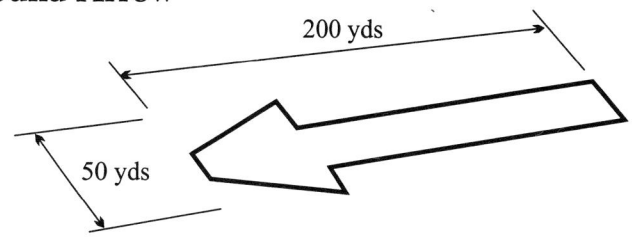

The precise construction details of this rather labour-intensive French system of 1915 have not come to light, but it would seem likely that the arrow was laid out with separate canvas panels which were rolled up when the signal was moved to pass on updated information to pilots as to the direction of enemy aircraft. It can be seen from the dimensions that a fairly large area would be needed to lay out the signal – certainly not on the designated landing area where, apart from taking up valuable landing space, it would need to be well pegged down flat and secure otherwise it would constitute a hazard to flying operations!

Ground Signals
(Some examples of the Ingram Code)

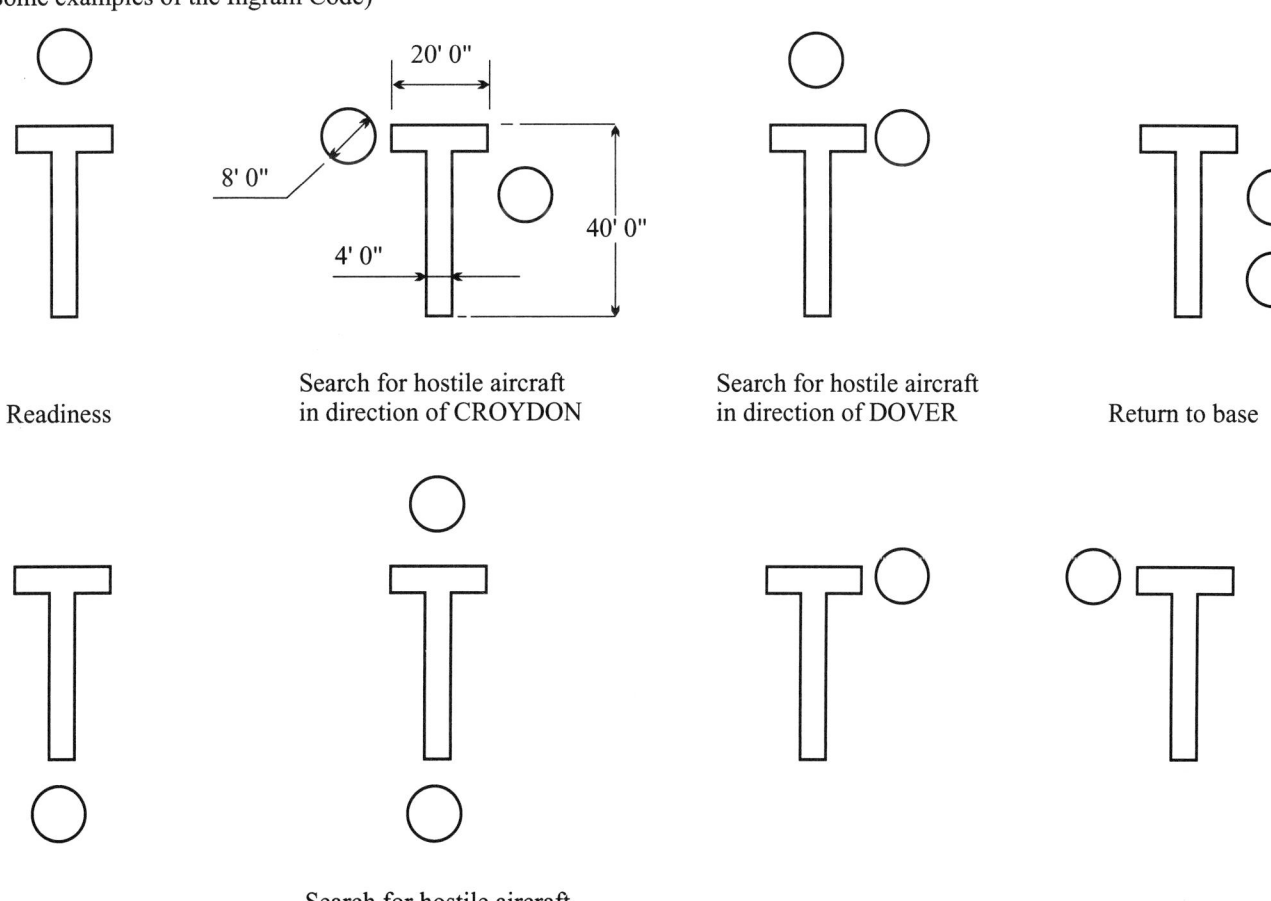

Flight Station Plans

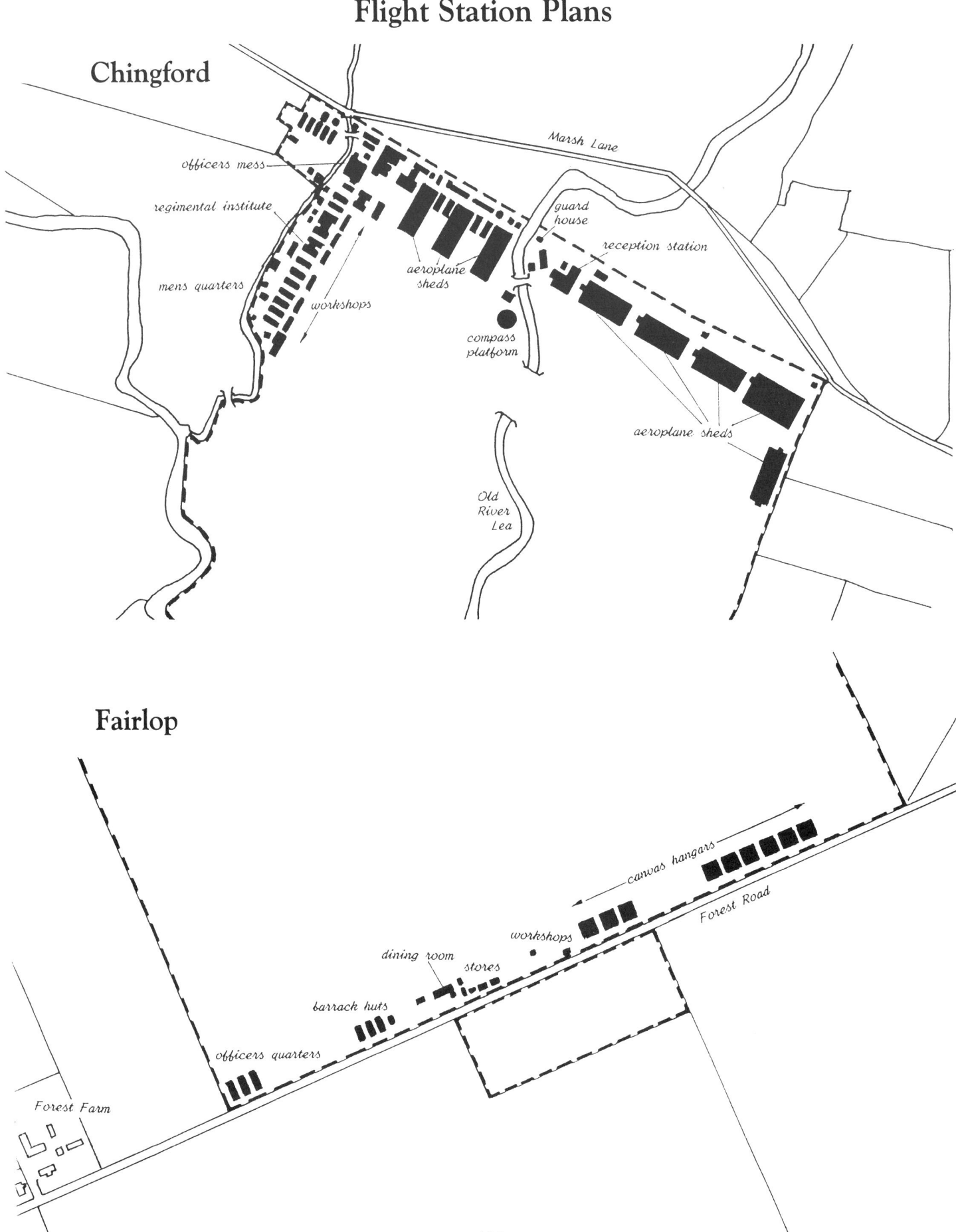

Chingford

officers mess

regimental institute

mens quarters

workshops

aeroplane sheds

Marsh Lane

guard house

reception station

compass platform

aeroplane sheds

Old River Lea

Fairlop

canvas hangars

Forest Road

workshops

dining room

stores

barrack huts

officers quarters

Forest Farm

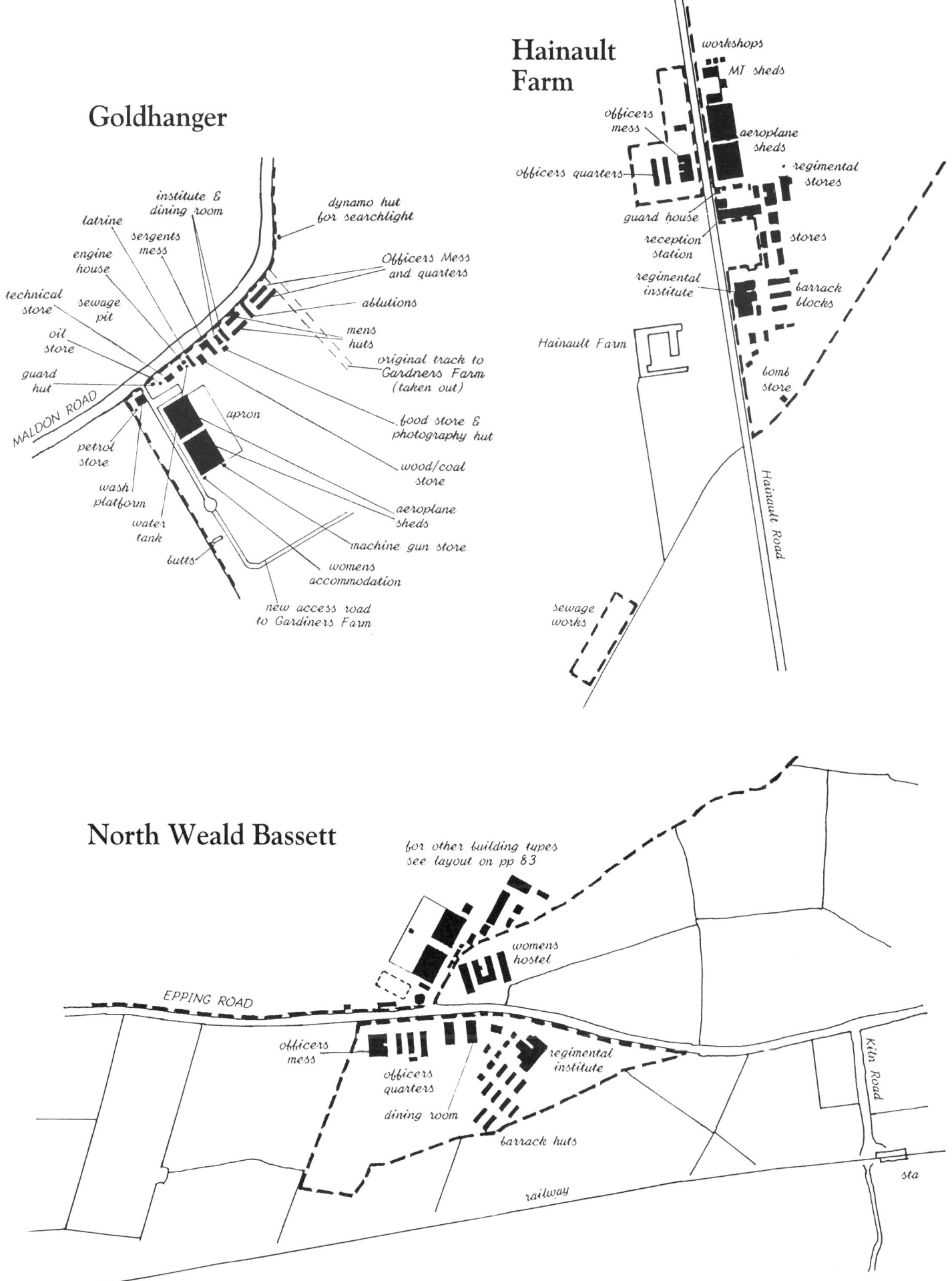

Goldhanger

latrine

institute &
dining room

engine
house

sergents
mess

technical
store

sewage
pit

oil
store

guard
hut

MALDON ROAD

petrol
store

wash
platform

water
tank

butts

new access road
to Gardiners Farm

apron

womens
accommodation

machine gun store

aeroplane
sheds

wood/coal
store

food store &
photography hut

original track to
Gardners Farm
(taken out)

mens
huts

ablutions

Officers Mess
and quarters

dynamo hut
for searchlight

Hainault Farm

workshops

MT sheds

officers
mess

officers quarters

guard house

reception
station

regimental
institute

Hainault Farm

aeroplane
sheds

regimental
stores

stores

barrack
blocks

bomb
store

Hainault Road

sewage
works

North Weald Bassett

for other building types
see layout on pp 83

EPPING ROAD

officers
mess

officers
quarters

dining room

womens
hostel

regimental
institute

barrack huts

railway

Kiln Road

sta

103

Rochford

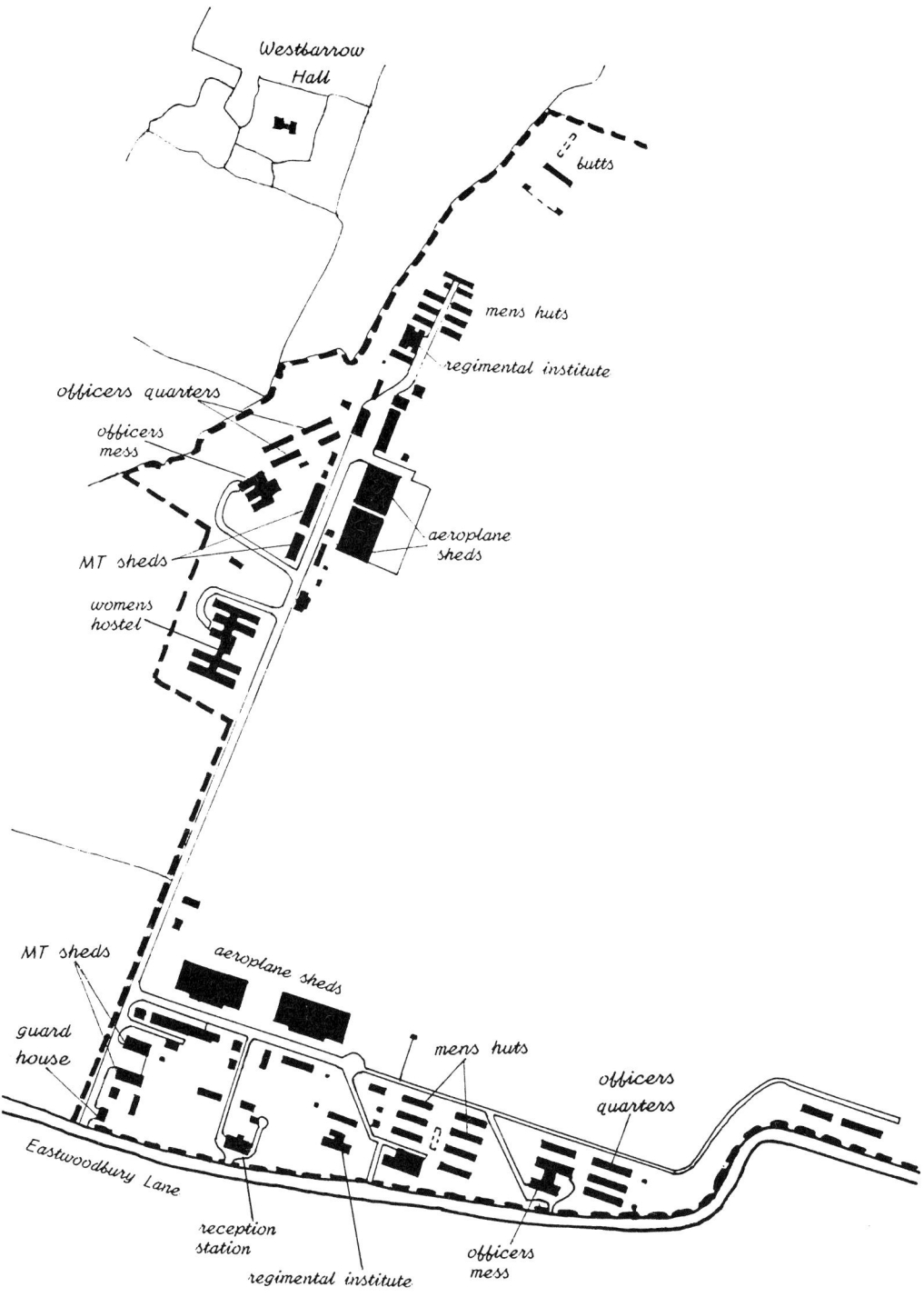

Westbarrow
Hall

butts

mens huts

regimental institute

officers quarters

officers
mess

aeroplane
sheds

MT sheds

womens
hostel

MT sheds

aeroplane sheds

guard
house

mens huts

officers
quarters

Eastwoodbury Lane

reception
station

regimental institute

officers
mess

Stow Maries

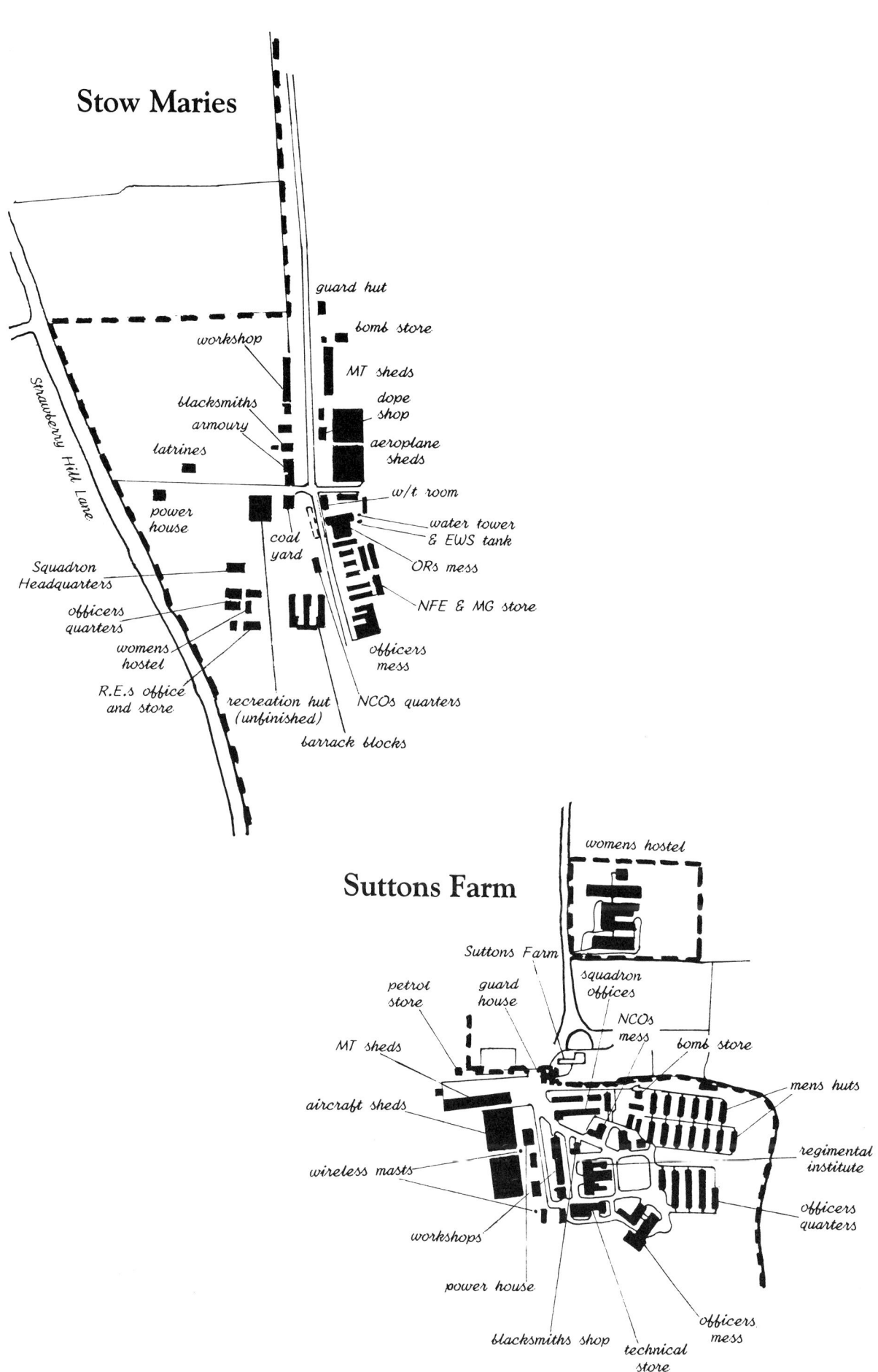

guard hut

bomb store

workshop

MT sheds

blacksmiths

dope shop

armoury

aeroplane sheds

latrines

w/t room

Strawberry Hill Lane

power house

water tower & EWS tank

coal yard

ORs mess

Squadron Headquarters

NFE & MG store

officers quarters

womens hostel

officers mess

R.E.s office and store

recreation hut (unfinished)

NCOs quarters

barrack blocks

Suttons Farm

womens hostel

Suttons Farm

petrol store

guard house

squadron offices

NCOs mess

bomb store

MT sheds

mens huts

aircraft sheds

regimental institute

wireless masts

officers quarters

workshops

power house

blacksmiths shop

technical store

officers mess

Drawings

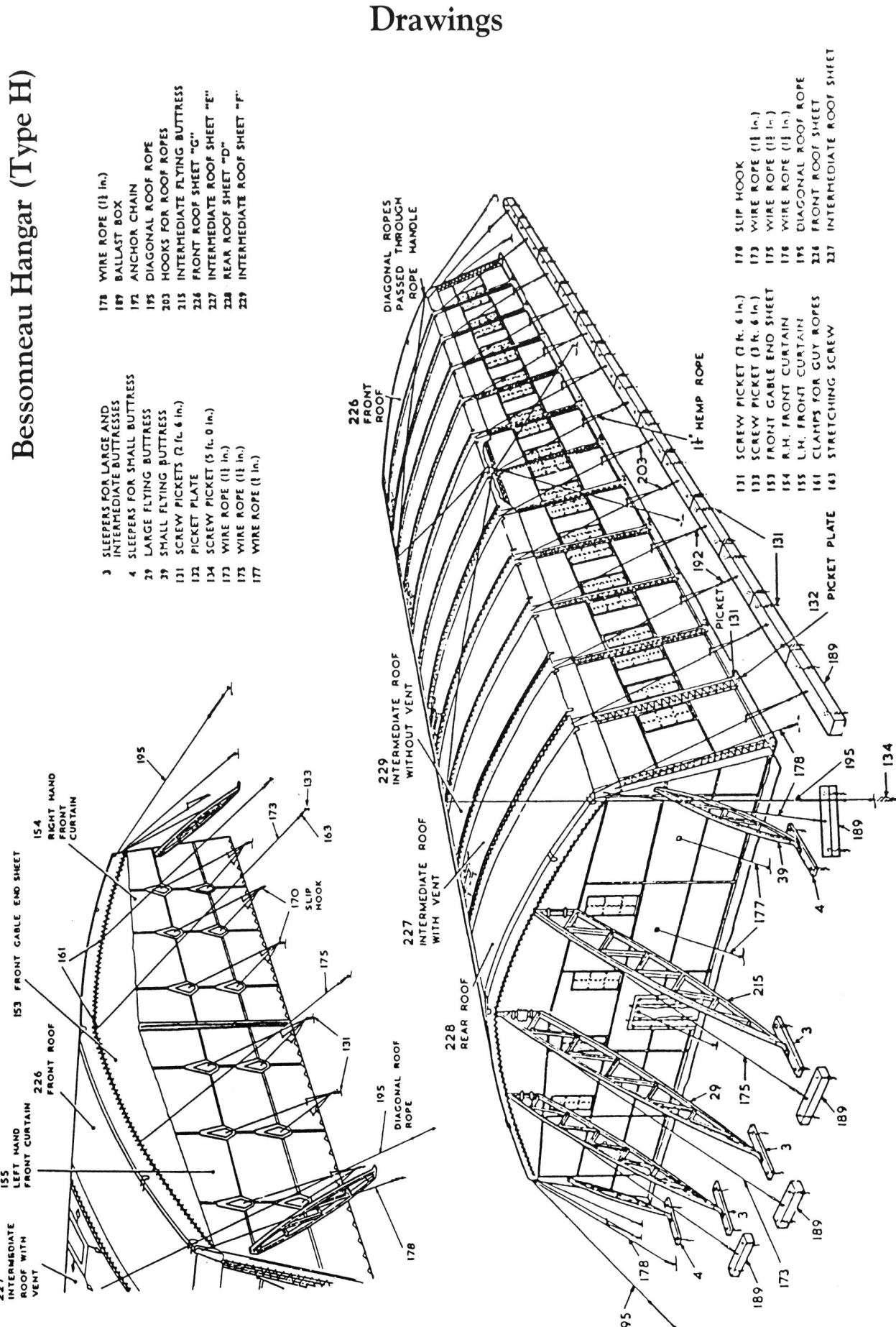

Bessonneau Hangar (Type H)

3	SLEEPERS FOR LARGE AND INTERMEDIATE BUTTRESSES
4	SLEEPERS FOR SMALL BUTTRESS
29	LARGE FLYING BUTTRESS
39	SMALL FLYING BUTTRESS
131	SCREW PICKETS (2 ft. 6 in.)
132	PICKET PLATE
134	SCREW PICKET (5 ft. 0 in.)
173	WIRE ROPE (1¼ in.)
175	WIRE ROPE (1½ in.)
177	WIRE ROPE (1 in.)
178	WIRE ROPE (1⅛ in.)
189	BALLAST BOX
192	ANCHOR CHAIN
195	DIAGONAL ROOF ROPE
203	HOOKS FOR ROOF ROPES
215	INTERMEDIATE FLYING BUTTRESS
224	FRONT ROOF SHEET "G"
227	INTERMEDIATE ROOF SHEET "E"
228	REAR ROOF SHEET "D"
229	INTERMEDIATE ROOF SHEET "F"
131	SCREW PICKET (2 ft. 6 in.)
133	SCREW PICKET (3 ft. 6 in.)
153	FRONT GABLE END SHEET
154	R.H. FRONT CURTAIN
155	L.H. FRONT CURTAIN
161	CLAMPS FOR GUY ROPES
163	STRETCHING SCREW
170	SLIP HOOK
173	WIRE ROPE (1¼ in.)
175	WIRE ROPE (1½ in.)
176	WIRE ROPE (1⅛ in.)
195	DIAGONAL ROOF ROPE
226	FRONT ROOF SHEET
227	INTERMEDIATE ROOF SHEET

Many buildings were constructed in rendered brickwork with timber trussed roofs for general purposes but the aeroplane sheds, or hangars, are the most interesting from an engineering aspect.

'RAF Hangar'

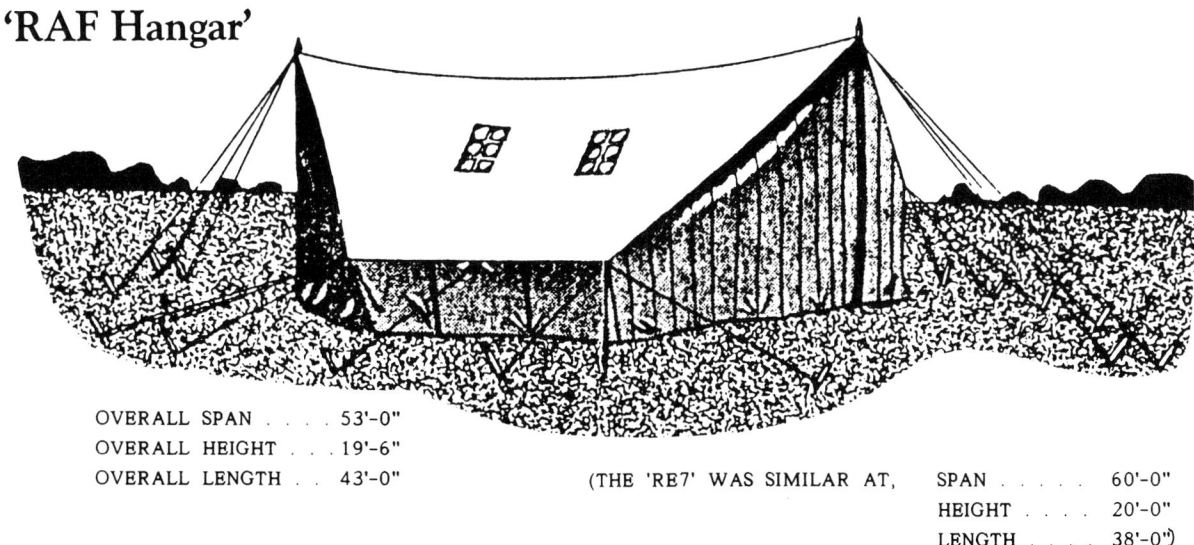

OVERALL SPAN . . . . 53'-0"
OVERALL HEIGHT . . . 19'-6"
OVERALL LENGTH . . 43'-0"

(THE 'RE7' WAS SIMILAR AT, SPAN . . . . . 60'-0"
HEIGHT . . . . 20'-0"
LENGTH . . . . 38'-0")

Aeroplane Twin-shed

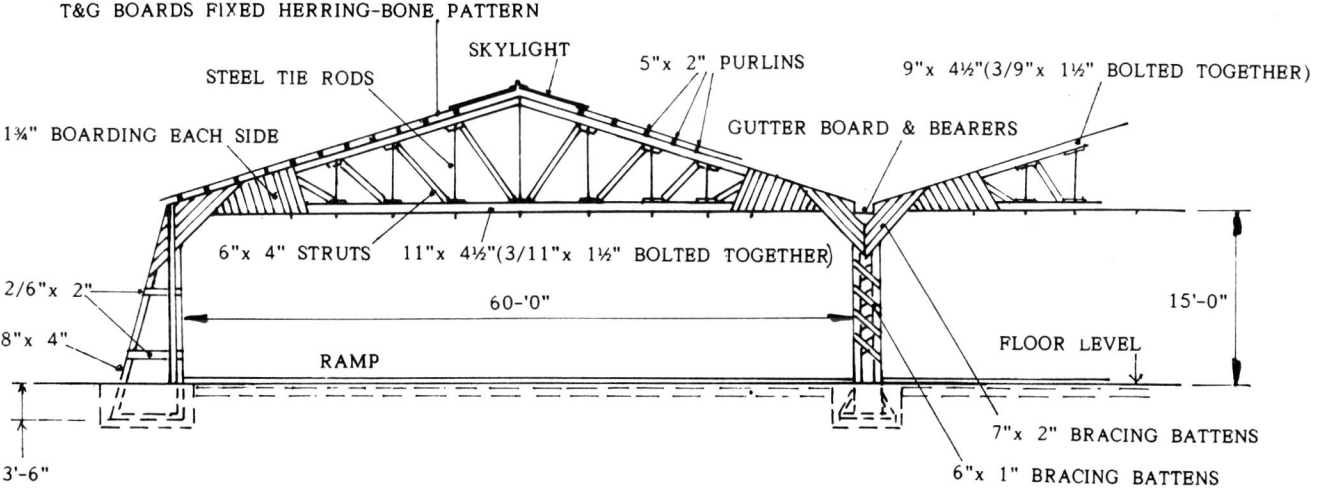

T&G BOARDS FIXED HERRING-BONE PATTERN
STEEL TIE RODS
SKYLIGHT
5"x 2" PURLINS
9"x 4½"(3/9"x 1½" BOLTED TOGETHER)
1¾" BOARDING EACH SIDE
GUTTER BOARD & BEARERS
6"x 4" STRUTS
11"x 4½"(3/11"x 1½" BOLTED TOGETHER)
2/6"x 2"
8"x 4"
RAMP
60-'0"
FLOOR LEVEL
15'-0"
7"x 2" BRACING BATTENS
6"x 1" BRACING BATTENS
3'-6"

HALF SECTION

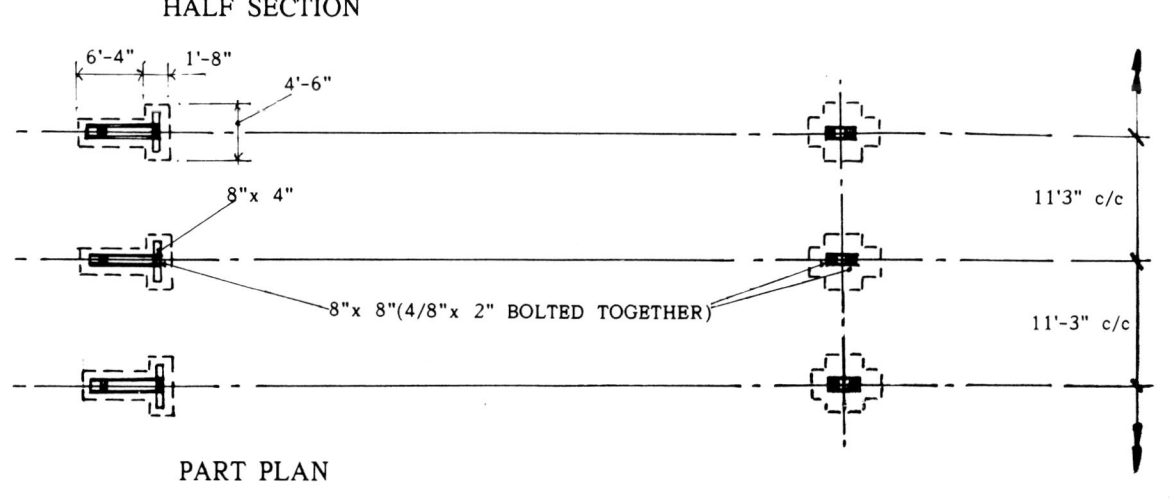

6'-4"
1'-8"
4'-6"
8"x 4"
8"x 8"(4/8"x 2" BOLTED TOGETHER)
11'3" c/c
11'-3" c/c

PART PLAN

107

Appendix 7

Cost of First World War fighter aircraft and engines

Aircraft	£ s d	Engines available	£ s d
(No. guns or instruments)		Beardmore 120 hp	825.00.0
B.E.2c/e	1,072.10.0	Beardmore 160 hp	1,045.00.0
B.E.12	990.00.0	B.R.1	643.10.0
Bristol Fighter F2b	1,350.19.0	130 hp Clerget	907.10.0
F.E.2b	1,521.13.4	Hispano Suiza	1,004.00.0
F.E.2d	1,540.00.0	110 hp Le Rhone	771.10.0
Maurice Farman Shorthorn	1,005.08.0	100 hp Monosoupape	696.00.0
Royal Aircraft Factory SE5a	862.08.0	R.A.F. 1a	522.10.0
R.E. 7	1,886.10.0	R.A.F. 3a	1,210.00.0
R.E.8	1,232.00.0	R.A.F. 4a	836.00.8
Sopwith Camel F1	874.10.0	Rolls-Royce Eagle 2,3 & 4	1,430.00.0
Sopwith 1½-strutter	842.06.0	Rolls Royce Eagle 5	1,721.10.0
Sopwith Pup (ships aeroplane)	770.00.0	Rolls Royce Eagle 6 & 7	1,919.10.0
Sopwith Snipe	945.17.0	Rolls Royce Eagle 8	1,622.10.0
		Rolls Royce Falcon 1,2 & 3	1,210.00.0
		Rolls Royce 4	1,617.00.0
		Wolseley Adder W4b	946.00.0
		Wolseley Viper W4a	814.00.0

Notes:

1. Position of engines in adjacent column does not relate to the aircraft type given horizontally opposite.

2. Aircraft and engine costs are at 1918 prices. Reference to the Retail Price Index for 1995 shows that the comparative purchasing power of the £ in 1918 would have been in the order of £26 12s 6d (£26.63p), or 3.76p at 1995 prices.

Appendix 8

Personnel and equipment numbers at Flight Stations

	Personnel		Transport	
Chingford	Officers	3	No records acquired	
	NCOs	2		
	Cpls	4		
	Rank & file	21		
	Women	13		
	Women (household)	8		
		51		
Fairlop	Officers	34		
	Officers under instruction	80	Touring cars	1
	NCOs under instruction	40	Light tenders	8
	WOs & NCOs	31	Heavy tenders	8
	Cpls	22	Motorcycles	6
	Rank & file	214	Sidecars	4
	Forewomen	5	Trailers	3
	Women	105		30
	Women (household)	42	+24 Camels, 24 Avros	
		573		

	Personnel			*Transport*	
Goldhanger	Officers	7		(see Stow Maries)	
	NCOs above Cpl	3			
	Cpls	2			
	Rank & file	<u>43</u>		+ 8 Camels ('C' Flt 37 Sqn)	
		55			

				Motor cars	1
Hainault Farm	Officers	28		Light tenders	7
	WOs & NCOs above Cpl	19		Heavy tenders	5
	Cpls	18		Motorcycles	6
	Rank & file	159		Sidecars	4
	Women	12		Trailers (Mk 1)	3
	Women (household)	<u>17</u>		Repair trailers	2
		253		Ambulances	<u>1</u>
					29
				+ 24 Camels	

				Motor cars	1
North Weald	Officers	48		Light tenders	7
Bassett	WOs & NCOs above Cpl	19		Heavy tenders	5
	Cpls	18		Motorcycles	6
	Rank & file	166		Sidecars	4
	Women	12		Trailers (Mk 1)	3
	Women (household)	<u>17</u>		Repair trailers	2
		280		Ambulances	<u>1</u>
					29
				+ 24 2-seater Bristol Fighters	

		61 Sqn	198 (Night) Sqn		61 Sqn	198 (Night) Sqn
Rochford				Motor cars	1	1
	Officers	28	17	Light tenders	7	3
	Officers under instruction	0	50	Heavy tenders	5	5
	WOs & NCOs above Cpl	19	15	Ford tenders	0	4
	Cpls	18	15	Motorcycles	6	6
	Rank & file	159	126	Sidecars	4	4
	Women	12	57	Trailers (Mk 1)	3	2
	Women (household)	<u>17</u>	<u>24</u>	Repair trailers	2	0
		253	304	Workshop trailers	0	3
				Trailers (plane carrier)	0	1
				Ambulances	<u>1</u>	<u>1</u>
					29	30
				+ (61 Sqn) 24 Camels and (198 (Night) Trg Sqn) 24 Camels & Avros		

				Motor cars	1
Stow Maries	Officers	21		Light tenders	11
	WOs & NCOs above Cpl	17		Heavy tenders	6
	Cpls	16		Motorcycles	8
	Rank & file	150		Sidecars	4
	Women	3		Trailers (Mk 1)	4
	Women (household)	<u>12</u>		Repair trailers	4
		219		Ambulances	<u>3</u>
					41
				+ 16 Camels (a portion allocated to Goldhanger)	

Suttons Farm Personnel and transport as for 61 & 198 (Night) Training Sqns at Rochford.
Equipment – (78 Sqn) 24 Camels, (189 (Night) Trg Sqn) 24 Camels & Avros

Bibliography

A History of Aviation in Essex (edited by K. Cole) Pub: RAeS (Southend branch) 1967
A History of the County of Essex, Vol 5 (edited by R.B. Pugh) Pub: OUP 1956
A Time To Fly (The memoirs of Sir Alan Cobham) Pub: Shepheard Walwyn 1978
AIR 1/452 & 453, AIR 2/4557 and various other files (Public Record Office, Kew)
Airfield Review magazine (various issues) Pub: Airfield Research Group (quarterly)
Airfields of the Eighth Then and Now (Roger Freeman) Pub: Battle of Britain Prints
International Ltd 1978
Aviation memorials of Essex (P.A. Doyle) *Flypast* magazine April 1989
Daily Sketch newspapers
Environmental and Planning Services records, Chelmsford Borough Council
Essex Countryside magazine series
Fighter Squadrons of the RAF and their aircraft (J.D.R. Rawlings) Pub: Macdonalds 1969
First Through The Clouds (F Warren Merriam) Pub: Batsford 1954
Claude Grahame-White (Graham Wallace) Pub: Putnam 1960
London Gas Museum archives, Bromley-by-Bow
RNAS Order of Battle, 1914 (Mike Goodall) Cross & Cockade Journal 1982
Southend Standard newspapers
Stow Maries (P.A. Doyle) *Flypast* magazine March 1994
The Air Defence of Britain 1914-1918 (C. Cole & E.F. Cheeseman) Pub: Putnam 1984
The Fire Brigade in Chingford, 1895-1985 (George Rider)
The War In The Air, Vols 3, 5 & 6 (H.A. Jones) Pub: Clarendon Press 1931-37
The Winged Bomb, History of 39 Sqn RAF (Ken Delve) Midland Counties Publications 1985
2MT Writtle, the birth of British broadcasting (Tim Wander) Pub: Capella 1988
Where the Lysanders were . . . (P.A. Doyle) Pub: Forward Airfield Research Publishing 1995
Woggle and Butter Harsies (George Clarke, Burnham on Crouch) Pub: Terence Dalton 1990
Grateful thanks are due to the successors of companies that produced Dr Liston's Essence, Parkinson's Health
Salt and Watson's Matchless Cleanser for their period advertisements.

How this book came about

The author, a member of the Airfield Research Group and the British Society of World War One Aero Historians (Cross & Cockade, UK), is employed as a construction engineer with the Defence Estates Organisation at RAF Mildenhall and flies with the Aero Club at RAF Lakenheath for relaxation. Currently living in North Weald Bassett, next to an airfield that had its origins in the First World War, prompted the chronicling of the Essex landing grounds used by all three services in that first great aerial conflict.

Although having had various pieces published in magazines this is only the author's second book, coming about as an offshoot of the previous work which was an in-depth study of a little-known but very active airfield site in Hertfordshire with a First World War history. Researching the local history aspect of each WW1 location was treated in the same way as before with fieldwork involving visiting the area and contacting as many of the long-time and elderly residents as could be found, in order that their personal memories of the First World War period could be recorded before they were lost with the passage of time, their stories proving to be so vital to the overall picture.

Having got around the lengthy problem of establishing the precise location and extent of each site, the next obstacle was the airborne mount to be used in photographing the state of the sites as they are now. The ideal choice would have been a machine from the WW1 period but as no 1918 PR types exist the Thruxton Jackeroo owned by Ian Oliver and Les Smith was instead made available as a camera ship. Built in 1943 as one of 7933 DH82 Tiger Moths it served with the RAF in the Second World War as a two-seater trainer and post-war went onto the civil register. In 1957 Thruxton Aviation converted it to the four-seat Jackeroo configuration and it is now one of only two of the type flying in the UK.

Normally based at Little Gransden (Cambs) it was employed on the photo sorties over two days by positioning at Andrewsfield to cover the northern group of sites and North Weald for the southern. The author is grateful to the owners for permitting it to be used, and in particular thanks are extended to Ian Oliver for flying many miles across the county from one grass field to the next and putting the aircraft into the best possible camera position.

The author and pilot Ian Oliver with Thruxton Jackeroo G-AOIR during a refuelling stop at The Squadron, North Weald over the course of the 1997 photo work. The Squadron is just outside what was the Northern boundary of the First World War Flight Station.   *(Anthony Hutton photo)*

Still available:–

Please use reference ISBN 0 9525624 0 5 when ordering through booksellers